HISTORY OF THE PUNJAB,

AND OF THE
RISE, PROGRESS, & PRESENT CONDITION
OF
THE SECT AND NATION
OF

THE SIKHS.

JAMES PRINSEP, HENRY THOBY PRINSEP

IN TWO VOLUMES

VOL. II

GYAN

Published by

Gyan Publishing House
5, Ansari Road
Daryaganj, New Delhi-110002
Phone: 011-47034999, 9811692060
E-mail: books@gyanbooks.com

Distribution Network
gyanbooks.com
India, USA, Canada, UK, Australia, France

ISBN: 978-81-212-8794-4 (SET)
978-81-212-8792-0 (PB)
First Published, 1846

2nd Impression 2023

Printed at: Gyan Press, Delhi.

HISTORY OF THE PUNJAB (VOL. II)
Author: James Prinsep, Henry Thoby Prinsep

HISTORY OF THE PUNJAB.

HISTORY OF THE PUNJAB,

AND OF THE

RISE, PROGRESS, & PRESENT CONDITION

OF

THE SECT AND NATION

OF

THE SIKHS.

IN TWO VOLUMES.

VOL. II.

LONDON:
Wm. H. ALLEN & CO.,
LEADENHALL STREET.

1846.

CONTENTS OF VOLUME II.

CHAPTER XII.

A.D. 1812 TO 1813.

CHAPTER XIII.

A.D. 1814 TO 1818.

CHAPTER XIV.

A.D. 1819 TO 1822.

CHAPTER XV.

A.D. 1823 TO 1829.

CHAPTER XVI.

A.D. 1829 TO 1831.

CHAPTER XVII.

A.D. 1832 TO 1837.

CHAPTER XVIII.

A.D. 1838 AND 1839.

CHAPTER XIX.

CHARACTER AND POLICY OF RUNJEET SINGH.

CHAPTER XX.

REIGN OF KHURUK SINGH.

A.D. 1839 AND 1840.

CHAPTER XXI.

REIGN OF SHER SINGH.

A.D. 1840 TO 1842.

CHAPTER XXII.

A.D. 1843 AND 1844.

CHAPTER XXIII.

REIGN OF DHULEEP SINGH.

A.D. 1843 TO 1845.

CHAPTER XXIV.

A.D. 1845 AND 1846.

CHAPTER XXV.

CAMPAIGN OF THE SUTLUJ.

APPENDIX.

HISTORY OF THE PUNJAB,

&c.

CHAPTER XII.

A.D. 1812 TO 1813.

In the beginning of the year 1812, the court of Lahore was occupied in preparations for celebrating with due magnificence the marriage of the heir-apparent, Koonwur Khuruk Singh, with the daughter of Jymul Ghunea, the same chief from whom Runjeet Singh had taken Puthan-Kot, in the Julendra Turaee. An invitation was sent to Colonel Ochterlony at Lodiana to honour the ceremonies with his presence, and an envoy being despatched to conduct him to Lahore, the colonel crossed the Sutluj on the 23rd of January, with a small escort, to which, by particular desire of Runjeet, a galloper gun was attached, the Sikh chief's curiosity to see how this branch of artillery was equipped in the British service being intense. Colonel Ochterlony was accompanied by the Rajas of Naba, Jheend, and Kytul, and on arriving near Amritsur, on the 28th, received the *istuqbal*, or meeting of honour, from the chief of the Sikhs, who had gathered to his court, on this occasion, all his sirdars, and indeed the whole nation appeared to be assembled to do honour to the nuptials.

The ceremony was performed at the residence of Sirdar Jymul Singh, in Futehgurh, and, after its conclusion, on the 6th of February, the whole party returned to Amritsur. Suda Koonwur alone was not present; indisposition was assigned as the reason of her non-attendance on the occasion, but her dissatisfaction at the failure of an attempt to procure from Runjeet, her son-in-law, the public acknowledgment, during these ceremonies, of the two boys she had brought up as twins born to her daughter, was generally believed to be the true cause of her absence.

Runjeet Singh received Colonel Ochterlony with marked distinction, appointed his principal officers to shew him every object worth seeing at Lahore, and pressed upon him an invitation to stay and see the festivities of the *Hooli*, which would be celebrated in March. The colonel declined this honour for himself, but the Sikh chiefs who had come with him gladly accepted it, and the Bhye of Kytul obtained by cunning and intrigue, during the orgies, a grant from the Lahore ruler of Goojurawul, on the protected side of the Sutluj. The frank confidence displayed by Runjeet in his present reception of Colonel Ochterlony was much in contrast with the suspicious mistrust with which Mr. Metcalfe had been treated. Runjeet shewed the colonel his troops, and particularly the new battalions he was raising; took him over the fortifications of Lahore, and inspected with him some new works he was constructing for their improvement, and to connect the Juma Musjid with the palace,

His prudent dewan, Mohkum Chund, and the Sirdar Gundha Singh, are reported to have remonstrated against the communication of such knowledge to a professional person of a nation that might have designs against him. Runjeet, however, observed with shrewdness, that if such were their sentiments, they should have advised his withholding the invitation altogether from the colonel.

After the conclusion of these ceremonies and festivities, the armies of Lahore resumed active operations. Koonwur Khuruk Singh was sent with a strong force against Bimbur and Rajaoree, where Sooltan Khan, the Musulman holder of the former territory, proved a formidable enemy, having recently overpowered and slain his relation, Ismael Khan, who had been left, as the result of previous operations, in the possession and management of a large portion of the territory. Dul Singh was at the same time sent with another force to plunder and levy tribute from Muzuffur Khan, at Multan; and a third, under Desa Singh, was again detached to Kangra. Runjeet in person made a tour into the Jalendra Doab, towards the Turaee, whither he summoned various hill chiefs, and made with them fresh arrangements, attended with increase of tribute. The resumption of Shujanpur from Boodh Singh Bhugut was the only operation of that kind effected on this occasion. Returning to Lahore, on the 23rd of May, Runjeet received intelligence there of the success of Khuruk Singh against Bimbur, Jummoo, and Aknur. The Koonwur was honoured with a grant of these places in jagir, and he placed them in the management of Bhye Ram Singh. Dul Singh had also succeeded in extorting a considerable sum from Mozuffur Khan, of Multan.

In August of the same year, Jymul Singh, the father-in-law of Khuruk Singh, died suddenly, and it was generally believed that his death was occasioned by poison administered by his wife. Runjeet constituted himself the heir to all the treasure accumulated by this chief during a long life of parsimony and usurious dealing. Much of his wealth was, at the time of his decease, out at interest with mahajuns of Amritsur, all of whom were called upon to account with the Lahore treasury. In the following month, the families of the two ex-Shahs of Cabul (Shah Zeman and Shah Shuja) sought an asylum at Lahore. After escaping from the unfortunate enterprise Shah Shuja had undertaken in September preceding, his person was seized by Juhan Dad Khan, the governor of Attock, by whom he was sent to his brother, Ata Mahomed, of Cashmere, who held him a close prisoner. The helpless Shah Zeman brought both families to the Sikh capital, where Runjeet Singh professed much interest in the misfortunes and fate of Shah Shuja, and seemed as if disposed to make an effort against Cashmere, to procure his liberation, and to obtain that province for him. He was then preparing an expedition against Bimbur, in the Pir-Panjal range of mountains, and the wife of Shah Shuja was led by these professions to believe, and to represent to her husband, that he would find a friend in the ruler of Lahore. The Shah made his escape from confinement during the operations subsequently undertaken against the valley by Futeh Khan Vuzeer, and was thus led to direct his flight towards Lahore. Finding an opportunity to join the force under Mohkum Chund, he came down with him to that city.

After the *Dussera*, at the close of the rains, the Sikh army was assembled, and led entire, by Runjeet in person, against the Musulman chiefs of Bimbur and Rajaoree, who, though pressed by the expeditions before directed against them, made head again, immediately the force was withdrawn, and were now assisted by a confederacy of chiefs and jagirdars of their faith, and by succour from the Governor of Cashmere. The possessions of these chiefs commanded the approaches to the Pir-Panjal mountains, and there is reason to believe that Runjeet Singh had, even at this time, an eye to the conquest of the valley of Cashmere, to which the occupation of both Bimbur and Rajaoree was a necessary preliminary. The Sikh army defeated the confederated chiefs with great loss, and Runjeet, pushing his success, occupied both Bimbur and Rajaoree in the early part of November, and received the submission of the discomfited Mahomedan chiefs of both places. The rest of the confederates were compelled to fly into Cashmere, where they were received by the governor, Ata Mahomed.

Futeh Khan, the vuzeer of Shah Muhmud, was at this time upon the Indus, whither he had come to punish the two brothers, who held Attock and Cashmere, for the assistance they had rendered to Shah Shuja, and to recover the two provinces for Cabul. He had sent forward a detachment of 8,000 Afghans to Rotas, and was already planning operations against Ata Mahomed of Cashmere, when Runjeet obtained his successes against the Bimbur and Rajaoree chiefs. It became essential that, engaged as the Lahore and Cabul forces were so closely upon the same field, the two leaders should come to a mutual explanation of their views and intentions; accordingly Runjeet Singh sent agents with an overture for this purpose, and invited the vuzeer to an interview upon the Jelum, in order that they might concert a joint expedition against Cashmere. Futeh Khan being no less desirous to come to an understanding with the Sikh, the meeting took place on the 1st December, when it was settled that Runjeet should place a force, under his dewan Mohkum Chund, at the vuzeer's disposal in the expedition he meditated, and should give every facility for the passage into Cashmere, by the passes of Rajaoree, which he had recently subdued. The aid of a detachment of Afghans, to be employed afterwards against Multan, and a share of the plunder of Cashmere, were the returns stipulated for this succour. Runjeet desired a portion of the revenues of the valley, but the politic vuzeer objected to any participation in the permanent resources of the province, and preferred agreeing to a nuzurana of nine lakhs from the spoil expected. Having on these terms secured the assistance of 12,000 Sikhs, under the Dewan Mohkum Chund, the vuzeer proceeded on his expedition, and the joint armies commenced their march, while Runjeet returned to Lahore. A heavy fall of snow impeded their progress, and the Sikhs, being less inured to the severities of a mountain winter than the northern troops, were outstripped by the vuzeer; who, penetrating into the valley in February, drove Ata Mahomed from his stockades, and in a short time reduced him to submission, and obtained all the strongholds in the province, without receiving much assistance from Mohkum Chund and the Sikhs.

Runjeet made great rejoicings at Lahore on receiving news of this success, treating the operation as a joint one, tending equally to his own as to the vuzeer's glory. A deep intrigue was, however, in progress, which the issue of the Cashmere expedition brought immediately to light. Juhan Dad Khan, the governor of Attock, despairing, after his brother's defeat in Cashmere, of his own ability to resist the vuzeer single-handed, and knowing he had little favour to expect from him, had previously placed himself in correspondence with Runjeet Singh, to whom he promised the fort of Attock for a jagir, in case he should be reduced to extremity. Runjeet, accordingly, when he returned to Lahore, left a detachment under Dya Singh in the vicinity of the Indus, to be ready to occupy that important fortress whenever it should be given up. In March, 1813, Runjeet heard that his officer had been admitted, and that the place was held and administered in his name. He accordingly lost no time in reinforcing the detachment, with a strong convoy, containing every thing necessary to place the fort in a complete state of defence, and Devi Das and Hakim Uzeez-ud-Deen were sent as commissioners to settle the country surrounding, which formed the dependency of Attock. Futeh Khan Vuzeer cried out against this usurpation, and deeming himself absolved by it from the conditions upon which he had obtained the co-operation of the Sikhs under the dewan, he dismissed them without any share of the booty obtained; and then nominating his brother, Uzeem Khan, governor in Cashmere, he marched to Attock, and made upon Runjeet a demand for its surrender. This was spun out into a negotiation—and, of course, evaded by the Sikh.

With the dewan Mohkum Chund, Shah Shuja came to Lahore, where a demand was immediately made upon him, and upon his principal wife, to surrender the famous diamond, called *koh-i-noor* or 'hill of light,' a jagir being promised with a fort as the condition of compliance. The Shah denied that he had it, and the Vufa Begum declared it had been placed in pawn with a mahajun to obtain supplies for the Shah in his distresses. Runjeet, disbelieving these assertions, placed guards round the Shah's residence, and allowed no access or egress without strict search. The exiled family, however, being proof against the severity of mere restraint, the prohibition of food was added, and for two days the Shah, with his wives, family, and servants, suffered absolute deprivation; but their firmness was even proof against this trial, and Runjeet, from a regard to his own reputation, determined to proceed with more art, and ordered food to be supplied. On the 1st of April, there were produced in his durbar two notes, purporting to be from the Shah to Futeh Khan Vuzeer, and to other Afghan chiefs, descriptive of his sufferings, and praying for their efforts for his deliverance. These were stated to have been intercepted, but were generally believed to have been fabricated. It was now assumed to be indispensable to take precautions against the intrigues and machinations of the Shah, and a guard of two companies of Sikhs, from the newly-raised corps, being added to that previously set over the premises where he resided, threats of a transfer of the Shah's person to Govindgurh, with treatment of the most galling and injurious kind, were resorted to, in order to enforce compliance with the demand for the jewel. Having tried remonstrance in vain, the Shah next resorted to artifice, and solicited two months' delay, to enable him to procure the diamond from certain mahajuns with whom it was asserted to be pledged, and he said that some lakhs of rupees must be expended to effect this. Runjeet reluctantly consented to allow the time solicited, and severities were accordingly suspended for a season. They were renewed, however, before the period expired, and Shah Shuja, wearied out by them, and seeing that the rapacity of the Sikh would not hesitate even at the sacrifice of his life for its gratification, agreed at last to give up the precious jewel.* Accordingly, on the 1st of June, Runjeet waited on the Shah, with a few attendants, to receive it. He was received by the exiled prince with much dignity, and both being seated, a pause and solemn silence ensued, which continued for nearly an hour. Runjeet then, getting impatient, whispered to one of his attendants to remind the Shah of the object of his coming. No answer was returned, but the Shah with his eyes made the signal to an eunuch, who retired, and brought in a small roll, which he set down on the carpet at equal distance between the chiefs. Runjeet desired Bhooanee Das to unfold the roll, when the diamond was exhibited, and recog-

* This diamond was one of those described by Tavernier, as adorning the peacock throne at Delhi. It is the largest known to exist, and is by Hindus supposed to have belonged to the Pandus of mythological celebrity, before it fell into the hands of the Mogul sovereigns. It is nearly an inch and a half in length, and an inch wide, and rises half an inch from its gold setting. Nadir Shah robbed the Delhi family of it, and Ahmed Shah Abdali got possession of it in the pillage of Nadir Shah's tents, after his assassination.

nized, and the Sikh immediately retired with his prize in hand. The Shah was now left more at liberty, his guard being withdrawn: a letter was, however, intercepted a few days after from Kazee Sher Mahomed, one of his followers, to Mahomed Uzeem Khan, the new governor of Cashmere, containing a proposition to assassinate Runjeet Singh, and advising the vuzeer Futeh Khan to make a simultaneous attack on Lahore. The Sikh sent for one of the princes of the exiled family, and through him transmitted the letter, with its writer, who had been seized, to the Shah. The ex-king sent both back, begging of Runjeet to punish the kazee as he might deem fitting. In the idea, that a confession of the Shah's privity would be extorted, the guard on duty were desired to beat the kazee with their shoes and with sticks. He fainted under the blows, declaring, however, to the last, his master's entire innocence. He was then committed to prison, whence Shah Shuja, after a time, purchased his release by a payment of 20,000 rupees.

Futteh Khan Vuzeer, after his return from

Cashmere, had sat down before Attock, and pending the negotiation at Lahore, upon his demand for its surrender, closely blockaded the fort. Dewan Mohkum Chund had been sent to the vicinity, and in the beginning of July, intelligence was received from him, that the garrison was reduced to such straits for supplies, that, unless very shortly relieved, they must surrender. Runjeet held a council upon this, and it was determined to relieve the fort, even at the risk of the attempt producing hostilities with the vuzeer. Orders to this effect were accordingly sent immediately to the dewan, who, being encamped at Boorhan, marched at break of day, on the 12th July, 1813, to execute them. On that day, he made a short march to an outpost on a rivulet, held by a piquet of the vuzeer's army, which retired in the night. The dewan marched again next morning leisurely along the rivulet, that his men might drink, and be always fresh for action, the weather being extremely hot. At ten in the morning, he came to the Indus, at about five miles from the fort. The Cabul army was here drawn up to oppose his further advance, its van being composed of a body of Moolkea Musulmans, supported by a body of cavalry under the since celebrated Dost Mahomed Khan. The dewan took up his ground, forming his cavalry in four divisions, and the only battalion of infantry that had yet come up, in square. The Moolkeas immediately made a resolute charge on the battalion, but were received with so heavy a rolling fire as to be driven back with severe loss. The dewan ordered up for the support of his battalion some fresh troops and artillery, under Ghousee Khan, which had come in sight; but his order was not obeyed. Dost Mahomed now attacked with his horse, and the Sikhs were sinking before him, when the dewan, in person, on his elephant, carried up two guns, which, discharging grape, checked the Afghans. By this time it was noon; the heat of the sun had become intense, and a strong hot wind blew the dust into the faces of the Afghans. Under these disadvantages, the vuzeer did not think proper to carry the troops he had in reserve into action, and those who had been engaged being exhausted, the battle ceased. The vuzeer retired across the Indus to Peshawur, leaving the dewan free to relieve the fort, which having effected, Mohkum Chund returned to Lahore in August, to receive the reward of his service, and to prefer his complaint against the officers, whose disobedience had so nearly proved fatal. They received the punishment attaching to correspondence with the enemy, which was detected as the motive of their so critically holding back from the action.

Toward the close of the rains of 1813, Runjeet commenced preparation for an expedition into Cashmere. In October he visited Juwala Mookhee and Kangra, and thence marched by Seal-Kot and Vuzeerabad to the Jelum, where he summoned all his jagirdars, and all the tributary hill chiefs, to be in attendance with their respective quotas. Strict muster was taken of each party as it arrived, and fines were imposed if the number was short, or the equipment in any respect deficient. Great preparation had also been made to bring an effective artillery into the field, and to improve that mounted on camels, and the whole having been reviewed, Runjeet Singh, on the 11th November, crossed the Jelum, and entered the town of Rotas. The vuzeer Futteh Khan was brought from Peshawur by these preparations to the Derajat, on the west bank of the Indus, which circumstance, added to intelligence, that the snow lay still deep on the Pir-Panjal mountains, induced Runjeet to suspend his proposed expedition until the following spring. He accordingly sent a detachment to occupy and seize the passes in the hills beyond Rajaoree, and to select places for grain and store-depôts, and then returned by Rotas to Lahore, where he arrived on the 26th of December.

The confiscation of the hill territory of Huripur, and its annexation to the Lahore Khalsa (fisc), was the first act which marked the return of the Sikh ruler to his capital. Bhoop Singh, the raja, whose treacherous seizure and confinement preceded the confiscation, received on its completion a small jagir for subsistence. The next act of Runjeet Singh was more shamelessly extortionate. Hearing that Shah Shuja had still some jewels of rare value, a demand was made for them;

and, on the Shah's declaring that he had none left, the Sikh determined to judge for himself, and sending Bhya Ram Singh, with a party of females, to search the interior apartments, caused to be brought into his presence every box or packet the Shah possessed. The Shah's head eunuch was then made to open them, and Runjeet seized and retained for himself all the most precious articles, with the swords, pistols, and two cart-loads of carpets, and women's dresses. The Shah was then ordered to remove from the Shahlemar garden and palace to a common house in the city, and was subjected there to strict surveillance. After experiencing every kind of indignity and discomfort, he determined to attempt an escape with his family. Towards the end of November, it was reported to Runjeet, that the begums of Shah Shuja were missing, whereupon the Shah's person was placed under a guard, and alternate threats and promises were employed to induce him to declare where they were gone. He denied all knowledge of their motions or intentions. The city was searched, and egress forbidden to all veiled women, and all merchants having property of the Shah's, or of any members of his family, in deposit, were ordered to surrender it into the Sikh treasury. These precautions were, however, taken too late. It was ascertained that the begums had left the house of Shah Shuja in the dress of Hindu females, and thence had been conveyed to the banking house of Baluk Ram, the agent or correspondent of Soogun Chund, a great banker at Delhi, and treasurer of the British residency there; that by him they had been assisted in passing out of the city, and provided with the means of making their way to Lodiana, where they had arrived safely, and making themselves known to Captain Birch, the assistant, in temporary charge of the station, were received with hospitality and attention. Baluk Ram was seized by Runjeet, and compelled to shew his books, and render up all property in his possession belonging to the Shah or his family. He received, however, no further punishment.

In April, 1815, Shah Shuja himself made his escape in disguise. His guard was disgraced, and a reward offered for recovery of the prisoner, who succeeded in reaching the hills, where he was hospitably received by the petty Raja of Kishtewar. Here he collected a body of 3,000 men, and in the winter season made an attempt on Cashmere: but the cold prevented his passing the Pir-Panjal range, and his troops dispersed. His condition was now desperate, but after a long and circuitous journey over the Kooloo mountains, with few attendants, and fewer comforts, he at last, in September, 1816, joined his family at Lodiana, and placed himself under the protection of the British government. A provision of 50,000 rs. per annum was assigned for the maintenance of the Shah in his exile, while he might remain in the British territory. He was afterwards joined at Lodiana by his sightless brother, Shah Zeman, whom with his family already in abject poverty, Runjeet took no trouble to detain. To this prince a separate allowance of 24,000 rs. per annum was assigned.

The chronological order of events has been somewhat anticipated, in order to bring the misfortunes of these princes into one connected relation. The first expedition of Runjeet against Cashmere will take us back into the year 1814. The events, however, which preceded or attended it, will more fitly form the subject of another chapter.

CHAPTER XIII.

A.D. 1814 TO 1818.

RUNJEET SINGH, having celebrated the *Hooli*, and bathed at Amritsur, moved his army, in April, 1814, into the hill country about Kangra, to enforce the collection of his tributes, and the personal attendance of the rajas with their contingents. Having thus strengthened himself with a large body of hill-men, he moved to Bimbur on the 4th June; and, advancing slowly from thence, was met by Agur Khan, the chief of Rajaoree, through whose territory lay the route to Cashmere. On the 11th June, the army arrived at Rajaoree, and disencumbering itself of heavy baggage, was equipped for mountain movements, preparatory to the passage of the famous Pir-Panjal range. An attempt had been made to gain the Poonch raja, Rooh-ullah Khan, to the Sikh cause; but he pleaded engagements with Cashmere, and the presence of his son as a hostage with Uzeem Khan, the governor. After a consultation of the principal officers, however, it was determined, nevertheless, that the main army, commanded by Runjeet in person, should pursue the Poonch route, and endeavour to penetrate by the Toshu Mydan pass, while a strong diversion should be made by Buhramgulla (or Baramulla), towards Soopyn, in the valley.

The cavalry being dismounted, and every man furnished with provisions for three days, a detachment was formed and sent forward, on the 15th June, under Ram Dyal, a grandson of Mohkum Chund Dewan, with whom were Dul Singh and other jagirdars. They appeared before the post at Buhramgulla on the 18th, and after a little negotiation, obtained possession of the pass, on payment to the defenders of the arrears due to them by the Poonch raja. Heavy rain set in on the 20th June, and the Sikh army beginning to suffer from the wet and cold, and the supplies already running short, the march of the main body was delayed until the 26th. On the 28th, however, Runjeet reached Poonch, and found it evacuated; the raja having given orders to his people to attempt no resistance, but to desert their towns and villages, to bury or remove the grain, and to hover in small parties on the flanks of the invaders. The consequences of this system had already begun to be felt, and compelled a halt at Poonch, for further supplies, until the 13th July. Thence advancing by Mundee, Runjeet reached Toshu Mydan on the 18th, where he found Mahomed Uzeem Khan, with the forces of Cashmere, drawn up to oppose his progress. The Sikh army took up its position in face of the enemy, and remained for some days inactive. Here Runjeet received intelligence from the detachment at Buhramgulla. On the 19th July, Ram Dyal and the jagirdars ascended the Pir-Panjal mountains, by the Surae and Mudpoor pass, driving before them the Cashmere troops left to defend it. Runjeet was uneasy at this precipitancy, thinking his detachment out of reach of support, and liable to be overpowered; he sent off immediately, therefore, a reinforcement under Bhya Ram Singh. The Rajaoree chief recommended an attack of

Uzeem Khan, as the best means of preventing his undertaking any thing against the detachment; but Runjeet, having reconnoitred the position, deemed the attack too hazardous. It is probably the only thing that would have prevented the disasters which followed.

In the mean time, Ram Dyal, having passed the mountain barrier, and debouched upon the valley at Heerapur, was attacked, on the 22nd July, by a party sent against him by Uzeem Khan. The Cashmerians were defeated and followed to Soopyn. On the 24th, Ram Dyal assaulted the town; but it was well defended by Shukoor Khan, and the assailants were repulsed; whereupon the Sikhs retired again to the Pir-Panjal mountains, to wait for reinforcements. Bhya Ram Singh, hearing of this discomfiture, deemed it necessary to halt at Buhramgulla, with the support he was bringing up, in order to secure the pass.

Mahomed Uzeem Khan, seeing matters in this critical position, thought the time favourable for offensive operations against the main army, which had already suffered much from sickness, and more from desertion. On the 29th of July, Roohullah Khan, the Poonch chief, approached, and commenced a desultory fire on the Sikh position. On the following morning, he renewed his attack with more vigour, and Runjeet was compelled to fall back on Mundee. Being pursued thither, he fired the town, and, directing his disciplined battalions to cover the retreat, continued his retrograde march to Poonch, which he reached on the 31st of July, with the loss of many men, and his principal officer, Mit Singh Buhranea, and stripped of nearly all his baggage. The army was now no longer in a state of organization or discipline, and, setting fire to Poonch, Runjeet quitted the camp and continued his flight to Bhoohi, whence he with a few attendants took the nearest route to Lahore, which he reached on the 12th of August.

Ram Dyal and the jagirdars serving with him, in the detachment which had penetrated into the valley, were surrounded, and their supplies were cut off; but the detachment was allowed by Uzeem Khan to retire, and was furnished with a safe conduct to the Sikh frontier, in consideration of the friendship professed by this governor for Dewan Mohkum Chund, its commandant's grandfather. That distinguished officer of Runjeet Singh had himself been prevented by indisposition from taking part in the expedition. He warned his master, however, of the difficulties he must expect if he allowed himself to be overtaken in the hills by the rainy season, and particularly pointed out the necessity of providing large depôts in Bimbur and Rajaoree, in anticipation of a determined opposition from the Musulman chief, and the whole population of Poonch. All had happened exactly as he predicted, and the ruler of Lahore returned to lament the want of his Dewan's experience and judgment, no less than of his tried skill and valour, in this important expedition. The illness, however, which prevented him from accompanying the Sikh army increased, and in the course of October, soon after the return of Runjeet to Lahore, he died, amidst the regrets and lamentations of all well-wishers to the power of the Sikhs, and to the dominion of Runjeet Singh. In his private character the Dewan was liberal, upright, and high-minded; he enjoyed the confidence of the troops placed under his command, and was popular and much respected amongst the entire Sikh community.

The losses sustained by Runjeet in this expedition required some time to repair. The Sikh army was not, therefore, in a condition to take the field at the close of the *Dussera* of 1814, as usual; but in April, 1815, a force was employed, under Ram Dyal and Dul Singh, ravaging the Multan and Bahawulpur territories, and exacting tributes and contributions in that neighbourhood. Runjeet himself passed the hot weather at Adenanugur, raising and disciplining new battalions; and especially recruiting men of the Goorkha nation, of whose valour he began to entertain a very high opinion, from having watched the operations which, during the season, had passed in the hill country east of the Sutluj. The British Government had engaged in hostilities with the Goorkhas, and Colonel (afterwards General) Ochterlony had taken the field there against Umur Singh, who, for six months, maintained himself at Ramgurh and Maloun, and baffled the known skill and superior forces of this experienced commander. His final discomfiture, and the dispossession of the Goorkhas from all the hill territory west of the Gogra or Kalee river, occasioned a breaking up of their power, which was highly favourable to Runjeet's views, and procured him many men of this nation particularly well adapted for hill warfare.

In the mean time, the defeat of the Sikh expedition against Cashmere encouraged the Musulman chiefs of Bimbur and Rajaoree to break out into rebellion, and towards the close of the year 1814, the son of the latter, who was detained as a hostage at Lahore, effected his escape and joined his father. The Bimbur insurgents were headed by the brother of Sooltan Khan, who, since he made his submission in 1813, had been himself detained by Runjeet Singh, and was now a close prisoner at Lahore.

In October, after the *Dussera* of 1815, the Sikh army was called out, and its rendezvous for muster appointed at Sealkot. A division was sent in advance under Ram Dyal and Dul Singh to punish the Bimbur and Rajaoree chiefs, and to ravage their territories with fire and sword. Poonch was saved from a similar visitation by its greater elevation, and by the setting in of winter with severity. Runjeet was not yet prepared for an attempt to retrieve his fortune and lost reputation, by another expedition against Cashmere. He was content, therefore, to employ the season in confirming his authority in the hills before subdued, and in punishing the disobedient and refractory rajas and chiefs on this side the Pir-Panjal range. He returned to Lahore on the 28th December, where he was waited upon by Beer Singh, the Raja of Noorpur, in the hills, who had failed to attend the summons to rendezvous at Sealkot. A heavy mulct was imposed, which being beyond the chief's means, he offered his thakoors, or household gods, of silver and gold, in pawn; but, these not sufficing, he was arrested at the door of the durbar, or hall of audience, on the 20th January, 1816, and next day was sent off in a palkee to witness the seizure and confiscation of his all, and to render an account to the sequestrators. He declined the petty jagir offered to him for subsistence, and, after a fruitless attempt to recover his fortress and territory by force, took refuge within the British territory. A second example was made of the Raja of Juswoul, Omed Singh, for a similar failure. Being stripped of his possessions, however, he accepted the jagir tendered.

After completing his arrangements in the hills, Runjeet, having bathed at Turun-Tarun, moved with his army into the territories of Multan and Bahawulpur, where the still unripe crops and abundant herds presented the means of enforcing contributions or inflicting irremediable injury. The Sikh detachments penetrated down the Indus, to the verge of the Sinde territory, and Mahomed Khan, chief of Bukur and Leah, of the family ejected by the meers of Sinde, having recently died, a demand of tribute was made on his successor, Hafiz Ahmed Khan. On his refusal, his forts, Khangurh and Muhmudkot, were occupied, and Phoola Singh

Akali was allowed to perpetrate there atrocities and insults to the Mahomedan population of the most revolting description. Hafiz Ahmed soon after paid down a sum of money to procure the withdrawing of the Sikh garrisons, and thus recovered his forts, with part also of the plunder extorted. Ahmed Khan, of Jhung, was now summoned to the presence, and called upon for a large contribution. On pleading inability, he was sent prisoner to Lahore, while three battalions proceeded to occupy and annex to the Khalsa the whole of his possessions, reckoned to yield about four lakhs of yearly revenue. They were farmed to Lala Sookh-Dyal for 1,60,000 rupees. Futeh Singh Aloowala was at the same time employed in seizing Ooch and Kot-Maharaja, the first held by Syuds, who had hitherto been respected, and were now provided with a jagir; and the second by a chief named Rujub Ali Khan, who was sent prisoner to Lahore.

Runjeet Singh returned from the south-west, and re-entered his capital on the 20th May. Here he learned that the Vuzeer Futeh Khan had employed the season in a march across the Pukholee and Dumtour hills, into Cashmere, where he aided his brother in enforcing the collections, and establishing his authority in the valley, and then returned by the same route. The Sikh detachment, under Ram Dyal and Dul Singh, had remained upon the frontier to watch his motions.

A domestic matter now occupied the attention of Runjeet. His second wife, the mother of Koonwur Khuruk Singh, was accused of scandalous improprieties, and particularly, of too notorious and close an intimacy with Bhya Ram Singh, the Koonwur's dewan. Runjeet had lavished much territory in jagir upon the heir-apparent, and the management was undertaken by his mother and the dewan, upon the usual condition of maintaining an efficient contingent of horse for service with the Sikh army. Complaint, however, was loud and frequent, that the jagirs were the scene of extortion and mismanagement, while the condition and equipment of the Koonwur's contingent was deemed by Runjeet highly discreditable. He first endeavoured to procure a reform by exciting the pride of his son, who was of age to take an interest in such things; but the influence of the mother and dewan preventing any amendment, the Sikh ruler was at length compelled to interfere more authoritatively. The Dewan Ram Singh was thrown into confinement, and ordered to account for his stewardship of the jagirs, and the Koonwur's mother was directed to fix her residence in the fort of Shekhoopur. Khuruk Singh was reprimanded for allowing such proceedings; and Bhooanee Das, of Peshawur, was assigned to him as a new dewan. Several lakhs of rupees, and some valuable jewels, were extorted from Ram Singh, whose banker, Ootum Chund, of Amritsur, was also called to account, and made to refund what he held for the ex-dewan.

After the *Dussera* in October, Runjeet's first journey was into the hills, where he paid a visit to Raja Sunsar Chund, at Nadoun, and collected his yearly tributes; thence returning, he effected the confiscation of the jagirs and territories of Beer Singh and Dewan Singh, two brothers of the late Jodh Singh Ramgurhea, valued at five lakhs of rupees yearly revenue. The persons of both chiefs were seized, as they came to the durbar to pay their respects, without suspicion that any design against them was entertained by the Lahore ruler. Amritsur was illuminated for the return of its sovereign, on the 13th of December.

The constitution of Runjeet, though it must have been excellent to have carried him so long through a course of life consisting of alternate toils and debaucheries, each extreme in degree, began now to yield to these incessant trials. His digestion failed, and with loss of strength, thinness of body and incapacity for much exertion were superinduced. Towards the commencement of 1817 his health was seriously impaired, and he submitted to a course of regimen prescribed by his native physicians, which continued for forty days, but produced in the end little permanent benefit. No military enterprise or other active operation was undertaken in this year. The Sikh ruler's principal source of anxiety, in the course of it, arose from an attachment to Ram Lal, the brother of his chamberlain, Khooshal Singh, upon whom such unlimited bounties had been lavished, and who had become the great court favourite, and the bottle companion of his master. Ram Lal could not be induced by the most seductive offers to give up his Braminical thread, and adopt the Sikh ritual and customs, as his brother had done. In order to avoid further importunity on the subject, he fled to his home east of the Sutluj, where he was beyond the reach of the Lahore ruler, who, provoked that he should have escaped, wreaked a real or pretended vengeance on his chamberlain, by removing him from office, and placing him under restraint. Ram Lal returned for his brother's sake, and ultimately received the *pahal*, or Sikh initiation, and changed his name to Ram Singh.

The following season was employed in preparation for an expedition against Multan, of which the resources had been annually drained by forced contributions, ravage, and waste, so as to lead Runjeet to hope that Mozuffur Khan's means of defence and preparation were now so impaired, as to make the city and fort an easy conquest. Before undertaking this enterprise, however, Runjeet gave liberty to Ahmed Khan, of Jhung, whom he had held in close confinement for nine months. A small jagir was assigned to him for subsistence. The Sikh army had been ordered to rendezvous, in the beginning of the year 1818, on the south-west frontier of the Sikh dominion. Koonwur Khuruk Singh was now appointed to the nominal command, aided by Misur Dewan Chund, who had risen by his merit and activity from a low situation to be commandant of the artillery, and who undertook to reduce the fort of Multan, if vested with the chief command during the siege. The jealousy of the jagirdars, who objected to serve under a man of yesterday, obliged Runjeet to adopt the plan of sending his heir-apparent in nominal command of the whole.

All the boats on the Ravi and Chenab were put in requisition to carry supplies and stores for the army; and the march was commenced in January, 1818. A demand was made of an exorbitant sum in cash and of five of Mozuffur Khan's best horses, and this not being immediately complied with, his two forts of Mozuffurgurh and Khangurh were stormed and taken. In the course of February, the city of Multan was occupied, and its citadel closely invested, without much loss. The approaches were made according to no consistent plan, but every jagirdar and chief erected his own battery, and a promiscuous fire was kept up from guns and small arms against every part of the defences. The means of the garrison were, however, so deficient, that even under this irregular method of attack, the wall of the citadel was, by the continual fire kept up, breached in several places, and the upper works and defences were nearly demolished in the course of the month of April. In May the approaches were carried close to the *dhool-kot*, or fausse braye of the works, and the army became eager to be led to the storm; but Runjeet, who, though absent, regulated every thing connected with the siege, forbade any risk being run, and continued his offer to the Nuwab of a jagir, if he would surrender. He was obstinate in his refusal, and seemed determined to hold out to the last extremity. While matters continued in this state, an

Akali fanatic, named Sadhoo Singh (drugged, it is said, with opium), on the 2nd of June, advanced without orders, with a few companions, and attacked, sword in hand, the Afghans in the dhool-kot, who, being at the time asleep or negligent, were overpowered. The men in the Sikh trenches, seeing this, advanced simultaneously, on the impulse of the moment, to support the attack, and the entire outwork was carried with a slaughter of those defending it. Flushed with this success, the assailants attempted the fort, and found ready entrance by the breaches made, the garrison not expecting assault, nor being prepared for a consistent and determined resistance. The citadel was thus suddenly carried, Mozuffur Khan, with his four sons and household, made a final stand at the door of his residence, but fell covered with wounds. Two of his sons, Shah Nuwaz Khan and Huq Nuwaz, were also killed on the spot, and a third was left badly wounded. Surfuraz Khan, the fourth, who had been vested by his father with the government under himself, was found in a vault, or cellar, and taken prisoner. The citadel was now sacked, and an immense booty fell to the troops engaged in the assault. Runjeet Singh, however, was not content that his treasury should be defrauded of the wealth known to have been laid up in this citadel, and which he had long coveted and hoped to have secured by a surrender on capitulation. He accordingly issued peremptory orders for the immediate return of the whole army to Lahore, with the exception of a detachment under Jodh Singh Kulsea, of sufficient strength to hold the place, and conduct the local administration. Sookh Dyal, who had taken the farm of Jhung, as above stated, was nominated to the civil government. Upon the arrival of the army at Lahore, proclamation was made, that the plunder of Multan was the property of the state, and all soldiers, officers, or jagirdars, possessing any article of spoil, or any money obtained in the sack of the fort, were ordered to bring the same in, and to account for the whole to the treasury, under penalty of heavy mulct, or confinement. It affords a strong proof of the awe, in which the power and sources of information possessed by Runjeet Singh, were held by his troops, that this order produced no outrage or general resistance. Most of the spoil was traced and collected for the treasury, and, though rendered up with much discontent, and with many efforts at concealment, still the severities practised on the obstinate, and the mutual jealousies and envy of their fellows, felt by those who had been compelled to disgorge, led generally to the discovery of all that was valuable; so that the *toshuk-khana*, or jewel-office, of the Lahore ruler, was enriched by this respoliation of the troops. There is but one example of similar audacity in a commander, and that was the terrible Nadir Shah, who, upon his return from India, when his army was crossing the Attock, placed a guard at the ferry, and as every one came over, searched his person and baggage, for every article of the spoil of Delhi, that the soldiers or followers of his army might have secured.

Surfuraz Khan, and his wounded brother, Zoolfikar Khan, were conducted to Lahore, where Runjeet assigned them a small stipend for subsistence. The capture of Multan was the only operation of the season, the whole Sikh army having been employed against the place since January, and the rains having set in as it fell. During that season, Govind Chund, Raja of Datarpur, in the hills, dying, his territory was annexed to the Khalsa, and his son was held in durance until he consented to accept a jagir.

This season of necessary inactivity produced, however, another event of great influence on the future fortune of Runjeet Singh. In the month of August, 1818, the vuzeer Futteh Khan, whose energy and talents had raised Shah Mahmud to the throne of Cabul, and who alone kept together the turbulent and discordant materials of which the Afghan empire had been composed, was plotted against by the Prince Kamran, the son of Mahmud, and, being treacherously seized, was first blinded, and soon after put to death by his order. The vuzeer had fifty brothers, all at the head of governments, or otherwise in the possession of power and wealth, and the cry to vengeance was general throughout the kingdom. Mahomed Uzeem posted from Cashmere, leaving a younger brother, Jubur Khan, in the valley. Taking the direction of the measures of resistance organized, he defeated the troops of Kamran, and dislodged his garrisons from the neighbourhood of Cabul, Ghuzni, and Candahar, so that in a few months the authority of the weak Shah Mahmud, and his rash, ill-advised son, was confined to the city and plain of Herat, and the rest of the Afghan territory was assumed and portioned out in separate governments and independent principalities, by the powerful members of this extensive family. The plea put forward by Kamran for his conduct towards the vuzeer Futteh Khan, was, his having plundered the property of Feroz-ud-deen, a prince of the blood royal, whom he expelled from the government of Herat, in order to recover it for Mahmud. The real cause, however, was jealousy of his power and reputation, and the vain conceit entertained by Kamran, that the vuzeer's abilities could be dispensed with, and affairs conducted as well by the household and family of the imbecile nominal sovereign.

The intelligence of these events determined Runjeet to carry his army across the Indus in the ensuing season, more especially as a detachment of Sikhs had recently been overpowered by the Khutuk Musulmans, and every motive of policy required that this should not pass unrevenged. The troops, having been called out in October, advanced to Attock, under Runjeet's personal command, and the river being forded with some loss, the fortress of Khyrabad, with Jugheera, and the territory on the opposite bank, were reduced and occupied. No immediate resistance was offered; Feroz Khan, the chief of the Khutuk tribe, made his submission, and Runjeet, having ascertained that no organized force was in the field to oppose him, directed an advance on Peshawur. The city was entered on the 20th November, Yar Mahomed Khan, the governor, retiring, as the Sikhs advanced, into the mountains occupied by the Yusufzai tribes of Afghans.

Runjeet Singh remained with his army three days in Peshawur, and then returned, leaving as governor on his behalf, Juhan Dad Khan, to whose treachery he was indebted for the possession of Attock, but whom he had left unrewarded hitherto, and without the promised jagir. He furnished him, however, with neither troops, nor money, to maintain the possession. Accordingly, the Sikh army had no sooner crossed the Indus on its return, than Yar Mahomed came down from the mountains with the Yusufzais, and expelled the Sikh governor: Juhan Dad Khan fled to the southward, and there fell in with Shah Shuja, whom the state of affairs in Cabul had tempted from Lodiana again to try his fortune. From him he received a free pardon, and joined his standard. The curse of Fate was, however, on every enterprise undertaken by this prince, whose character, though amiable in many respects, and irreproachable in all, possessed not the energy to inspire awe and attach followers in troubled times, or to give confidence to those disposed otherwise to favour his cause. Shah Shuja returned destitute to Lodiana, after a few months of vain wandering, and fruitless negotiation with the Meers of Sinde, and other quondam tributaries and dependants of the Afghan empire; and Juhan Dad Khan then made his peace with the court of Herat, and proceeded thither, despairing of obtaining favour or advancement at that of Lahore.

CHAPTER XIV.

A.D. 1819 TO 1822.

In February and March, 1819, Desa Singh Majhitea was employed by Runjeet Singh, with Raja Sunsar Chund, in collecting the hill tributes. In the course of their operations they came in contact with the Raja of Kuhlur, whose capital, Belaspur, is on the British side of the Sutluj, but who held at that time extensive possessions north and west of that river. This chief refusing the tribute demanded, Desa Singh marched to occupy his territory, and having dispossessed him of all he held on the right bank of the boundary river of British protection, sent a detachment across it against Belaspur. Captain Ross, the political agent in the adjoining hills, and commandant of a battalion of Goorkha light troops, stationed at Subathoo, marched immediately to the point threatened, and was joined there by a detachment from Lodiana, ordered out by the resident at Delhi. This promptitude alarmed the Sikh ruler, and Desa Singh was ordered not only to recall his detachment, but to wait upon Captain Ross, and offer every explanation and apology in his power.

Nothing material occurred in the early part of this year, but the season was occupied in preparation for a second expedition against Cashmere. To this Runjeet Singh was encouraged partly by his recent success against Multan, which had given him confidence in his troops, and had added largely to their reputation, but mainly by the state of the Afghan power, and the knowledge, that Mahomed Uzeem Khan was absent and had carried with him the most efficient troops in the valley, to forward his other designs. Misur Dewan Chund, the conqueror of Multan, was selected by Runjeet to command the present expedition, the Sikh ruler being determined to remain within his own frontier, influenced partly by his bodily infirmities, partly by a superstitious notion that fortune and fate were against his personal success in the valley, but mainly perhaps by the knowledge, that the more important task of expediting supplies, and supporting the armies operating in advance, could best be performed by himself.

In the month of April, the Sikh army marched towards the frontier, and a select and strong division was formed there, under the Misur's command, to lead the advance. A second army, to support this officer, was placed under the command of Koonwur Khuruk Singh; while Runjeet kept with himself a reserve, to be employed as occasion might require in expediting stores and supplies.

By the beginning of June, Misur Dewan Chund had occupied Rajaoree and Poonch, and all the hills and passes south of the Pir-Panjal range. The supporting division was accordingly advanced to Rajaoree, to keep open the communications. The chief of this last place was in rebellion, and acting with the Raja of Poonch in the defence of the Pir-Panjal passes. Runjeet, however, had given liberty to Sooltan Khan, of Bimbur, after a confinement of seven years, and had secured his advice and co-operation, by holding out hopes of extensive benefit to him from the success of the enterprise. On the 23rd June, the Misur attacked the Rajaoree and Poonch rajas, in their position at the Dhaki Deo and Maja passes, and carried them, thus securing to himself a road over the Pir-Panjal. Khuruk Singh, with his division, advanced now to Surdee Thana, and Runjeet, with his reserves, came up as far as Bimbur, while Misur Dewan Chund, crossing the barrier mountains, descended into the valley, and took up a position at Surai Ali, on the road to Soopyn.

Jubur Khan, who had been left by Mahomed Uzeem governor in Cashmere, was at Soopyn, with 5,000 men, to make his stand for possession of the valley. The troops he had, however, were raw, and unable to compete with the disciplined battalions led by Misur Dewan Chund, which besides outnumbered them greatly. On the 5th July, having been furnished with supplies and reinforcements from the rear, the Misur advanced to Soopyn, and immediately on coming in view of the Cashmerian army, ordered an attack, which, after a few hours of smart fighting, attended with considerable loss on both sides, was completely successful. The Afghans and troops of Jubur Khan fled at once across the mountains, towards the Indus, leaving the valley to be occupied without further opposition by the victorious army of Runjeet Singh. Great was the joy of this chief at his success. The cities of Lahore and of Amritsur were illuminated for three nights, and Motee Ram, son of the late Dewan Mohkum Chund, was sent as governor of the valley, accompanied by a strong body of troops, for the reduction of Derbend and other strongholds; and with instructions to spare no effort to bring the Poonch and Rajaoree chiefs to make their submission.

The arrangements consequent upon the subjugation of Cashmere occupied Runjeet for the remainder of the year 1819. Towards its close, the Sikh army was again called out, and led by him in person to Multan, whence operations were directed for ravaging the territories of the Nuwab of Bahawulpur, and southward as far as Bukur, belonging to the Meers of Sinde, with a view to extort augmented tribute and contributions. Dera Ghazee Khan, on the west bank of the Indus, was at the same time wrested from its governor, Zeman Khan, and, in the settlement made with the Bahawulpur chief, the place was given to him in farm at a heavy rent.

Runjeet returned to Lahore in April, 1820, bringing with him a horse of high repute, that he had extorted from Hafiz Ahmed Khan of Munkera. Many subsequent enterprises were undertaken for similar animals; the love for them, and the desire to possess all of any repute for excellence, being a growing passion carried by the Sikh chief almost to folly. The horse acquired in this instance bore the name of *Soofed-puri*.

In Cashmere the troops were employed in petty operations against isolated chiefs. One of these, Sher Zeman Khan of Gundgurh, having risen in rebellion, Ram Dyal, the governor's son, and the grandson of the late Dewan Mohkum Chund, was employed against him, and unfortunately met his death in an action, which was a source of deep regret to Runjeet Singh, no less than to his father Motee Ram, and of general sympathy with all; for he was a rising officer of great promise in the Sikh army. The Raja of Rajaoree, Agur Khan, was in May made prisoner by Golab Singh, brother of Meean Dheean Singh, the *deohrewala*, or lord of privy chambers, of the Lahore court. For this service, the family obtained, in jagir, the principality of Jummoo, with which they had long been connected. In June, the troops employed in Cashmere, having suffered much from sickness, were relieved, and the governor, Motee Ram, who was of pacific devotional habits, was changed for a more martial chief, Huree Singh Nalooa, a Sikh jagirdar, who had killed a tiger single-handed on horseback, with the sacrifice, however, of his horse.

In this season, the court of Lahore received two visitors, one the ex-Raja of Nagpoor, Moodaji Bhoosla, commonly called Apa Saheb, who escaped as a fugitive, in disguise, after the campaign which ended in the capture of Aseergurh and reduced the last Mahratta opponent in arms of the British supremacy in India. He resided some time at Amritsur, while Runjeet was with his army to the south-west, but on his return, the fugitive was required to quit the capital and dominions of the Sikh, whereupon he retired to seek refuge in the hills with Raja Sunsar Chund. There, engaging in some intrigue with the Cabul princes at Lodiana, he was required by the Raja to leave his court, and he proceeded to Mundee, where the chief, Eeshuree Sein, gave him temporary protection. The other visitor was the superintendent of the Company's studs in India, the adventurous British traveller, Mr. Moorcroft, who passed through Lahore on his route to Ladakh, as a merchant proceeding to purchase horses in Bokhara. He was received with much civility and attention by the Sikh, and from Ladakh, which he reached by way of Mundee, made good his route across the northern mountains into Cashmere.

After October the muster of the Sikh army was taken at Seal-kot, whither Runjeet proceeded by the route of Batala. Thence, skirting the hills, and sending detachments against the turbulent Chib-

Bhao tribe, to ravage their possessions, he proceeded to Rawul Pindi, and dispossessing the chief, Nund Singh, annexed it to the Khalsa. He returned to Lahore on the 13th of December, and for the rest of the season was occupied chiefly in domestic arrangements.

Sher Singh, the eldest of the children brought forward by Suda Koonwur, had been adopted, and brought up by her with great expectations. He was now approaching man's estate, and began to be clamorous for a jagir and separate establishment. Runjeet encouraged him in this, hoping that the Rani would make a suitable provision from the possessions of the Ghunee Sirdaree, in her management. She, however, desired to force the recognition of Sher Singh, and the provision, on Runjeet, who obstinately refused, and craftily fomenting the dispute between Sher and his adoptive mother, gained over Bysakh Singh, an old and highly confidential retainer of the Ghunees, who was in great trust with Suda Koonwur. After this intrigue had been carrying on for some time, and Sher Singh's complaints had made an impression unfavourable to Suda Koonwur, Runjeet thought matters ripe for an authoritative act of interference on his part. He accordingly sent to his mother-in-law an order, in October, 1820, to set apart half of her own jagir for the maintenance of the two youths, Sher Singh and Tara Singh, whom she had brought up with such high expectations. She remonstrated in vain, and being herself in the Sikh camp, then at Shah-Dehra, and consequently in the power of Runjeet Singh, she felt the necessity of complying so far as to execute a deed, making the assignment required. But she had no sooner done so, than she plotted the means of escape, and after a time left the camp secretly in a covered carriage. Intelligence of her evasion was conveyed to Runjeet by Bysakh Singh. Desa Singh was accordingly sent with a detachment of horse to bring her back, and she was committed, by her son-in-law's order, to close confinement. Not content with this punishment, Runjeet ordered a division of his army to march and sequester all her wealth and territory, and this was effected, after a resistance of a few weeks, by one of her female attendants, who was in charge of the fort of Attul-gurh, her principal stronghold. Thus, after an influence maintained for nearly thirty years, fell at last this high-spirited woman. She had been serviceable to Runjeet Singh, indeed was the main stay of his power, in the early part of his career, and it was through her intrigues and aid that he was able to assume authority so early, and to put aside his mother and her dewan. The independence she asserted, and the high tone she was accustomed to assume, had for some time been irksome to the Sikh ruler in his growing fortunes, and her ruin was prepared by the course of events, no less than by her own unbending disposition. She bore the restraint of her confinement with great impatience, continually beating her breast in lamentation, and venting imprecations on the head of her ungrateful son-in-law.

Another domestic event, which preceded the catastrophe of Suda Koonwur's fall, was the birth of a son to Koonwur Khuruk Singh. The event took place in February, 1821, and was the occasion of great festivity and rejoicing; the child was called Nou-Nehal Singh. In April, Runjeet moved to Adenanugur, and remained there till July, occupied in collecting the hill tributes. The two petty territories of Kishtewar and Man-Kot were, in this interval, annexed to the Khalsa. The harshness of Huree Singh having made him unpopular and obnoxious to the inhabitants of Cashmere, he had been removed in December, 1820, and the mild and peaceable Motee Ram was re-appointed governor.

The above events having occupied the hot season and rains of 1821, the Sikh army was called out, as usual, after the Dussera, and Runjeet, taking the command in person, led it to the Indus, into the possessions of the chief of Munkera, Bukur, and Lea, south of Multan. Annual contributions and forced presents had for some time been extorted from Hafiz Ahmed, the nuwab: it was now determined to assume possession of the whole of his country. With this view, the army, marching by Ram-Nugur, Nur-Meanee, Pind-Dadur-Khan, and Bhera-Khooshab, reached the Indus at Meeta-Thana, and on the 5th November was encamped opposite to Dera-

Ismael-Khan. A detachment of 8,000 men was sent across, and the place was surrendered on the 9th by Manik Rae. Bukur, Lea, Khangurh, and Moujgurh, were then successively reduced without resistance. Munkera, fortified with a mud wall, and having a citadel of brick, but protected more by its position, in the midst of a desert, was now the only stronghold remaining. It was situated amongst sand-hills, in which it was difficult to supply a besieging army with water. A division was advanced for the investment of this place on the 18th, and beeldars were set to dig wells, the troops being supplied with water, in the first instance, at great expense, by land, from Moujgurh, on camels, ponies, or bullocks. By the 25th November, wells having been sunk, a further division was advanced to complete the investment of the place, and Runjeet moved there himself soon after, to superintend the conduct of the siege. Each jagirdar, as usual, was allowed to conduct his own approaches, and an active rivalry and spirit of competition was kept up amongst them by Runjeet. Between the 26th November and the 7th of December, the works were carried close to the ditch, but not without suffering from the continual fire of the besieged. The Nuwab Hafiz Ahmed, conceiving that enough now had been done for his honour, proposed terms, and stipulated for the surrender of Munkera, under condition of his being allowed to march out with his arms and personal property, and of receiving the town of Dera-Ismael-Khan, with a suitable jagir. Runjeet granted the terms, and desired to be put in possession of one of the gates of the fort. Solemn pledges were exchanged, and rich dresses sent to the nuwab, and every means taken to allay his suspicions. On the 14th December, 1821, he admitted a Sikh detachment, and surrendered the gates to it; and on the 18th, he came out with 300 followers, and encamped at a spot assigned to him within the Sikh position. On the 20th, he waited on Runjeet Singh, and was received with marked attention. An escort was sent with him to Dera-Ismael-Khan, and the treaty, as a new example of Sikh faith, was observed to the letter, and fully executed.

An engagement for tribute was now enforced on the Balooch Musulmans of Tonk and Sagur, west of the Indus, and the Sikh army then moved to Dera-Deen-Punah. Runjeet here embarked on the Indus, sending his army by land to Multan. At Dera Ghazi Khan, he arranged with the Nuwab of Bahawulpur for an increase of tribute, and of rent upon the farms he held of that place, and Mittun Kot. On the 10th January, 1822, he rejoined his army at Multan, but on the 16th posted on to Lahore, leaving it to follow. On arriving at his capital, on the 27th, he learned that one of his principal sirdars and jagirdars, Jy Singh Utarewala, had gone over to the Afghans west of the Indus.

It was in March 1822, that the first European adventurers presented themselves at Runjeet Singh's durbar, seeking military service. There arrived in that month two French officers, one M. Ventura, an Italian by birth, and the other M. Allard. Both had left Europe to seek their fortunes in the East upon the death-blow given at Waterloo to the hopes of the military youth of France. They had since been employed in Persia, but not liking the subordinate place they were there required to fill, they made their way, after a time, through Candahar and Cabul, to Lahore.* Runjeet was at first very suspicious of their motives, and could not at all understand what could have induced two young men to leave their native country, and travel so far. He could not believe that employment in his service was a sufficient object to have induced such a journey. They had stated their views verbally, and had besides given several representations in Persian, but these failed to satisfy the suspicious chief. He accordingly desired them to write down their views and wishes in their own language, and having thus obtained a paper in the French language, Runjeet sent it to his agent at Lodiana, to be there literally translated for him. On obtaining this satisfaction, Runjeet gave to the two French

* Major Lawrence states (Adv. in Punjab, vol. i. p. 42) that they are said to have suffered great distress on their travels, and even to have officiated in the great mosque of Peshawur or Cabul as criers to the morning prayers. M. Jacquemont (Letters from India, vol. i. p. 327) states that M. Allard was formerly aide-de-camp to Marshal Brune.

officers assurance of employ; and houses in Lahore, with handsome salaries, were at once assigned to them. M. Ventura was an infantry colonel in the French service; M. Allard had similar rank in the cavalry. They were both set to instruct troops in the European method of exercise and manœuvre. The native commandants were at first extremely jealous of the favour shewn to these Europeans, and of their exercising any authority or command; more especially because, on Runjeet's asking their opinion of the troops in their present condition, they had expressed themselves very slightingly as to their state of discipline and drill. At first they were employed on the troops at the capital, which were under Runjeet's own eye and M. Allard received orders to raise a corps of dragoons, to be disciplined and drilled like the cavalry of Europe. These officers by their conduct won further confidence in the course of time, and others, particularly M. Court, who was brought up at the Polytechnic Institution at Paris, have followed, and joined them in subsequent years.

Towards the beginning of April, Runjeet

went to Aknur, in the Jummoo hills. His army was in the field, under Misur Dewan Chund, watching the movements of Uzeem Khan, who had come down to Peshawur; where, being joined by the fugitive jagirdar, Jy Singh Atarewala, he was pushing back the Sikh posts and garrisons towards the Indus, and even threatened Khyrabad, the principal station held by them on the western bank. In June, Runjeet returned to his capital, without achieving any enterprise of note.

Amongst the possessions of Suda Koonwur, was a small territory, called Himmutpur Wudni, lying south of the Sutluj, and held by her under grant from Runjeet, made in September, 1808, in consideration of a payment of 15,000 rupees. This territory, being on the protected side of the Sutluj, could not be confiscated with the rest. Runjeet, however, compelled his mother-in-law to execute in his favour a deed of relinquishment of right to the territory, and, armed with this, his agent proceeded to take forcible possession. Upon resistance, however, by Suda Koonwur's manager, and complaint to the British authorities, this deed was at first not admitted as valid, and the lands were ordered to be left in the former management. They continued thus to be preserved from the grasp of the Lahore ruler, until 1828, when, upon further representation, the supreme government consented to Runjeet Singh's assuming them under his management. Suda Koonwur's position was not in the least improved by this result; she continued to be held a close prisoner.

The rule of Runjeet in Cashmere was at this period oppressive. Mr. Moorcroft, writing from thence in 1822, says, "Runjeet Singh slackens not his impositions, but rack-rents the unfortunate Cashmerians to the last farthing he can extort. Rapacious as were the Duranis, they were irregular in their oppression, and many escaped through a careless scrutiny, mixed with something like feeling; but the raja is a systematic grinder, oppressing most mechanically. If Mahomed Uzeem Khan were immediately to make a vigorous attack from Peshawur, across the mountains, upon Cashmere, he would almost certainly succeed in driving out the Sikhs, from the aversion to the Singh existing not only in the Musulman but amongst the Hindu population."

CHAPTER XV.

A.D. 1823 TO 1831.

IN October, after the Dussera of 1823, the Sikh army was assembled at Rotas, and muster taken of the jagirdars' contingents. Runjeet was on this occasion more than ordinarily severe in taking account of the numbers and equipment of the men, and amongst other chiefs who fell under his animadversion for neglect, was Dul Singh Miherna, an old jagirdar, who had served with much zeal and honour. He was threatened with a heavy mulct, and treated disparagingly; whereupon he took poison at night, and so relieved himself from further trouble. The army moved, in December, towards Rawul Pindi, whence Hukeem Useez-ud-deen was sent forward to Peshawur, to demand tribute from Yar Mahomed Khan, the governor. This chief, being unprepared for resistance, collected some valuable horses, and forwarded them as tribute, which satisfied Runjeet for the time; he returned to his capital in January, making the pilgrimage of Kitas on his route.

Mahomed Uzeem Khan disapproved of the compromise made by his brother of Peshawur, and marched from Cabul to superintend the affairs of this quarter in person. He arrived at Peshawur on the 27th January; and Yar Mahomed, fearing to meet him, sought a temporary refuge in the Yusufzai hills. Runjeet now ordered his army to cross the Indus, and the river was forded on the 13th March. Feroz Khan, chief of the Khutuks, being dead, a sequestration was made of all his possessions. On the 14th March, the army entered Akora, where it was joined by the fugitive, Jy Singh Atarewala, who was now anxious to make his terms, and be re-admitted to favour. His pardon was granted. Intelligence was soon after brought, that Mahomed Zeman Khan, nephew of Uzeem Khan, with Sudeeq Khan, son of the deceased Khutuk chief, Feroz Khan, were in position at Noushuhur, near the camp, with about 4,000 men, and had already cut off some parties of foragers. Runjeet ordered his army to be formed, directly he learned this intelligence, and marched forthwith to attack the Musulmans. The battle commenced with a furious charge, led by Phoola Singh Akali, a Sikh desperado,* who was in the habit of rushing forward, with some followers of like zeal, at the commencement of action. The Musulmans, however, also felt their battle to be a religious one, and met the fanatic Sikhs with corresponding zeal, so that the latter were completely destroyed, and their leader slain. Fresh troops were now ordered up by Runjeet, but the Mahomedans stood firm, and resisted every attack until sunset, by which time they had lost nearly half their originally small number, but still maintained

* When Mr. Moorcroft visted Amritsur, in May, 1820, this man expressed to him his contrition for his conduct towards Mr. Metcalfe (vol. i. p. 289), his dissatisfaction with Runjeet, his determination to attach himself to the English, and his readiness to carry fire and sword wherever Mr. Moorcroft should bid him. "I declined the interview which he solicited," says Mr. Moorcroft, "and recommended him to entertain more prudent and loyal purposes."—Travels, vol. i. p. 110.

their ground on two insulated hills. Runjeet now ordered his cavalry to surround the whole position of the enemy, and directed his Nujeeb and Goorkha battalions to charge and dislodge them. Twice did these troops advance to the charge, and twice were they repulsed by the determined body opposed to them; nor could the utmost efforts of Runjeet's army dislodge them from their position before nightfall. In the course of the night, the remnant of the band cut their way through the surrounding posts of the Sikhs, and so made good their retreat to the mountains.

There were not more of the Musulmans engaged on this occasion, than between four and five thousand men, and these were mere mountaineers and villagers, who turned out for the *Ghazi*, that is, to fight the religious battle against the infidel Sikhs. Disciplined professional soldiers there were none amongst them, yet did they resist, for a whole day, the entire army of Runjeet Singh, who had in the field against them not less than 24,000 men, and all his best troops. There were upwards of 1,000 men (Sir C. Wade says

2,000) killed and wounded on the side of the Sikhs, and amongst them four officers of distinction, Phoola Singh, Akali, Ghurba Singh and Kurum Singh, Chahul, two jagirdars, and Bulbhudur Singh, Goorkhali. The last named was the officer who had defended Nalapani, with so much determination, against Generals Gillespie and Martindell, at the commencement of the British war with Nepal. After peace was re-established, he formed an ill-fated connection with the wife of another, and, by the law of Nepal, his life became forfeit to the injured husband. This led to his expatriating himself, and taking employment from Runjeet Singh, where, after serving with distinction, he died in a manner worthy of his military reputation.

Mahomed Uzeem Khan was, during this action of the Ghazi, at Chumkawa, about four miles and a half east of Peshawur. He made no effort to succour or support the warriors, and was watched in his position by a Sikh force under Kripa Ram, Sher Singh, and Huree Singh, which had advanced by the opposite bank of the river. Upon learning that the party was overpowered, and had dispersed, he retired to Jelalabad, on the Cabul road, leaving the field clear to Runjeet and the Sikh army.

On the 17th March, Runjeet Singh made his entry into Peshawur, and advanced the army to Khybur Durra, where it was employed in pillaging and destroying the cultivation. It suffered much, however, from the activity and bigoted spirit, with which the Musulman population attacked its parties and cut off all stragglers; and the camp was kept during the night continually on the alert by their daring skirmishes. In April, Runjeet Singh secured the submission of Yar Mahomed Khan, who came with some fine horses, including the far-famed Kuhar, and with a request to be allowed to hold Peshawur as a tributary of Lahore. The Sikh was well content to make a settlement for the city and surrounding territory on this basis. He accordingly divided the country into five portions, or fiefs, between Nawab Summund Khan, Yar Mahomed Khan, Sooltan Mahomed Khan, Syud Mahomed Khan, and Pir Mahomed Khan, who contracted to send him annually a tribute of horses, rice, and fruits. Having effected this arrangement, he returned to his capital on the 26th April.

Mahomed Uzeem Khan died in the following month, and the event contributed to produce further confusion in the affairs of Afghanistan; for, while he lived, he was looked upon as the head of the family in succession to Futeh Khan, whereas, after his death, the numerous brothers and nephews of that chief acknowledged nobody, and their quarrels and contentions involved in disturbances the fairest portion of the Afghan territory. Mahmud and his son Kamran were confined to the fort and city of Herat, beyond which their name was nowhere respected, nor could they exercise any authority.

After the Dussera, in October, the Sikh army, being again called out, was led by Runjeet down the Indus, with the professed design of an attack upon Sinde. The river was crossed in November, and the whole of that month was occupied in reducing Bhutee villages, and exacting contributions from the Balooch and other jagirdars, whose possessions lay on the extreme northern frontier of the Sindian territory. The Lahore chief was, however, content with having thus felt his way this season, and in December moved his army homeward. At the close of the year, Raja Sunsar Chund, of Kangra, died, and was succeeded by his son Unrodh Chund. A nuzurana was demanded on the succession; and, upon the young raja demurring to the payment, Runjeet summoned him to attend in person at his summer residence of Adenanugur. He was persuaded by the Fakir Azeez-ud-deen to obey the summons, and met the court at Juwala Mookhee. On his arrival, an exchange of turbands took place, and mutual pledges were interchanged, between him and Khuruk Singh, on the part of the durbar; and, after much negotiation, a lakh of rupees was at last settled, and paid, as the nuzurana of accession, by Unrodh Singh.

Huree Singh Nulooa, who had been left with a force to overawe the turbulent Musulman population of the mountains about Gundgurh and Derbend, contrived, by harsh and vexatious proceedings, and particularly by the seizure of a Syud's daughter, to drive the whole into insurrection. The insurgents collected in such force, as to compel Huree Singh to stockade himself, and remain on the defensive, and he wrote to Runjeet Singh, representing the difficulties of his situation, and soliciting reinforcements. Runjeet ordered him to put on a bold face, and maintain himself as he could, but sent no immediate reinforcements, indeed, the rains having set in, it was not easy to do so. Huree Singh, in the mean time, being attacked, suffered a severe loss, and was compelled to retire before the insurgents. The Sikh army was, in consequence of this disaster, called out earlier than usual, and directed against the hills between the Indus and Cashmere, in the early part of October. By the 19th Runjeet had penetrated with a division of his troops to Gundgurh, but found the population dispersed, and nothing but empty walls and deserted houses. The place, with all the surrounding villages, was burnt and pillaged; the unripe crops were used for forage to the army; and Runjeet, following the deserters, determined to ford the Indus after them, an attempt in which many lives were lost, but the object was effected on the 3rd November. When the army was well across, Mahomed Yar Khan was summoned to attend from Peshawur, which, after some hesitation, he did on the 16th November, bringing a present of horses, which was accepted, and the terms on which Peshawur had been assigned were renewed, with fresh protestations and oaths of allegiance on the part of the Afghan chief. On the 30th November, the Sikh army re-crossed the Indus, not without further loss, from the depth and bad footing at the ford. On the 10th December, Runjeet re-entered his capital, by no means satisfied with the result of the expedition, for he had incurred heavy expenses, and yet had been able to inflict no blow on the turbulent body of Mahomedans in insurrection, and had levied very little in the way of tribute and contribution.

No further expedition was attempted in 1824, or in the early part of the following year. Indeed, the Burmese war had been commenced by the British Government, and Runjeet seemed to watch with intense interest all the events and operations of it. The most exaggerated reports were spread at first of the successes of the Burmese, and there were not wanting counsellors to instil into the ear of the Lahore ruler, that the time was approaching when the field would be open to him to the east. It was at this period, that Mr. Moorcroft forwarded to Calcutta a letter of Prince Neselrode, the Russian Minister for Foreign Affairs, addressed to Runjeet Singh, purporting to introduce an agent, named Agha Mehdee. The agent, it seems, was endeavouring to make his way by the difficult route of Tibet, and either died, or was murdered, some few stages from Ladakh. There Mr. Moorcroft obtained his papers, and amongst them this letter, which he procured to be translated afterwards by M. Ksoma de Körös, with whom he fell in on his travels. The letter, except as introductory of the agent, was merely one of compliment, with assurances of protection to any merchants of the Punjab who might penetrate to the Russian dominions.

No military enterprise was undertaken in the season 1824-1825; but, in April, 1825, sequestration was made of all the jagirs and possessions formerly assigned to Dewan Mohkum Chund, and now managed for Motee Chund by Kripa Ram, the dewan's grandson. The bad management of the jagirs, and the inefficient contingent kept up by this agent, were the assigned reasons, Motee Ram himself being left in his government of Cashmere, and subjected to no indignity or diminution of favour, consequent upon the sequestration. In the Dussera of 1825, the army was called into the field, with the avowed purpose of an expedition against Sinde. With this view, Runjeet marched the troops to Pind-Dadur-Khan; but learning there, that the Sinde country was suffering from scarcity and famine, he gave up the design, and returned to Lahore on the 24th November. An agent he had sent into Sinde, to demand tribute, returned with vakeels from the ruling Meers, and they for some time continued to reside at Lahore. It was at this period that Runjeet's close associate and turband brother, Futeh Singh Aloowala, conceived some suspicions as to the safety of his position at the durbar, and suddenly left Lahore, to place himself in security within the possessions held by him on the protected side of the Sutluj. Runjeet was much vexed at this sudden step of his old ally, and made great efforts to induce him to return. The British officers, while they confirmed him in the assurance of the inviolability of his territory on the protected side of the Sutluj, advised him not to yield to vague suspicions, as a ground for breaking a friendship of so long standing as had subsisted between himself and Runjeet. Guided by this advice, Futeh Singh, some time after, that is, in April, 1827, yielded to the invitations of the Lahore ruler, and, returning to his durbar, was well received, the Maharaja sending his grandson, Nou Nehal, to give him the meeting of honour. He soon, however, became an object of rapacity, being called upon to pay tribute, or take in farm, at no easy rent, much of the territory he had hitherto enjoyed free, by the assignment of his turband brother.

Sadiq Mahomed Khan, the Nuwab of Bahawulpur, died in April, 1826, and was succeeded by Bahawul Khan, who renewed his father's leases and engagements with Runjeet, for the territory he held west and north of the Sutluj. In September, a question arose upon the application of Kootub-uddeen of Kasoor to be received under British protection, as holder of Mundot and Rumnawala on the left bank of the Sutluj; but the feudatory relations this chief had come under to Runjeet Singh for these, as for his other possessions, forbade the British Government from holding out the hope that he could be received under protection as an independent chief. An unsuccessful attempt by Beer Singh, ex-Raja of Noorpur, in the Hills, to recover the territory from which he had been ejected since 1816, is the only other event recorded in this year. He was defeated and made prisoner by Desa Singh. A main cause of the inactivity of the Sikhs arose from the increasing infirmities of Runjeet. His indispositions and ailings increased upon him so much, towards the end of the year, that he applied to the British Government for a medical officer, and Dr. Andrew Murray was sent over from Lodiana to attend his highness.

In the early part of 1827, the reformer, Syud Ahmed, raised the green standard of Mahomed in the mountains inhabited by the Yusufzais, and commenced a religious war against the Sikhs. This individual was originally a petty officer of horse in the service of Ameer Khan. Upon the breaking up of the military establishment of that chief, in 1818-19, Syud Ahmed took a fanatical turn; and fancying he had received special revelations, went to Delhi, and associated himself with some muluyis of sanctity in that city. One of them collected these revelations into a book; and from it the Syud, and his associates and followers, commenced preaching against many irregularities that had crept into the practice of the Mahomedan religion. Amongst the principal were, the reverence paid by the Moslems of Hindustan to the tombs of saints and relations, the manner of their celebrating the death of Husun and Hoosein, the sons of Ali, and other similar customs, which these reformers denounced as idolatrous, and as deviations from the pure precepts of the *Koran.* In 1822, Syud Ahmed came down to Calcutta, and was there much followed by the Musulman population. Thence he took ship to make the pilgrimage of Mecca. On his return, he travelled through Hindustan, and declared his intention of devoting himself to the service of his religion, by waging an interminable holy war against the Sikh infidels. Many zealots and fanatics joined him, and subscriptions of money were poured in upon him from all parts of the British possessions. Thus armed and prepared, he made his way to the hills near Peshawur, and raised the Mohumdee Jhenda, as above stated, amongst the Yusufzai Musulmans. Runjeet was compelled, by the formidable character of the insurrection thus organized, to send a strong force across the Attock, for the protection of Khyrabad and his interests in that quarter. In March, 1827, the Syud, at the head of a countless irregular host, ventured to attack this force, which was commanded by Budh Singh Sinduwalea, an old warrior, and had thrown up works to strengthen itself in its position. The assailants surrounded the works, and the Sikhs were in great distress for some days. At length Budh Singh, losing patience, proposed to the sirdars to attack the enemy, and invoking his guru, headed the assault. The Sikh discipline and superior equipment secured them an easy victory (each Sikh killing fifteen to twenty of the runaways), and the Syud, being entirely defeated, retired with his followers into the hills, whence he kept up a desultory and annoying warfare with the Sikhs, directed against their convoys and small detachments.

Lord Amherst passed the hot season of the year 1827 at the station of Simla, near Subathoo, in the hills east of the Sutluj. The proximity of this position to Lahore induced Runjeet Singh to send a mission of compliment to his lordship, with presents, and amongst others, a handsome tent of shawl for the king of England. The mission was received with distinction, and a return compliment made of the same kind. Captain Wade, the officer at Lodiana, through whom the correspondence with the Lahore ruler was conducted, and some officers of the Governor-General's personal suite, were deputed to Lahore, with return presents, and a suitable retinue, to express the Governor-General's satisfaction at the terms of cordiality and friendship which subsisted between the two states. In 1828, the British Commander-in-Chief, Lord Combermere, passed the warm season at Simla, and a complimentary vakeel was sent over by Runjeet Singh to offer his congratulations. It was his lordship's desire to procure an invitation in person to Lahore, but the wily chief evaded compliance with this wish.

At the durbar of Lahore, at this time, the entire favour of the chief was engrossed by Raja Dhean Singh, the chamberlain, and his brothers Golab Singh and Soochet Singh, Meeans of Jummoo, where their influence had been re-established under Runjeet Singh's authority, by the grant of the place in jagir in 1819, as before related. Heera Singh, a boy of about twelve years of age, son of Raja Dhean Singh, was the object of particular favour, Runjeet Singh seldom suffering him out of his sight, and seeming to delight in humouring all his whims and caprices. In common with his father and uncles, he was created Raja, and Runjeet studied to procure him a high matrimonial alliance. It was about this time that Raja Unrodh Chund, son of Sunsar Chund, of Kangra, paid a visit to Lahore, with his family, on his route to attend the nuptial ceremonies of the Aloowala's son, Nehal Singh. He had with him two sisters, on whom Rajah Dhean Singh cast his eyes, desiring them to be joined in matrimony with his family. The pride of the hill chief was roused at the proposition of so degrading an alliance, but the influence of Runjeet procured from him a written promise, that the two young women should be at his disposal. The mother of Unrodh Chund, however, succeeded in carrying them off, and took refuge with them in the hills under British protection, whither Unrodh Chund himself soon followed, leaving his possessions on the other side of the Sutluj at the mercy of Runjeet Singh, who sequestered the whole, and received the surrender of them without any resistance from Futeh Chund, Unrodh's brother. A *khawas*, or concubine, of Raja Sunsar Chund, named Guddun, was enticed away from the family, and fell on this occasion into Runjeet's hands, with several children she had borne to the late raja. Two of the daughters the Sikh married himself, and upon a son he conferred the title of Raja, with a considerable jagir. The nuptials of Heera Singh were at the same time celebrated with great pomp, though not with a member of the Kangra family.

In the course of 1829, Syud Ahmed again appeared in the field in great strength, and his vengeance was directed against Yar Mahomed Khan, who, he declared, had sacrificed the cause of his religion by swearing allegiance to, and accepting service from, the Sikhs. As the Syud approached Peshawur, Yar Mahomed moved out with such troops as he could collect for its defence. In the action which followed, however, he received a mortal wound, and his troops dispersed. Peshawur was saved to Runjeet Singh by the opportune presence there of M. Ventura, who had gone with a small escort to negotiate with Yar Mahomed Khan for the surrender of a famous horse, called Lylee. The horse had been demanded in the previous year, but the Afghans declared it was dead.

The falsity of this declaration being discovered, a written engagement had been extorted from Yar Mahomed, pledging himself for its delivery, and M. Ventura was deputed to enforce the execution of this deed. Upon the death of Yar Mahomed, he took upon himself to make dispositions for the defence of Peshawur, and wrote to Runjeet for instructions as to his further proceedings. The Sikh directed the city to be delivered over to Sooltan Mahomed Khan, brother of the deceased Yar Mahomed, but urged the securing possession of the famous horse Lylee, as an indispensable preliminary. M. Ventura succeeded fully in this negotiation, and brought away Lylee, leaving Sooltan Mahomed in possession of the government of Peshawur.

M. Ventura had not been long gone, when Syud Ahmed appeared again, with his host of Yusufzais before Peshawur, and Sooltan Mahomed, venturing an action, was defeated, so that Peshawur fell under the temporary power of the fanatic chief. Runjeet took the field with his army, in the early part of 1830, to punish this pretender.

On his crossing the Attock, however, and approaching Peshawur, the insurgent force dissolved before him, and he returned to Lahore, leaving a strong detachment across the Indus, to act as occasion might offer, having restored Sooltan Mahomed to his government. This chief, after the departure of Runjeet Singh, found it convenient to come to terms with Syud Ahmed, who again came down, and by a sudden attack carried Peshawur. The governor consented to allow free passage to men and money proceeding to join the reformer ; to place the administration of justice in Peshawur in the hands of a Kazee, and officers of the reformed faith and principles, and to pay monthly to the Syud 3,000 rupees. The city was on these conditions restored to Sooltan Mahomed, but the Syud had no sooner retired, than the Kazee and two Moolvees, left to administer justice according to his reformed principles, were slain in a popular tumult. Syud Ahmed's difficulties increased, for the Yusufzais took offence at some innovations he desired to introduce into the marriage ceremony, and were alarmed by his announcing the doctrine, that a tenth of all income or revenue should be subscribed for religious and state purposes. The wild untutored mountaineers rose against the preacher's authority, and not only rejected these doctrines, but compelled the Syud and his immediate followers to leave their mountains. He fled across the Indus, and found a temporary refuge in the mountains of Pekhli and Dhumtour. Runjeet Singh, however, sent a detachment against him, under Sher Singh, and in the early part of 1831, the detachment was fortunate enough to fall in with him, when, after a short but smart engagement, the Syud's force was dispersed and himself slain. His head was cut off, and sent in to be recognized and identified. His followers in Hindustan have, however, difficulty in believing yet, that he is dead, and still hope to see him display himself in some great action, for the permanent benefit of the faith, and for the extension of the dominion and power of its professors.

CHAPTER XVI.

A.D. 1829 TO 1831.

WHEN Lord Amherst returned to Europe in 1828, he carried with him the shawl tent presented by Runjeet Singh to the king of England, and it was determined to send from England a return present, and a very extraordinary selection was made; upon whose advice, has not transpired. It was resolved to send to Runjeet, on the part of his Majesty, a team of cart-horses, four mares and one stallion, upon some notion that, in his love for horses, Runjeet must be a breeder of the animal, and would be well pleased to have mares of large size to cross with the breeds of the Punjab. The fact, however, is, that Runjeet had no breeding stud nor establishment, and cared only for entire horses of high courage, well broken in to the *manége* of Hindustan, that he could ride himself, on parade or on the road, or set his choice sirdars and favourites upon. The result shewed this; for when the cart-horses arrived at his court, the stallion was immediately put into the breaker's hands, and taught the artificial paces usual. This animal, with its enormous head and coarse legs, stood always in the palace-yard, or before the tent of the chief, decorated with a golden saddle and necklaces of precious stones, and was sometimes honoured by being crossed by Runjeet Singh himself. The mares were never looked at, and were matters of absolute indifference to the Sikh. It is, however, an anticipation to state what happened on the arrival of the animals, their adventures on the road to Lahore involved matters of higher interest.

It was resolved to make the transmission of this present a means of obtaining information in regard to the Indus, and the facilities, or the contrary, it might offer to navigation. The recent successes of Russia in Persia, and the probability of that power entertaining further designs, either present, or hereafter, when the succession of Abbas

Meerza to the throne of Persia * might render that kingdom a province of Russia, made it desirable that intelligence should be collected, as to the frontier states of India, and the means of defence offered by this great river barrier in particular. The dray-horses were accordingly sent out to Bombay, and the supreme government instructed Sir John Malcolm, the governor of that presidency, to take measures to have them forwarded under charge of an intelligent and prudent officer, in boats up the Indus. Some demur was anticipated on the part of the rulers of Sinde to allowing them a passage through the Delta and lower part of the river; but it was assumed that the governing Meers, situated as they were relatively to Runjeet Singh on one hand, and the British Government on the other, would not readily incur the risk of offending both powers, by refusing a passage, if it were insisted upon.

Sir John Malcolm, having received the horses, forwarded them to Cutch, and appointed to the mission to Lahore, in charge

* Abbas Meerza died in 1834.

of them, Lieutenant (afterwards Sir Alexander) Burnes, then assistant to Colonel (now Sir Henry) Pottinger, who was in political charge of that district and of the British relations with Sinde. The young officer thus selected had been in the Quarter-Master General's department, and was in every respect qualified for the duty. Sir John Malcolm added to the dray-horses the present of a carriage of his own, as useless an article to Runjeet as the mares. The highly ornamental carriage sent to him by Lord Minto, in 1810, after being used for a few days as a novel plaything, had ever since remained neglected in the great arsenal at Lahore. The carriage and horses, however, were despatched from Cutch towards the end of the year 1830, and Sir John Malcolm thought the most politic course would be, to send them without previous notice or correspondence with the Meers of Sinde, thinking the necessity they would thus be under of deciding suddenly would be likely to contribute to the success of the expedition.

Lieutenant Burnes accordingly started, carrying with him the letters announcing the purpose of his coming, and entered with his fleet one of the mouths of the Indus. Passing up to the first inhabited town, he forwarded his despatches to Hyderabad. After a detention of some days, he was, on the 1st February, met by an officer and guard from Darajee, who requested him to wait at the mouth of the river till orders should arrive from Hyderabad. With this he complied, but there experienced so much incivility from the Kurachee people, who relieved the guard from Darajee, that he resolved to return and wait in Cutch till the Meers should decide upon his coming. The consent of the Meers was not, however, obtained till after a negotiation of nearly six weeks; at length Lieutenant Burnes sailed again on the 10th March, and on this occasion entered the Ruchel mouth by Kurachee Bundur, the extreme western channel of the river. Here difficulties were made, and delays interposed, so as to induce Lieutenant Burnes to start by land for Hyderabad, in the hope of removing them by personal negotiation. He had proceeded no further than Tatta, when, after much chicanery he received the required permission to pass by the route of the Indus. Boats of the country were now furnished to him, and every possible assistance rendered for his conveyance to Hyderabad, no effort being spared to obliterate the effects of the previous unfriendly treatment he had experienced. At the capital he was received in Durbar with great distinction, a chief of rank was appointed to attend him on his journey, and the best accommodation-boats on the river, even those of the ruling Meer himself, were assigned for his conveyance. Everywhere in Sinde he met with the same attention, and proceeded on his voyage by Tatta to Hyderabad, and thence after a short stay to Bukur. The mission reached Tatta on the 15th, and Hyderabad on the 18th April, 1831, and the month of May had closed before it left the Indus, and entered the Chenab. The river was then at its lowest, but nowhere was there the slightest difficulty or obstruction to the nagivation.

Sinde was then divided into three independent governments: the first, and by far the most considerable, was Hyderabad, ruled at this time by Meer Moorad Ali, last survivor of the four brothers, who, in 1780, effected the revolution which transferred the dominion of the country to the Talpoor family. The second division was that of Khyrpoor, to the north of the first, and lying on both sides of the river Indus. Its ruler was Meer Roostum Khan, the eldest son of Meer Soohrab Khan. The third division was that of Meerpoor, lying towards Cutch, and ruled by Meer Ali Moorad Khan. These subdivisions of the country had their origin in a partition made amongst the principal conspirators, by whose exertions the Talpoors obtained power.

Having passed through the Hyderabad territory, Lieutenant Burnes was received with even increased attention and kindness by the ruler of Khyrpoor, who professed a strong desire to cultivate a more intimate relation with the British Government, and made Lieutenant Burnes the bearer of a communication to this effect to the Governor-General. By this chief the mission was carried forward to the territory of the Nuwab of Bahawulpur, without experiencing the smallest obstruction or difficulty of any kind: there was found nowhere less than eight feet of water, and the current was moderate, and easily overcome, even where, from rocks, or hard soil at the banks, the water-way was contracted. The month of May was now passing, during which the navigation of the Ganges is much obstructed by strong westerly winds, and by the want of water, but no difficulty of the kind impeded the passage up the Indus at this season. The Bahawulpur chief was already in political relation, both with Runjeet Singh and with the British Government; from him, therefore, Lieutenant Burnes was sure of receiving every kindness. On the 30th May, the fleet reached Mittunkot, and embarking on other boats provided by the chief of the Daoodputras (Bahawul Khan), entered the Punjnud, being the united stream of the waters of the Punjab. A little below Multan, the escort and party sent by Runjeet to receive and conduct the royal* present, met

* It is a singular circumstance, that Sir J. Malcolm, in all the instructions he gave Lieutenant-Colonel Pottinger and Lieutenant Burnes, in regard to this mission, never

Lieutenant Burnes with boats of the Punjab, adapted to the navigation of the winding Ravi. In these Lieutenant Burnes and his party embarked on the 12th June, and soon reached Multan. The mouth of the Ravi is further up the Sutluj, and he did not enter that branch till the 23rd June. The rainy season overtook the mission while in that river, and the progress up it was tedious, being dependent entirely on the track-rope.

On the 17th of July, Lieutenant Burnes reached Lahore, where his arrival with the present from the King of England, and with the letter of Lord Ellenborough which accompanied it, was a source of great pride and rejoicing to Runjeet Singh. The attention he paid to Lieutenant Burnes was very

never mentioned, nor gave the smallest intimation to either officer, that the dray-horses were a present from the King of England. They made the discovery after the difficulties in respect to the passage through Sinde had been overcome, when a direct correspondence with the mission was opened by the Governor-General. Up to this time, they had believed, and had represented, the present to be sent from the British Government in India.

marked, and he had invited Captain Wade over from Lodiana, to assist at the ceremonial of reception. From Lahore, Lieutenant Burnes proceeded to Simla, to render to the Governor-General an account of his mission, and to lay before his lordship the valuable information obtained during it. This enterprising and zealous officer obtained his lordship's permission to return to his presidency of Bombay through Persia, and to explore the route of Balkh and Bokhara, after first crossing the Punjab and Cabul territory, in order that he might be the means of adding information of this little-known route to the stores of intelligence already contributed by him.

The very favourable disposition in which the ruler of Lahore seemed to be at this juncture encouraged Lord William Bentinck to hope, that a proposition for a personal meeting between himself and Runjeet Singh would be well received. He accordingly instructed Captain Wade, when at Lahore, to sound the chief's confidential advisers on the subject. As anticipated by his lordship, Runjeet shewed great desire for the meeting, but some difficulty was at first started in respect to the etiquette of a previous return mission, Runjeet Singh having paid his lordship the compliment of sending one, similarly composed to that which waited on Lord Amherst. The mission had been received by Lord William Bentinck in April, soon after his arrival at Simla; its members were the Dewan Mootee Ram, son of Mohkum Chund, Huree Singh, sirdar, and the secretary, Fakir Uzeez-ud-deen. They had been treated by the Governor-General with much distinction, and a return mission of some of the principal officers of his lordship's suite had been promised, or rather held out in expectation. The personal meeting between the heads of the two states would necessarily deprive Runjeet Singh of this compliment; for, in the first place, the time would scarcely allow of both, seeing that the intended journey of the Governor-General to Ajmer and Rajpootana required, that, if arranged at all, the interview should take place before the end of October, and in the second, if a formal mission were sent, immediately before the meeting, it would have the appearance, in the eyes of the world, of being sent to supplicate or induce the ruler of the Sikhs to come to the interview, whereas the rank and position of the head of the British Government required that the honour of a personal conference with him should be sought.

With a liberality, not inconsistent with his general character, Runjeet Singh, having made up his mind to the interview, gave up the point of etiquette, and preparation was made on both sides for the meeting to take place on the Sutluj about the 20th of October, without any previous return mission; the neighbourhood of Roopur was subsequently fixed upon as the most appropriate and convenient spot for the meeting.

In order to give éclat to the occasion, and to form a suitable escort, the Governor-General ordered up to Roopur, from Meerut and Kurnal, two squadrons of European lancers, with the mounted band of the regiment (H. M. 16th Lancers), an European regiment (H. M. 31st foot), two battalions of native infantry (the 14th and 32nd), and eight guns of horse artillery, with two squadrons of Colonel Skinner's irregular horse. The escort was thus composed, in order to exhibit to Runjeet Singh, whose curiosity was much excited as to the formation and equipment of the various arms and corps of our military force, as much variety as possible. In marching the Europeans through the Sikh territory, the population was somewhat scandalized at ascertaining that beef was killed in camp for their rations. The slaughter was made in the night, as secretly as possible; still the fact transpired, and became matter of complaint from the Sikh sirdars. The reply to them was, that it was no business of theirs to inquire what was done within the precincts of a British camp; that our customs prevailed there, and these could not be yielded to their scruples, though every care should be taken to prevent the obtrusion of any thing that was offensive. There is no doubt that the prejudices of the Sikhs were much outraged by the slaughter of oxen, but it would have been extremely bad policy to yield the point in this instance; for were it conceded, and the necessity to arise hereafter (as it has arisen), of bringing a considerable force of Europeans into the country, a similar concession would be expected when it would be impossible to grant it, and the population would be excited, from the want of previous knowledge and preparation, and the recollection that heretofore the concession had been made to their religious feelings.

The troops having arrived at Roopur, the Governor-General, who had left Simla on the 19th October, entered the camp on the evening of the 22nd. Runjeet Singh came into his camp, on the opposite side of the Sutluj, on the morning of the 25th, escorted by 10,000 of his best horse, and about 6,000 trained infantry. He was immediately waited upon by a deputation from the Governor-General, headed by Major-General Ramsay, brother to the Commander-in-Chief, Lord Dalhousie, and by his lordship's principal secretary. Koonwur Khuruk Singh, with six principal sirdars of the Sikhs, came at the same time to present the Maharaja's compliments to the Governor-General. It was arranged that Runjeet Singh should visit the Governor-General next day in the morning.

As the time approached for the meeting, Runjeet began to entertain an apprehension that some treachery or foul play must be designed: late overnight, he sent M. Allard to say that he should not attend the meeting of the morrow. M. Allard waited upon him immediately, and exerted himself to remove these suspicions and restore confidence, offering to stake his own head that nothing would happen that was disagreeable. He left the Maharaja still irresolute, and the astrologers were summoned. They consulted the *Grant'h* and declared the result favourable, but told his Highness to take with him a couple of apples, and to present them to the Governor-General and to his secretary: if they were at once taken without demur, he was to consider it as a good omen, and might proceed in full assurance that the result of the meeting would give him satisfaction. On the morning of the 26th October, a deputation went to conduct the Maharaja to camp, and he started at sunrise. A bridge of the flat-bottomed ferry-boats of the Sutluj had been constructed for the convenience of communication. Runjeet Singh made to cross over before him 3,000 of his best Ghorchur cavalry, dressed in new yellow silk quilted coats, also about 800 of M. Allard's dragoons; he then took his breakfast of a highly spiced cordial, and sent over the chiefs he meant should attend on their elephants. This occupied some time, for the boats were fragile and would allow but few elephants to be put on the bridge together. Lastly, his Highness passed over in person, and then, to prevent all confusion, ordered the guard at the bridge to permit none else from his camp to cross over. With the escort and attendance thus formed, the Sikh chief crossed the open plain, at the further end of which lay the camp of the Governor-General, from the centre of which a street was formed of the British troops collected. On reaching the end of the line, the Maharaja stopped to examine each corps, and put an infinity of questions as to their equipment, asking the use and cost of every strange article that caught his eye. In the middle of the street he was met by the Governor-General, and presented the apples as enjoined by the astrologers: they were freely and at once taken. His Highness then crossed into the Governor-General's houda, and the two chiefs proceeded together to the tents of audience that had been prepared. In an outer tent, all the European gentlemen were collected, and Runjeet Singh was detained in it a short time, that several of them might be presented to him, standing, as he passed through. In a further tent chairs were laid out, and the Maharaja, with the chiefs of his nomination, and some select officers of the suite, was led thither by the Governor-General for a more private conference. It was amusing to see the pains taken by Runjeet in the arrangement of his part of the ceremony. He waited at the door of the outer tent, and himself called and told off the chiefs that were to proceed to the inner, making them precede himself in order to prevent confusion or crowding. They were all, like himself, dressed in yellow, that and light green being the favourite colours of his court, and called *Busuntee*, or the colours of spring. Some wore elegant, highly-polished armour, with scarfs of this colour, and the splendour of the attire of all was very striking. The inquisitive and apparently frank manner of the Sikh chief made the conference pass off with more liveliness than is usual on such occasions of ceremony. Presents of every variety of manufactured stuffs, which had previously been sent for, from Calcutta, Dacca, and Benares, with guns and jewels of value, a fine Burmese elephant, and two select thorough-bred young horses from the Hissar stud, were laid out or passed in review before his Highness. Dresses of honour and presents were also laid out for the heir-apparent, and other chiefs, according to a list obtained from his Highness. The Maharaja examined carefully every article of his own present, and then sent for the keeper of his wardrobe, and desired him to receive charge and pack up the articles forthwith. He took his leave, apparently highly pleased with the interview, and at the door of the tent, called up and paraded before the Governor-General, his own favourite horses, telling the names and merits of each. Again, as he passed through the street of troops, he stopped to examine the different corps, and his inquiries into every minute particular were renewed. It was noon before he reached his own camp in returning.

On the following day, the Governor-General returned the visit, and was met at the bridge of boats by Runjeet Singh. His lordship was escorted by the lancers, who, with their mounted band, preceded the cavalcade. Runjeet was much struck with their appearance, particularly with that of the band; and, after they had crossed and drawn up on the farther side of the river, he went up to them and listened for some time to their playing, while the suite crossed. The Sikh troops formed line, from the bridge to the Maharaja's tents, which, consisting chiefly of *kunats* and *sumeeanas*, tastefully arranged, were of red colour, and covered a large space. The lining of all the sumeeanas, under which the chairs were placed for the Governor-General and his suite, was of shawl, beautifully worked, and that under which sat the Governor-General and his Highness himself, was a sheet of inlaid pearls and jewels of great value. The Maharaja, after the party were seated, introduced his chiefs in succession, and each, as he came forward, presented nuzurs of Dutch gold sequins, both to his Highness and to the Governor-General. The horses were again brought forth, and exhibited in superb trappings, and after an hour passed in lively conversation, the presents for the Governor-General were laid out, and his lordship took his leave.

Evening entertainments were afterwards exchanged, and reviews held of the troops collected on both sides. The Maharaja seemed particularly struck with some of the evolutions exhibited before him by the British regiments, and sent his sirdars up to the ranks to examine particularly how they were executed. He himself also went up to the squares formed by the infantry, to see how many ranks knelt, and how many kept up fire, shewing in all things a most insatiable curiosity.

On the 31st October, the last day of the interview, the Maharaja came across the river to witness some artillery practice with grape and spherical-case shot. His astonishment at the effect on the curtain at different distances, from four hundred to one thousand paces, was extreme. After amusing himself afterwards with firing at a chutur, or umbrella, with one of the six-pounders, and exhibiting feats of horsemanship and dexterity, by his sirdars, he was presented by the Governor-General with two nine-pounder horse artillery guns, with horses and equipments complete.

The evening of this day was that of the parting interview, which it was arranged was to take place at the entertainment given by the Governor-General. At Runjeet's particular request, a paper was executed and delivered to him on this occasion, promising perpetual friendship from the British Government. A complete model of an iron suspension bridge, made up at Calcutta for the purpose, was also presented to his Highness, and excited his applause and admiration. On the following morning, the 1st November, 1831, both camps broke ground, and commenced their march in opposite directions, after a week of magnificence and mutual display, reminding one of the days of "The Field of Cloth of Gold."

No business of importance was transacted at this interview; Runjeet Singh, however, invited the two officers he thought most in the Governor-General's confidence to his tent, and in the midst of much desultory conversation, put to the official secretary, who was one of them, several questions in respect to Sinde, as if desirous to open a negotiation, and concert measures, in relation to that state; or at least to come to an understanding, as to the views of the British Government in respect to it. He said the vukeels of Sinde were in attendance in his camp, and he asked if he might introduce them to the Governor-General. Upon being answered in the affirmative, he added, that it was a very rich country, and much treasure had been accumulated there, ever since Nadir Shah's invasion of Hindustan; that there was no standing army, or any soldiers, except the population at large, who would be called from the plough to take the field against an invading force. He then made allusion to the Meers having sent back Lieutenant Burnes, and to their general character for pride and haughtiness. It appeared evident that the Maharaja had learned, or at least suspected, that the British Government had some further views in respect to Sinde; also, that nothing would be more gratifying to him than to be invited to co-operate in an attack upon that state. Notwithstanding, however, the desire thus shewn to come to an understanding on the subject, it was not thought advisable to make any communication yet to the ruler of Lahore, for it was conceived, that, if made aware of the intentions of the British Government, he might, with every profession of a desire to forward them, contrive by intrigue and secret working to counteract the negotiation.

On the very day before his Highness arrived at Roopur, instructions had been issued to Lieutenant-Colonel Pottinger, to prepare for a mission to Sinde, with a view to the negotiation of a commercial treaty, having for its object to open the navigation of the Indus to the trade of Europe, and of India.

The negotiation was to be separate with each of the three independent Meers; but Colonel Pottinger was directed to proceed first to Hyderabad, to arrange with Meer Moorad Ali for a free passage for vessels and merchandize through the mouths and delta of this great river. The basis of the negotiation was to be, to obtain guarantees against the levy of irregular duties, or wanton obstruction of any kind to boats and merchandize; to offer a guarantee against loss of revenue to the Sinde Government from the adoption of the scheme, and so to procure that the river Indus should become again the channel for extensive commerce, and be frequented securely by the craft and vessels of all the adjoining districts, and even of Europe. The object of entering upon this negotiation, at the particular juncture, was perhaps in some measure political, having reference to the necessity of being prepared against the possibility of designs on the part of Russia, should she succeed in establishing her influence in Persia. The Governor-General, however, was not prepared to make any avowal or display of such motives, and a commercial treaty, stipulating for the free navigation of the river, seemed to him the better form in which to open relations with the governments and chiefs who occupied its banks.

The result of this mission was, that, in April, 1832, treaties were made between the British Government and the Meers, stipulating that a free passage should be afforded to the merchants and traders of Hindustan, by the river and roads of Sinde, upon payment of moderate duties.*

* This chapter closes the historical part of the work written by Mr. Prinsep, from the materials prepared by Captain Murray. The succeeding portion of the history is compiled from other sources.

CHAPTER XVII.

A.D. 1832 TO 1837.

FROM this period Runjeet appears not only to have dismissed from his mind all distrust of the British Government, but to have cherished sentiments of the most cordial friendship towards it, evinced by the manner in which he received English visitors at his court, and especially by the frank and unsuspecting tone of his communications in all political discussions. In the negotiations for opening the navigation of the rivers,—a measure which the British Government had much at heart, but to which an eastern potentate, in the position of Runjeet, might naturally have had some repugnance,—he entered into all our views; and at a later period (January, 1835), a treaty was concluded between the two governments, by which moderate tolls were established upon the Indus and Sutluj, in conformity with the treaty of 1832.

The notoriety of his friendly relations with the only other independent state in Hindustan contributed, no doubt, to strengthen his power and influence, with which henceforward no formidable enemy ventured to contend, and even his tributaries, however restless under his supremacy and exhausted by his oppressions, were discouraged from rebellion, the only resource in the East against the abuse of power, and which even oriental despots cannot prevent. In July, 1832, an attempt at insurrection was made in the hills, headed by Payindah Khan, of Derbend, aided by some neighbouring zemindars; but it was promptly put down by Huree Singh, though not without loss on both sides.

Runjeet this year exhibited another proof of that contempt of public decency which has been already mentioned as a trait in his character, by formally marrying and raising to the gudi a dancing-girl, named Gulbahar, celebrating their nuptials with great pomp, and conferring high titles upon her relatives, which gave umbrage to many of his chiefs and ministers.

In the early part of 1833, the deposed and expatriated King of Cabul, Shah Shuja-ul-Moolk, made another attempt to recover his throne; and with this view, understanding that he had no hope of direct aid from the British Government, he entered into a treaty with Runjeet Singh. In September, 1831, the Shah had opened negotiations with the Maharaja, proposing, through his agent at Lahore, as the price of the Sikh's assistance, the cession, to Runjeet and his successors, of Cashmere, Peshawur, and other possessions of Cabul, which the Sikhs had acquired by arms or stratagem. Runjeet appears to have entered with alacrity into the scheme, with the design of extorting as much as possible from the necessities of the unfortunate prince, and his counter-project affords proof of his encroaching and rapacious disposition. He required that the Shah should meet him at Amritsur or Lahore, where he would have been a prisoner as long as it suited Runjeet's policy to detain him; that the Shah's heir-apparent should attend the Sikh court, and always accompany the Maharaja wherever he went, whereby he would have been a hostage for his father's conduct; that the Shah should disclaim for himself and his successors all right and title to the places acquired not only by the Maharaja, but by his dependants and tributaries, which opened a large avenue to future usurpations; that the Shah should pay down at once three lakhs of rupees (30,000*l.*), and send 102 horses of the finest description annually to Lahore—"the Maharaja's passion for horses being well known"—besides other valuable presents; that whenever the Maharaja was in want of troops, the Shah should send his army to him, with one of his sons; that the abomination of killing kine should be prohibited throughout the Cabul dominions, and in the Afghan armies; that whatever money, jewels, or cannon should be taken from the Barukzye chiefs, should be divided equally between the Shah and the Maharaja, and "that the portals, made of sandal, which had been carried away to Ghuzni, from the temple of Juggernat (Somnat), shall be delivered to the Maharaja, when the Shah's government is well established." These hard and unfeeling terms, to which other humiliating conditions were annexed, must have convinced the Shah how little sincere friendship he could expect from a man whom his agent, nevertheless, saluted as "one of the greatest persons of the age."

In his reply to these demands, the Shah courteously eluded the proposal for a meeting, as well as that for the attendance of the heir-apparent at the Sikh capital, "because the world would consider the prince in the light of a hostage;" but with respect to the other conditions, he either assented to them in terms, or tacitly, by agreeing to make them matters of negotiation hereafter; excepting two, namely, the prohibition of the slaughter of kine, and that relating to the gates of sandal wood. The Shah's observations upon the latter demand furnish an amusing specimen of the dexterity of Asiatic diplomacy. His Majesty declared the proposition inadmissible on two grounds: "First, a real friend is interested in the good name of his friend; the Maharaja being my friend, how can he find satisfaction in my disgrace? Secondly, there is a tradition, that the forefathers of the Sikhs have said that their nation shall, in the attempt to bring away the portals of sandal, advance to Ghuzni, but having arrived there, the foundation of their empire shall be overthrown. I am not desirous of that event; I wish for the permanence of his highness's dominion."

With these two exceptions, the treaty actually concluded between the parties, on the 12th March, 1833, embraced all the severe conditions required by Runjeet. The Shah disclaimed all title, on the part of himself, his heirs and successors, to whatever territories were in the possession of the Maharaja on either bank of the Indus, viz. Cashmere (including its limits east, west, north, and south); the fort of Attock; Chuch (an extensive plain to the east of Attock); Khebel (N.E. of Attock); Amb (or Ambar, a town on the right bank of the Indus, southward of Dera Ghazi Khan), with its dependencies on the left bank of the river; Peshawur, with the Yusufzai territory;* Kheteks; Husht-

* This "territory" is of great extent, being bounded N. by the Hindu Coosh; S. by the river of Cabul; E. by the Indus; and W. by the Otmunkhail mountains.

nugur, a town and fortress twenty miles N. of Peshawur; Muchnee (N.W. of Peshawur, commanding a ferry over the Cabul river); Kohat, and all places dependent upon Peshawur, as far as the Khybur pass; Bennoo (a very extensive plain, full of villages, adjoining Dour); the Vezeree territory;* Dour (a long, populous valley, full of villages, below Kalabagh); Tonk, Gorauk, Kalabagh, and Kushalghur (places conquered by Runjeet in 1825), with their dependent districts; Dera Ismael Khan, and its dependencies; Dera Ghazi Khan, Mittunkote, and Omerkote, with their dependent territory; Singhur (in the Soliman mountains); Heren, or Hurund (a district on the route from Dera Ghazi Khan to Cutch Gandava); Dajel (a district in the same route to Bhag); Hajipur and Kajinpur (districts taken from Shah Newaz Khan, the representative of the Calora family of Sinde); the three Keeches, or Kuchis (districts S.W. of Multan, on the Punjnud and Ghara rivers);

* This is a large country lying between the Soliman range on the W., and Kalabagh on the E.; on the N. it is bounded by the Sufeed Koh, and from that range extends 100 miles south.

Munkerah (in the Sind-sagur Doab), and the province of Multan. The original draft of the treaty contained an agreement for the equal division " of the territories of the Sindians and others;" but in the executed treaty there is a stipulation that, "regarding Shikarpore, and the territory of Sinde lying on the right bank of the Indus," the Shah shall abide by "whatever may be considered as right and proper, in conformity with the happy relations of friendship subsisting between the British Government and the Maharaja, through Captain Wade." The treaty further pledges the Shah to allow no one to cross the Indus without the Maharaja's permission, and stipulates that each party shall address the other on terms of equality.

This treaty (which was renewed in the tripartite treaty of 1838), although dated in March, was not ratified by Runjeet Singh till August, when the temporary success of the Shah seemed to render it the policy of the former to do so, and it was artfully kept from the knowledge of the British agent till June, 1834, when its provisions became, for the present, nugatory. It secured to the Sikh ruler, as Captain Wade observes,* "not only the entire sovereignty of the Punjab, but also of the river Indus, and the territories that immediately bound it on either side, after its escape from Little Tibet, to the confluence of its tributaries at Mittunkote."

Whilst the Shah was thus parting with large tracts of territory and making liberal promises of treasure, he was so poor in credit as to be unable to raise a loan of 20,000*l.*, even on the pledge of his jewels. He made application to the British Government of India for money to equip, as well as military officers to lead, his army; but Lord William Bentinck, then Governor-General, peremptorily refused compliance with either request, distinctly declaring that "the British Government religiously abstains from intermeddling with the affairs of its neighbours when this can be avoided."† His suit to the Meers of Sinde was at first

* Papers relating to the Expedition of Shah Shuja, 1839, p. 30.

† Letter to Shah Shuja, 20th Oct. 1832. Papers *ut supra*, p. 8.

more successful. These princes were not released from their former nominal dependence upon the kingdom of Cabul, and they agreed to assist the Shah, upon condition that he should relinquish all claim of sovereignty over Sinde and Shikarpore, and confer it upon them. The Shah does not appear to have bound himself by treaty with the Meers to make this cession; but in their subsequent negotiations with the British Government, they produced releases, written in *Korans*, signed by Shah Shuja, conferring Sinde and its dependencies upon the Meers, as their property, for ever, and renouncing all claim or pretension to the territory on the part of Cabul.

Having at length raised some funds and collected a small force, the Shah, in January, 1833, emerged from his retreat at Lodiana, crossed the Indus, and established himself at Shikarpore. The Meers having declined to assist him with a large sum of money, which he demanded, the Shah treated them as foes, and defeated the Sindian army, which had marched to drive him from Shikarpore, with great loss. In May, 1834, he advanced towards Candahar, and routed the force of the Sirdars of that city in a pitched battle. The operations of the Shah at this juncture were facilitated by the success of the Sikhs at Peshawur, which drew off the attention of Dost Mahomed Khan of Cabul, and prevented his march to the succour of his brothers. By virtue of the treaty, an army was despatched by Runjeet Singh to Peshawur, which was occupied by Hurée Singh, the commander, with little difficulty. According to one authority,* this was accomplished by artifice and stratagem. It is said that Huree Singh made his appearance near Peshawur, apparently for no other purpose than to collect the usual tribute from the Sirdars, which was immediately paid; but he delayed his departure on various pretexts, and finally obtained permission for Prince Nou Nehal Singh, who was in the rear, to make a friendly visit to the city. In the character of attendants, a large body of the Sikh army was admitted, and the Sirdars being unprepared, the place

* Mr. Masson, Journey in Beloochistan, &c., vol. iii. p. 225.

was taken. Other accounts, however, state that the capture of the city was favoured by the disaffection which was then entertained by many persons of influence towards Sooltan Mahomed Khan, who had become embroiled with the family of one of his wives, by whose means, moreover, the Sikhs established themselves in Kohat, and other parts of the country.

In June, 1834, Dost Mahomed Khan marched to Candahar, then besieged by Shah Shuja, whom he attacked and totally defeated, and this unfortunate monarch, the very plaything of fortune, after encountering many perils, and enduring severe privations, returned to his asylum at Lodiana.

Flushed with his success over the Shah, and highly exasperated at the treacherous capture of Peshawur, the Ameer of Cabul uttered threats of vengeance against the Sikh ruler, vowing to expel his troops beyond the Indus, and even to invade the Punjab. He endeavoured to rouse the passions of the Mahomedans against the infidels, and to embitter the contest by mingling religious antipathies with political rivalry. Runjeet, on his part, made formidable preparations, and reinforced his army at Peshawur, which now amounted to 25,000 men.

Whilst the Maharaja was thus extending his authority beyond the Indus, he was not without disquietude respecting Cashmere, where the severity of his exactions, and the abuses to which they gave rise in a remote dependency, had produced withering effects, and at length excited an insurrection, in which the Sikh governor, Meean Singh, was killed. Runjeet had meditated a journey to the valley in 1833, in order to reform the administration there; but his health had now become precarious; rheumatism settled in his limbs and he laboured under general debility. His French officers, General Ventura and General Allard, apprehensive probably of his approaching dissolution, desired to return to Europe at this time, but he refused to part with them.

In the early part of 1835, Dost Mahomed Khan commenced his operations against Peshawur. A strong body of Afghans, under Mahomed Akhbar Khan, marched to Jelalabad, whence parties were despatched into the Peshawur and Kohat districts. Various encounters took place, in one of which Huree Singh,* one of Runjeet's ablest generals, a man of fierce temper, who had rendered himself peculiarly obnoxious to the Musulmans, was worsted with severe loss. No serious affair, however, occurred, neither party being anxious, apparently, to bring the contest to an issue. Runjeet, having proceeded with some reinforcements, in April, 1835, to Rotas, hearing there that the Ameer of Cabul had arrived before Peshawur, crossed the Indus, and marched thither. The two armies were drawn up in order of battle, when Dost Mahomed Khan, finding that his force was inferior in numbers, as well as discipline, to that of his antagonist, deemed it prudent not to risk a battle, and retired (11th May), hastily and ingloriously, pursued by the Sikhs to the mouth of the Khybur pass. His brother, the ex-Sirdar of Peshawur, upon this, made terms with Runjeet, who settled jagirs upon him

* His personal prowess is mentioned p. 55. Mr. Vigne says Huree shewed him the sword with which he killed the tiger.

and his family, but required that he (Sooltan Mahomed Khan) should accompany him to Lahore, holding out hopes that, if he did so, he should be reinstated in his former authority. But Runjeet, when at Peshawur, made arrangements for the permanent occupation of the country, and left General Avitabili* in command there, whose vigorous

* General Avitabili, a Neapolitan, according to Baron Hügel, formerly an officer of Murat's army and court, and a pupil of the Polytechnic School at Paris, entered Runjeet's service in 1830, and was at first appointed governor of Vuzeerabad; while there, he almost rebuilt the town in the European style, making the streets wide enough to admit a carriage with four horses, and introducing other improvements, to the astonishment of the natives. His government of Peshawur is thus spoken of by Major Lawrence (Adv. in the Punjab, vol. i. p. 43): "Of Avitabili the most lenient view that can be taken is, to consider him as set in authority over savage animals,—not as a ruler over reasonable beings; as one appointed to grind down a race, who bear the yoke with about as good a grace as 'a wild bull in a net,' and who, catching their ruler for one moment asleep, would soon cease to be governed. But the ground of complaint alleged against him is, that he 'acts as a savage among savage men,' instead of shewing them that a Christian can wield the iron sceptre without staining it by needless cruelty; without following some of the worst fashions of his worst neighbours. Under his rule, summary hangings

have

administration maintained the place against the reiterated attempts of the Afghans, who

have been added to the native catalogue of punishments, and not a bad one either when properly used; but the ostentation of adding two or three to the string suspended from the gibbet, on special days and festivals, added to a very evident habitual carelessness of life, lead one to fear that small pains are taken to distinguish between innocence and guilt, and that many a man, ignorant of the alleged crime, pays with his life the price of blood. It is the general's system, when, as often happens, a Sikh, or any other of his own men, disappears at or near any village in the Peshawur territory, to fine that village, or to make it give up the murderer or murderers. The latter is the *cheapest* plan; a victim or victims are given up, and justice is satisfied. He might be as energetic and summary as he pleased, and no one would object to his dealing with a lawless people in such a way as to restrain their evil practices; but such scenes as frequently occur in the streets of Peshawur, equally revolting to humanity and decency, might be dispensed with. Still, General Avitabili has many of the attributes of a good ruler; he is bold, active, and intelligent, seeing every thing with his own eyes; up early and late. He has, at the expense of his own character for humanity, by the terror of his name, *saved* much life. It is but just to state, that the peaceful and well-disposed inhabitants of Peshawur, both Hindu and Mahomedan, united in praise of his administration, though all with one voice declared that mercy seldom mingled in his decrees. Believed to fear neither man nor devil, Avitabili continued to harass the Sikh garrison for years afterwards. It is said that Runjeet made an offer to Dost Mahomed Khan of a jagir of 30,000*l*. a year, on condition that he would relinquish all claim to Peshawur, and cease to molest the Sikh troops, and that this offer was at first received favourably, though afterwards declined.

The possession of Peshawur, except as a step to further acquisitions, does not appear to have been advantageous to Runjeet Singh. According to Burnes, it was a drain upon the finances of Lahore, with the additional evil of

Avitabili keeps down by grim fear what nothing else *would* keep down—the unruly spirits around him, who, if let slip, would riot in carnage; his severity may, therefore, be extenuated, as the least of two evils. Avitabili's whole system of morals is oriental, avowedly eschewing force, when artifice can gain the point, and looking on subjects as made to be squeezed. In person he is tall and stout, with bushy beard, whiskers, and moustache, marked with the small-pox, and with a countenance exhibiting at times the workings of human passion, but again lighted up into even a pleasing expression. With little education, but strong natural sense and ability, he has acquired a good knowledge of Persian and of the Punjabi dialect. Strangely influencing those around him, and influenced by them, his history is a curious study, and, when his own generation has passed away, will hardly be believed."

leading the Sikhs into constant collision with the fierce tribes in the neighbourhood.

In July, 1835, the constitution of Runjeet sustained severe injury from an attack of paralysis, from which, however, he partially recovered before the *Dussera*. These successive bodily affections did not impair the mental energies of this extraordinary man. He renewed his negotiations with Shah Shuja for placing him upon the throne, or rather for employing him as an instrument of annoyance to Dost Mahomed Khan. He disclosed the hostile design he had long entertained against Sinde. He demanded from the Meers a tribute of ten lakhs of rupees (100,000*l.*); and a force was sent in advance, which captured Rojhan, the chief town of the Mazari tribe of Balooches, and carried by assault a fort garrisoned by Sindian troops in the neighbourhood of Shikarpore. Preparations were made by him for opening the campaign on a more extensive scale, when the British Government interposed, offering the Meers its mediation, and, upon certain terms, its protection against the Sikhs, and intimating to Runjeet Singh, in explicit terms, its sentiments respecting his aggressive policy. Far from resenting this interference, the Maharaja immediately abandoned his designs, assuring our agent, in terms evincing his usual cordiality and confidence, that he would give immediate orders for the discontinuance of hostilities with Sinde, and for withdrawing his troops from the country. He was suffered, however, to retain the town of Rojhan.

Meanwhile, Runjeet was pushing his conquests in the hill country. By means of Gholab Singh, the Raja of Jummoo, he made encroachments upon the state of Iskardo (Little Tibet), Ladakh, and almost to the confines of the Chinese empire, which exercises a nominal authority as far as the sources of the Punjab rivers.

In 1836, General Ventura was invested with the title of Commander-in-Chief of the Sikh army. His appointment was galling to the great sirdars, but in fact the general's authority was little more than nominal. In the same year, Runjeet gave satisfaction to the British Government by issuing an order abolishing slavery throughout his dominions.

He, however, retained to the last female slaves in his own establishment, as singers and dancers.

With the view of engaging our Government indirectly to support his dynasty, in the early part of the succeeding year, Runjeet Singh invited the Commander-in-Chief of the British forces in India (the late Sir Henry Fane) to be present at the nuptials of his grandson, Nou Nehal Singh, son of Khuruk Singh, which were celebrated with great magnificenee at Amritsur, on the 7th of March. Sir Henry went, accompanied by two squadrons of lancers, ten companies of infantry, and six pieces of horse artillery, and met with a princely entertainment from the Sikh sovereign, who went through, in the presence of his guest, the imposing ceremony of receiving the compliments and offerings of his great vassals. The bride, who was ten years of age, brought a royal dower (though her father was only a sirdar), consisting of eleven elephants, 101 horses, the same number of camels, with carriages, shawls, jewels, &c. An important part of the marriage ritual consisted in placing over the bridegroom's head a rich veil of pearls and gems strung on gold thread, in which the British commander was invited to afford his auspicious assistance. The Maharaja was in high spirits, active, energetic, and inquisitive, and in spite of his infirm health, indulged in potations of strong drink to an extent which astonished his English visitors.

The hostilities between the Sikhs and Afghans had continued in Peshawur, with varying success. In 1836, Sher Singh, the son of Runjeet, had a sanguinary encounter with the chief of Lalpoora, in which both parties suffered severely; and in June an action took place between a large body of Kuzzilbashes and Ghiljies, under Dost Mahomed Khan, and a Sikh army, under Nou Nehal Singh, in which the Afghans were victorious, the Sikhs being completely beaten. But in June, 1837, a more serious affair occurred.

Huree Singh, the commander of the Sikh forces at Peshawur, commenced the erection of a strong fort at Jumrood, in the mouth of the Khybur pass, with the view of bridling the tribes which guarded that terrific inlet, and of securing a passage to Cabul. Dost

Mahomed Khan perceived that an effort must be made to stop the progress of this work, and, if possible, to crush his dangerous neighbours; he accordingly prepared a force of 8,000 (some accounts say 15,000) horse and foot, with fifty pieces of artillery, which he placed under the nominal command of his son, the since well-known Mahomed Akhbar Khan; but the operations were directed by Abdul Summund Khan. The fierce mountain tribes were ready to co-operate with this force, and the courage of the troops was stimulated by fanaticism to an unusual degree of ferocity. The Sikhs appear to have been nearly equal in numbers to their antagonists; nevertheless, they intrenched themselves; but on the 22nd of June, they marched out to battle. The conflict was severe, and the victory for some time balanced; cannon was taken and retaken on both sides; the Afghans, however, acknowledge that on this day they were worsted. The success of the Sikhs was counterbalanced by the loss of their commander, Huree Singh, who was mortally wounded, and died the day after. Both armies passed the night on the battle-field; and on the 23rd, the attack was renewed by the Sikhs, who took several pieces of cannon from the Afghans, and threw them into disorder; but, according to the Sikh reports, the soldiers, believing the victory to be won, could not resist the temptation to plunder; whereupon a reserve corps, under a young Englishman, named Rattray,* with

* Lieutenant Wood (Journey to the Oxus, p. 159) gives the following account of Lieutenant-Colonel Rattray: "We wound up the pass to the fort of Ali Masjid, and were there received by its commandant, an ill-conditioned, dissipated-looking Englishman; slipshod, turbaned, and robed in a sort of Afghan dishabille, having more the look of a dissipated priest than a military man. His abode was a cave in the mountain, from which he and his hungry followers levied black mail on the passing kafilas. *Lieutenant-Colonel* Rattray received us at the head of his *column*, which, drawn up for the occasion, had something approaching to a military look; but no sooner did the commandant attempt a manœuvre, than a most ludicrous scene ensued. In utter hopelessness of restoring his scattered legion to order, he disbanded it forthwith, and then the *Lieutenant-Colonel* commenced whacking his men with a cudgel; but he was soon overwhelmed by numbers, and compelled to desist. Some time after this, when we were in Cabul, this man became a convert to Mahomedanism, much against the wish of Dost Mahomed Khan, who

artillery, seized the critical moment, rushed upon the enemy, and the disordered and retreating Afghans, being thus enabled to rally, the Sikhs were broken and fled to their intrenchments. Here they were enabled to maintain themselves against reiterated assaults for four days, till the arrival of General Allard, who advanced by forced marches, with reinforcements (Runjeet having made great preparations apparently for conquests in Afghanistan, which he had pushed forward); and upon his junction with the Sikh army, the Afghans retreated through the pass to Jelallabad. Both parties suffered severely in this conflict; about 7,000 men are said to have fallen. The Afghans acknowledged their loss to be 1,500, including a son of Dost Mahomed Khan, and several

who thought him a disgrace to any creed, and expressed in strong terms the contempt he felt for men who could change their religion to improve their fortune. The Khybur commandant was altogether a singular character; void of all principle, but clever and well-informed. His autobiography, written at the request of Captain Burnes, affords another proof how often the real events of life exceed in interest the wildest conception of fiction."

chiefs; that of the Sikhs was much greater, but the accounts are irreconcilable. The savage rancour of the belligerents towards each other, inflamed by religious antipathies, permitted no quarter to be given on either side; all who surrendered were put to death on the spot. When Lieutenant Wood entered the pass a few months after this event, he beheld Sikh scalps exhibited in the middle of the road, trophies of the field of Jumrood.

The news of this disaster, which, however, had no other result than to elate and intoxicate the Afghans,* and still further to exasperate the parties against each other, confounded Runjeet Singh, who told Captain Wade that he would be glad to give up Peshawur if he could save his *purdah* (honour); and Mr.

* Although Dost Mahomed Khan entertained a deep hatred towards Runjeet Singh, as a rival and a Sikh, he appears, from the despatches of Captain Burnes, to have acknowledged his own inferiority. "My sons and people," he said to Captain Burnes, "may speak in exaggerated terms of our late success, but it is too evident that our power is not one-tenth of that of the Punjab."

Masson* says that, in September, 1837, Captain Wade wrote to him that the Sikh ruler was ready to come to an amicable adjustment on reasonable terms. The Maharaja proceeded in person to the frontier, but, finding that his presence was unnecessary, he returned to Lahore, much incensed against his generals, to whose misconduct and cowardice he attributed the disgrace of his arms. It has been stated that he seized all the property left by Huree Singh (eighty lakhs of rupees, or about 800,000*l.*), whose family was suffered to fall into poverty.†

About this time, in imitation of European customs, Runjeet adopted the cheap expedient of rewarding military merit by establishing a military order, called the "Auspicious Star of the Punjab," the decorations of which he conferred upon some

* Journey in Baloochistan, &c. vol. iii. p. 424.

† Calcutta Review, No. 2, art. 5. The writer adds, that the children of Meean Singh, who was murdered in the government of Cashmere, were also thrown upon the world.

British officers. Towards the end of 1837, he was prevailed upon to redeem his pledge of nominating the Barukzye sirdar, Sooltan Mahomed Khan, ruler of Peshawur, or rather, his representative there.

CHAPTER XVIII.

A.D. 1838 AND 1839.

WE now approach the period of an important transaction, the restoration of Shah Shuja, by the joint aid of the British Government and the Maharaja of the Punjab. It is unnecessary to discuss in this place the policy of that measure, or the motives which prevailed with those who were intrusted with the guardianship of British interests in the East, to depart from the non-intervention principles which forbade Lord William Bentinck to countenance the expedition of Shah Shuja in 1833, and led them to consider that "we owed it to our own safety to assist the lawful sovereign of Afghanistan in the recovery of his throne."* It may be sufficient to say, that the anti-English feelings cherished by the Shah of

* Correspondence relative to Affghanistan, 1839, No. 4, p. 7.

Persia, the supposed designs of Russia, the activity of the agents of that power in Central Asia, and the predilection of Dost Mahomed Khan for a Russian alliance, in opposition to the views of England,—in which the Ameer was greatly biassed by our intimate relations with his bitter enemy, Runjeet Singh,—appeared to warrant the enterprise, in order to "arrest the rapid progress of foreign intrigue and aggression towards our own territories," and to secure our western frontier, by having there an ally who is interested in the maintenance of tranquillity, "in the place of chiefs ranging themselves in subservience to a hostile power, and seeking to promote schemes of conquest and aggrandizement."* The Declaration of the British Indian Government, which assigns these motives, adverts likewise to the "sudden and unprovoked attack," recently made by Dost Mahomed Khan, upon the territory of "our ancient ally, Maharaja Runjeet Singh;" the Dost's virtual refusal of our mediation, and the "most unreasonable pretensions" set up by him (namely, for the relinquishment of

* Simla Declaration of 1st October, 1838.

the Peshawur territory), as the basis of an arrangement between them, "such as the Governor-General could not, consistently with justice and his regard for the friendship of Maharaja Runjeet Singh, be the channel of introducing to the consideration of his highness."

After the rupture of the negotiations carried on with Dost Mahomed Khan, through the intervention of Captain Burnes, but before the retreat of the Persians from Herat, Lord Auckland, in a Minute* which preceded the Declaration, took a view of our past policy in respect to Afghanistan, which shews the importance he attached to the preservation of friendly relations with Runjeet Singh, a consideration which, no doubt, had great influence in the choice of the alternatives, namely, adopting the cause of Shah Shuja, or that of Dost Mohamed Khan. His lordship observed, that more direct aid to Herat was not in our power, and direct interference would have been opposed to the positive engagements of treaty; that arms supplied to the Barukzye chiefs of Cabul and Candahar

* Dated Simla, 12th May, 1838.

would have been, more probably, used against the Sikhs than against Persia; that the Ameer of Cabul would not move but on condition of the cession of Peshawur; and that relations with him, whilst such pretensions were advanced, would have destroyed the cordiality of our alliance with "the most powerful and valuable of our friends, Runjeet Singh."

The original design of our Government seems to have been to promote the success of the Shah by every means short of direct interference, but to leave the military operations in the hands of the Sikh ruler. It has been asserted, that Runjeet evinced some reluctance to enter into the project, and that he was at last induced, very unwillingly, to become a party to the tripartite treaty. Be that as it may, in August, 1838, Lord Auckland determined "to give the direct and powerful assistance of the British Government to the enterprise of Shah Shuja, in a degree which was not at first contemplated by him, from a conviction, confirmed in the most decided manner by every opinion of authority on the subject, that the measure could not be trusted mainly to the support of the Sikh ruler and army, without imminent hazard of failure, and of serious detriment to the reputation of the British name amongst the Afghan people."*

The project was first opened to Runjeet Singh. A complimentary deputation having been sent by the Maharaja to the Governor-General at Simla, consisting of some of the most distinguished Sikh chiefs, Lord Auckland resolved to send a mission, ostensibly to reciprocate the compliments, but really to treat respecting the state of affairs beyond the north-west frontier of India. This mission† was conducted by Mr. (the late Sir William) Macnaghten, who proceeded to the court of the Maharaja, and reached his camp, at Adenanugur, on the 28th May. Two marches from this place, the mission was met by Pertab Singh (a boy of seven years of age), son of Sher Singh, and grandson of Runjeet, who had been sent by his father to accompany the mission through his district.

* Letter to Secret Committee, 13th August, 1838.

† An account of this mission is given in the Hon. W. G. Osborne's "Court and Camp of Runjeet Singh."

According to precedent and custom, Sher Singh himself should have been sent; but it is supposed that Runjeet was jealous of European influence over his family and chiefs, and, according to Mr. Osborne, an excuse was assigned for this breach of etiquette which is highly characteristic of the manners of the Lahore court; namely, that the Shah-zadeh Sher Singh, in consequence of having been overcome at a drinking party with the Maharaja, on the evening before, was unable to travel.

The negotiations, it appears, went on less smoothly than was expected; Runjeet made the proposal a pretext for demanding a variety of concessions which could not be complied with. It is understood, that he insisted so pertinaciously upon having Shikarpore, as the price of his co-operation, that the negotiation was on the point of being broken off, till at length he was prevailed upon to accept a payment of two lakhs of rupees by the Shah, guaranteed by the British Government, in lieu of the cession. Accordingly, in the tripartite treaty, amongst the additions to the treaty of 1833, is an article under which Shah Shuja engaged to pay, after his restoration, two lakhs of rupees,* from the date on which the Sikh troops may be despatched for the purpose of reinstating the Shah, in consideration of the Maharaja stationing a force of 5,000 men (Mahomedans) in the Peshawur territory, for the support of the Shah. Another additional article stipulates that, of the tribute to be paid by the Meers of Sinde to Shah Shuja, fifteen lakhs should be made over to Runjeet Singh.

Upon the return of the mission from Lahore, a communication was made to Shah Shuja, who readily executed the tripartite treaty of 26th June, 1838, which was the same as that of 1833, with the additions just mentioned.

Preparatory to the commencement of the campaign, an interview took place between the Governor-General of British India (Lord Auckland) and the Maharaja of the Punjab, on the 29th November, 1838, at Feroze-

* The words "per annum" are omitted in the official copy of this treaty laid before Parliament. Indian Papers, 1839, No. 1.

pore. Runjeet Singh paid the first visit, crossing the Sutluj with his court in all the pomp and splendour of an Eastern potentate. He was met by the representative of the British nation, accompanied by Sir Henry Fane, the Commander-in-Chief, and a numerous suite. At the meeting, Lord Auckland received his royal visitor into the houda of his elephant, and embraced him, under a royal salute; and they proceeded to the tent of the Governor-General, through an avenue of 4,000 British troops, the scene realizing (says an eye-witness) all the fabled descriptions of Oriental magnificence. Upon reaching the inclosure, Lord Auckland and Sir Henry Fane, dismounting, handed down the Maharaja, whose feeble motions contrasted strongly with his quick eye and earnest and intelligent expression. Entering the Durbar tent, Runjeet took a seat on the same couch with the Honourable Miss Eden (the sister of Lord Auckland), having the Governor-General on his right, and addressed the lady on a few topics happily chosen, Major Wade interpreting. The tent presented an extraordinary scene, being filled almost to suffocation with

English generals and Sikh sirdars, ladies and matchlock men, English civilians in plain dresses, and Punjabi ministers in chain and plated armour, all crammed together. After enduring the agony with polite patience for some time, Runjeet was at length escorted by Lord Auckland and Sir Henry Fane to an audience-tent, where only a select number was admitted. Here the presents were exhibited, and amongst them a portrait of Queen Victoria, painted by Miss Eden, in a frame of solid gold. On receiving this picture, Runjeet bowed his head, and, in a graceful manner, pressed the portrait to his lips, declaring that it was the most acceptable gift he could receive,* and that he should suspend it in his tent under a salute of 101 guns.

The Maharaja was then conducted from the tent to view the elephants, horses, camel battery, howitzers, and other artillery, forming part of the presents; and here an incident happened, which the superstitious Asiatics interpreted as an unfavourable omen. Some

* According to report, he gave the picture to one of his sirdars soon after.

spherical cases had been piled up in front of the howitzers, which, owing to the confusion and crowd, were not observed, and over them the Maharaja stumbled and fell, Sir Henry Fane doing the same. The latter soon recovered himself, and raised Runjeet, who treated the matter as a trifle, notwithstanding his bodily infirmities, as well as the ominous aspect of the occurrence.

At the conclusion of the interview, which lasted two hours, the Maharaja returned with the same pomp and honours as he came.

On the following day, the visit was returned, and it is admitted that the Sikhs fairly outshone the representative of the English court. A body of British cavalry (including the 16th Lancers) crossed the Sutluj, and took up a station on the right bank of the river, at the foot of the bridge of boats. Lord Auckland, accompanied by his suite of civil and military officers, left his tents at sunrise, and proceeded on their elephants, under a salute of artillery, towards the river, a distance of about three miles. The procession had not moved more than a few hundred yards before it was met by Sher Singh (Runjeet's second son), with Dheȧn Singh, the prime minister, several rajas and sirdars, attended by a body of cavalry and infantry. The march was extremely picturesque, from the variety, as well as richness, of the different costumes and arms. When the procession crossed the river, and moved up an avenue formed by the British cavalry, it presented a grand spectacle, whilst batteries were firing, drums beating, and trumpets sounding. A discharge of distant artillery announced that the Maharaja had left his tents, and in a few minutes the opposite pageant came in sight, when the scene is represented to have been beyond the power of verbal description, and surpassing all that European imagination had conceived of even oriental luxury and splendour. Between the ranks of horsemen gorgeously arrayed, with steel casques and glittering appointments, moved in majestic order towards each other two masses of elephants, bearing in rich houdas the two greatest rulers in India, surrounded by their ministers and warriors. Columns after columns of troops were seen, in every variety of gay colours, covered with a profusion of ornaments, preserving a steadiness which the best European discipline could not excel, whilst to the east and west stretched an extensive encampment, in the centre of which were numerous tents, glittering in crimson and gold. At viewing distance from the Sikh legions, were dense masses of spectators of the humble classes, maintaining a silence and decorum scarcely ever shewn in the most civilized countries of Europe, as if the rules of military discipline had made some impression upon the habits of civil life. No tumultuous shouts rent the air; none of those bursts of rude, though hearty, exultation, which are not repressed in Europe; the silent awe or breathless astonishment of the masses was only occasionally broken by the licensed tongue of an Akali or a fakir. The processions met and mingled. The Maharaja, on a ponderous elephant, was habited, as on the day before, in a dark crimson shawl-cloth tunic, trowsers, and turban, without any trinkets, and was thus, as well as by his flowing white beard, distinguished from his richly-clad sirdars and attendants. Lord Auckland, who wore the blue and gold uniform of an English minister of state, entered the Maharaja's houda, amidst the clangor of trumpets and the roar of cannon, and the united procession moved on, in a majestic pace, to the durbar-tents. Upon their arrival there, bands of Sikh musicians, admirably trained, struck up our national anthem. The tents were inclosed within a vast area of crimson cloth walls, nine feet high, decorated with yellow lace (Runjeet's favourite *bussuntee* colour); and within this inclosure were drawn up in order about 2,000 of the Maharaja's household troops, in crimson silk, or elegant kingcaub dresses, armed with polished matchlocks and shields. Alighting in this magnificent inclosure, where the order and silence presented a striking contrast to the confusion and pressure which had been permitted in the English tents, the Maharaja conducted Lord Auckland and Sir Henry Fane, and their suites, to the durbar-tent, which was a splendidly carpeted floor, on which were numerous gold and silver chairs, covered in by a spacious *sumeeana*, lined with shawl-cloth. Here the introductions took place, and when they were over, a band of nautch-girls, covered with jewellery and glistening with silver-dust, performed their singular movements, and then the presents were produced. The departure of the Governor-General was honoured with a royal salute.

Shortly after this interview, Lord Auckland visited Amritsur and Lahore. At the former place, the Maharaja's hospitality and confidence were unbounded. The party were admitted into the chief temple, where Lord Auckland (the first European who had been so indulged) sat side by side with Runjeet Singh on the same carpet, listening to the lecture of the *Grant'h*, the secretaries, generals, and suite (including the Misses Eden), sitting or standing around. Amongst other ceremonies, an offering was made to the temple on that occasion.* The Maharaja conducted his visitor to Govind-gurh. It was not expected by Lord Auckland that he

* A report of this visit, in the Indian papers, having led to the misapprehension that the offering was made by Lord Auckland, the matter was noticed in the Court of Proprietors of East India Stock, on the 19th June, 1839.

would have been admitted within this important fortress; but, to the surprise of all, and the chagrin and anger of many Sikhs, Runjeet threw open the gates, and led the party over the whole, pointing out the vaults which contained his treasures (reported to be £12,000,000 sterling), which had been hitherto concealed from all but initiated Sikhs of high rank. It was observed that Runjeet had strengthened the walls both of the city and the fort, substituting brick for mud in the curtains and bastions.

At Lahore, where Lord Auckland arrived on the 21st December, the entertainments were on a scale of princely magnificence and truly oriental luxury. Runjeet insisted that his lordship should take his part in drinking, requiring each time that he should drain the cup of fiery liquid* he presented to the

* This wine was extracted from raisins, a quantity of pearls being ground to powder and mixed with it. It was made for Runjeet alone, and though he sometimes gave a few bottles to some of his favourite chiefs, it was very difficult to be procured even at the enormous price of a gold mohur for a small bottle. "It is as strong as aquafortis," Mr. Osborne says (p. 189), "and as at his parties he always helps you himself, it is no

easy

dregs. The excess committed by the Maharaja on this occasion,—he had been prevailed upon by his English medical attendant to live abstemiously,—produced a severe fit of apoplexy, and when Lord Auckland took leave of him, he was lying on his couch, scarcely able to articulate. It is said that when his lordship presented his host with a valuable jewel, his eye lighted up with all its wonted fire.

Prior to the meeting at Ferozepore, attempts were made by those about Runjeet, who were adverse to the British, to infuse distrust and suspicion into his mind, and doubts were expressed whether he would visit the Governor-General at such a distance in the British territory, the place of meeting being three miles from the river. His confidence in British honour, however, resisted these efforts, and he even went two miles further to be present at a review of

easy matter to avoid excess. The only food allowed you at these drinking bouts is fat quails stuffed with all sorts of spices, and the only thing to allay your thirst, naturally consequent upon eating such heating food, is this abominable liquid fire."

13,000 of our troops, forming part of the army of the Indus, on the 3rd December, when he appeared much struck with the manœuvres of this fine force.

The friendly feelings, which this personal intercourse confirmed, removed the reluctance, if it ever existed, in the mind of the Maharaja, to allow our troops a passage through the Punjab, in their march to Afghanistan. In the course of this year he gave a fresh proof of his sentiments, by refusing in open durbar to receive a communication from the Nepal Raja, on the ground that he and the British Government were friends, and that their enemies were his enemies.

Runjeet appears to have heartily cooperated in the execution of the tripartite treaty; and the inefficiency of the services rendered by his troops at Peshawur, where, however, the resistance was much greater than at Candahar and Ghuzni, is attributed to disobedience of his orders, and the jealousy of his son and sirdars. Captain (now Sir Claude Martin) Wade was appointed by the British Government to act with the Sikh army at Peshawur, whither Runjeet sent an imposing force, under Nou Nehal Singh, leaving his own Sutluj frontier open to us; whilst all his stores of cattle and grain were at the disposal of the British.

The life of Runjeet Singh was now drawing to a close. Although the remaining vigour of his wonderful constitution had partially recovered the paralytic attack which had seized him during Lord Auckland's visit, he lost the power of speech, though he retained his other faculties. "A curious and interesting sight it was now," says one authority,* "to behold the fast-decaying monarch, his mind still alive, by signs giving his orders; still receiving reports, and, assisted by the faithful fakir Uzeez-ud-deen,† almost as usual, attending

* Calcutta Review, No. II. p. 476.

† Uzeez-ud-deen, by birth a barber, became first attached to the household of Runjeet in this capacity, as well as in that of hakim, or doctor, the two functions being united in the East as formerly in the West. Being a smart, bold young fellow, intelligent and of insinuating manners, he gained Runjeet's notice, and obtained a small jagir. When Mr. Metcalfe came to the Sikh durbar, on an unpalatable errand, in 1808, all Runjeet's

to affairs of state. By a slight turn of his hand to the south, he would inquire the news from the British frontier; by a similar turn to the west, he would demand tidings from the invading army; and most anxious was he for intelligence from Afghanistan, doubting the success of the English measure, seeing his own advantage in their

councillors advised an appeal to the sword, except the hakim and one Purupteal (who died soon after), and they strenuously dissuaded him from a collision with the British. Runjeet followed their advice, and ever after gave Uzeez-ud-deen his fullest confidence, which he retained for thirty years. Being descended from the Ansari Arabs, and his family being fakirs, he took that title, and became the most confidential adviser of Runjeet, as well as his physician, possessing more influence over him than even Dhean Singh. He is a fine-looking man, with agreeable features, and now about fifty-five. His next brother, Noor-ud-deen, was intrusted with the command of the city of Lahore, and likewise enjoyed Runjeet's confidence. He was the owner of the manufactory of distilled waters, essences, and medicines, and superintended the magazines and public buildings. A younger brother, named Imam-ud-deen (who is now blind), was made governor of Govind-gurh, an office which, after his blindness, was executed by his son, Taj-ed-deen. All three brothers are men of remarkable intelligence and very agreeable manners.

failure, and yet unwilling or afraid to withdraw from his engagements." So deep were the feelings of respect he had inspired, that the most implicit obedience was paid to every wish he expressed, though his end was evidently near. Several times he was taken from his charpae (bedstead) and laid on the floor to die, but he rallied again. In the hot weather of 1839, he had applied for a British physician, and Dr. Steele was sent; but his case was a hopeless one; dropsy, attended by fever, had made rapid inroads, and defied the power of medicine.

When Runjeet became aware of the fatal character of his disorder, he seemed for days to struggle with death, and still clang with mad tenacity to an existence which had now no enjoyment to offer him that he had not exhausted. He had recourse to priests and holy men, whose effectual intervention with heaven, by a perversity of which all countries, in all ages, have furnished examples, he hoped could be purchased by gold. Even his avarice yielded to this exigency, and he lavished with almost wanton prodigality his immense treasures amongst sordid pundits, fakirs, and devotees of all sorts, who flocked from every quarter to Lahore, allured by the liberal prices he paid for prayers. His alms were distributed, without discrimination, amongst Hindus and Nanuk-Shahis, Bramins and Sodees; Gya and Juggernat participated in the spoil with Amritsur and other Sikh shrines. The nearer the dreaded moment seemed to approach, the more eager was his hankering for life, and the more undistinguishing and boundless his profusion. Jagirs were assigned to temples; his elephants, even his beloved horses, were parted with; steeds with jewelled saddles, cows with gilded horns, golden chairs and golden bedsteads, were sent to propitiate the various deities; his pearls and gems, even the jewels which had been recently presented to him by the representative of the British nation, were bartered for even the chance of a few additional moments of existence. It has been computed that, on the day of his death, the wealth bestowed by Runjeet in pious gifts amounted to more than a million sterling. As a last resource, two hours before his death, that matchless diamond, the Koh-i-noor, for the possession of which he had violated the laws of hospitality and perpetrated a cruel robbery, was sent for, to be despatched as a gift to adorn the image of Juggernat; but now his successor, and his ministers and courtiers (who were invaded by fears that nothing would be left for their cupidity), interposed, and represented that such a jewel, which the whole revenue of India could not re-purchase, was an alms too precious to be conferred upon Bramins. The other gifts, however, continued till the evening of the 27th June, 1839, when, after a succession of fainting fits, his mental faculties remaining unimpaired till the last, the Maharaja expired, at the age of fifty-eight.

His death was concealed by the Koonwur (or Prince) Khuruk Singh, Raja Dhean Singh, the minister, and Jemadar Khooshal Singh, until they had taken measures, during the night, for securing the city. In the early part of the month, he had directed his son, Khuruk Singh, to hold durbar, and Dhean Singh, in conjunction with Khuruk Singh, to regulate the affairs of the state, the

Vuzeerat being conferred upon the minister, as the second person in the state. On the night of the 20th, the condition of Runjeet being hopeless, it had been resolved that the heir-apparent should be proclaimed successor to the throne, which was done on the following morning, when Khuruk Singh and Dhean Singh took nuzzurs from the commandants of the troops and officers. On the morning of the 28th June, trusty officers having been placed in charge of the ghats on the Sutluj, and patrols disposed about the city, the death of Runjeet and the accession of Khuruk were announced. Raja Dhean Singh acted a strange and unaccountable part on this occasion. He declared his resolution to burn with the body of his late master, and was with difficulty persuaded, after some hours' entreaty, to forego this resolve, the prince and sirdars throwing their turbands at his feet, and declaring that, without him, the affairs of the state would be deranged. He gave way to their importunity only on condition that he should be permitted to visit Benares.

Although the practice of suttee forms no

part of the institutions of the Sikhs, and is rare amongst them, upon this occasion, the four ranis of Runjeet, Koondun, daughter of Raja Sunsar Chund; Hinderee, daughter of Meean Puddum Singh, of Noorpur; Rajkoonwur, daughter of Sirdar Jey Singh, of Chynpur, and Baant Ali, determined, in spite of the entreaties and remonstrances of Khuruk Singh and his ministers, who guaranteed their rank and property, to burn.

The corpse of the late Maharaja having been washed with Ganges water, and placed on a bier of sandal wood decorated with gold flowers, was carried, the day after his death, to the place of cremation, before the gates of the palace Hazaree Bagh, followed by the four ranis in their richest dresses, loaded with jewels of immense value, walking in a measured step, attended by Bramins and Sodees (Sikh priests), singing the holy hymns of Nanuk, in the same form, and with the same ceremonies, which were beheld in these very parts (on the banks of the Ravi) by the army of Alexander the Great more than 2,000 years before, and which are described by the Greek and Roman writers* with a minute fidelity, which would suit a modern suttee. The funeral pile was made of sandal wood, and when the procession reached it, an affecting scene took place. Rani Koondun, the principal widow, took the hand of Dhean Singh, and placing it on the breast of the corpse, made him swear never to betray or desert Khuruk Singh, or his son Nou Nehal Singh, or forget the interests of the Khalsa; and Khuruk Singh, in like manner, swore not to betray or desert Dhean Singh. Besides the fatal curse of a suttee, the torments incurred by the slaughter of a thousand cows were imprecated on the head of him who violated his oath.

Rani Koondun then mounted the pyre, sat down beside the body of her late husband, which was in a sitting posture, and placed his head in her lap. The other ranis, two of them only sixteen years of age, and of

* Diodorus Siculus, lib. xvii. c. 91; lib. xix. cc. 32, 33. Strabo, *Geogr.* lib. xv. Cicero, *Tusc. Quæst.* lib. v. c. 27. Propertius, lib. iii. El. xi. Valerius Maximus, lib. vi. c. 14.

extraordinary beauty, with five, some say seven, Cashmerian slave-girls (one of them the lovely Lotus, who had attracted the admiration of the mission in 1838), followed the example, seating themselves around the corpse, with every token of satisfaction in their countenances. At the hour fixed by the Bramins, in the presence of all the troops at the capital and an immense crowd of spectators, including several English officers, the pile was lighted, one account states by Khuruk Singh, another, by the Rani Koondun, and, without a shriek or groan being heard, the living and the dead were reduced to ashes. It is said that Raja Dhean Singh made four several attempts to jump upon the burning mass, but was withheld by the people about him. A witness of this appalling spectacle relates that a small cloud appeared in the sky over the pile, and that he saw (perhaps thought he saw) a few drops fall upon the smouldering embers, as if the very elements wept at the closing scene of this dismal tragedy.

The ashes were conveyed in a palanquin of gold, in grand procession, accompanied by Khuruk Singh (in a plain white muslin dress), Dhean Singh, and Khooshal Singh, to the Ganges, and committed to that holy river.

Nature was not liberal to Runjeet Singh in personal gifts; one of his disadvantages was a mean-looking aspect, and which, at first sight, was almost repulsive, though this impression speedily wore off. His stature was below the middle size; to Burnes (who says his height did not certainly exceed five feet three inches), he appeared diminutive, and to Major Lawrence, stunted; but as latterly he had an habitual stoop, he probably seemed shorter than he really was. None, however, represent his height as more than five feet seven inches. He was meagre, but had been vigorous and active in youth. His shoulders were broad; his head was square, large in proportion, and somewhat sunk in his shoulders; his neck was thick and muscular; his forehead remarkably broad; his face oval, and much marked with the small-pox, the scars not running into one another, but forming dark pits. The disease had closed the left eye; the remaining eye was large and brown; his nose was short and slightly *re-troussé*, or swollen at the tip; his lips were thin and stretched tight over his teeth, which were good to the last; his complexion was a dark brown; his voice, latterly rough and unpleasant, had been soft and agreeable. When necessary, he could assume a fascinating tone, which operated upon those about him like enchantment. A long white beard and moustaches, latterly thin and matted, gave him an appearance of greater age than he had. "Altogether," says Baron Hügel, "he is the ugliest man I saw throughout the Punjab, and the most forbidding human being I have ever seen." Others (and Mr. H. T. Prinsep in the number) have described his appearance as far from unprepossessing, his countenance having been full of expression and animation.* When, however, the first ill-impression disappeared, no one admitted

* The difference of age, at the periods of interview, will account for much of this inconsistency. The likeness of Runjeet, given by Captain Osborne, from a drawing by Miss Eden, fully justifies the Baron's description; while that in Mr. H. T. Prinsep's Life of Runjeet, from a painting by a native artist, warrants his more favourable portraiture.

to the presence of Runjeet Singh could fail to be struck with his extraordinary qualities, his intelligence and acuteness. His penetrating look, the restlessness of his fiery eye, which seemed to dive into the thoughts of the person he conversed with, and the rapidity of his laconic but searching questions, denoted the activity of his mind and his insatiable curiosity. "His conversation," M. Jacquemont says, "was like a night-mare; he is," continues the lively Frenchman, "almost the first really inquisitive Indian I have seen, and his curiosity balances the apathy of the whole of his nation." When he sat in an arm-chair, with his feet drawn under him, the position was peculiarly unfavourable for him; but as soon as he mounted his horse, which he managed with ease, even after his right side was affected with paralysis, his whole form seemed animated by the spirit within, and assumed a grace of which no one before thought it susceptible. When he had become weak, he adopted a singular method of mounting the tall horses on which he loved to ride. A man knelt down before him, and he threw his leg over his neck, when the man rose, with the Maharaja upon his shoulders, and approached the horse. Runjeet then, putting his right foot into the stirrup, and holding by the horse's mane, threw his left leg over the man's head and the back of the horse into the stirrup on the other side. He dressed plainly, wearing few ornaments, though he took pleasure in seeing his courtiers and dependants in rich dresses, and his durbar was very splendid. He did not use a gudi or throne; "my sword," he observed, "procures for me all the distinction I desire, and I am quite indifferent to external pomp." He was quite unreserved in all his habits; his diet consisted of high stimulants, of which he partook sparingly. His deportment was easy and dignified, and his manners, generally speaking, were polished. M. Jacquemont has recorded * a gross act of impropriety, of which, he says, Runjeet was guilty, in the presence of Lord William Bentinck and his whole court.

The character and policy of this remarkable personage deserve to be considered in a separate chapter.

* Letters from India, vol. ii. p. 223.

CHAPTER XIX.

CHARACTER AND POLICY OF RUNJEET SINGH.

RUNJEET SINGH has been likened to Mehemet Ali and to Napoleon. M. Jacquemont terms him, "a Bonaparte in miniature." There are some points in which he resembles both; but, estimating his character with reference to his circumstances and position, he is, perhaps, a more remarkable man than either. The worst parts of his personal character may be traced to the accidents of country and education, or rather want of education; his best qualities belonged to himself.

He was not only uninstructed in any branch of learning or science, but absolutely illiterate; he could not even read or write; whilst unlimited means were afforded to him by his mother, in early youth, of plunging into dissipation, gratifying every passion, and even the most irregular desires, at a court and amongst a sect notorious for immorality; licentiousness and sensuality, of the lowest and basest kinds, being the rule, and sobriety and decency the rare exceptions. At the age of seventeen, whilst pleasure and luxury spread their seductions before him, the affairs of his sirdaree fell into his hands, and the consummate skill with which he overcame the difficulties of his situation, defeated or foiled every antagonist, converted enemies to friends, and made friends subservient to his own purposes, must inspire the reader of the preceding chapters with surprise and wonder, if not with higher emotions. It is difficult to suppress admiration, in contemplating the career of such a man, who, with so many disadvantages, succeeded, with so few crimes, in elevating himself from a simple sirdar, to be the sovereign of a large kingdom, including Hindus and Mahomedans, as well as Sikhs, the only state in India not substantially under British dominion. The character of all Eastern princes must be judged, not by the European, but by the Asiatic standard of morals; according to which, craft, cunning, artifice, treachery, are reckoned talents, rather than vices, in a statesman; and even barbarous cruelty is pardoned as a means to a politic end.

Although he was unable to read or write in any language, the habit of hearing papers read in Persian, Punjabi, and Hindi, and great assiduity in attention even to the minutiæ of business, gave Runjeet a facility in following and understanding for the most part what was submitted to him; so that, although quite unable to appreciate elegancies of style, or to dictate word for word what should be written, he transacted business rapidly, was ready with a short and decided order upon any report or representation read to him, and when the draft of his instruction was prepared in due form, he saw at once whether it fully corresponded with his views. Confidential secretaries were perpetually in attendance, and frequently called up in the night, to expedite orders, as the sudden recollection or caprice of the Maharaja suggested them. With great natural intelligence, and a wonderfully quick apprehension, his memory was excellent, and stored with minute, as well as important, circumstances.

He audited all the revenue accounts, and the tenacity of his memory enabled him to follow the most complicated statements. In his annual circuits through the country, he kept in his mind a register of what he had seen. His disposition was at the same time watchful, and his eye quick and searching, so that nothing escaped his observation; while the perspicacity displayed in his appreciation of character, and in tracing the motives of others' actions, gave him a command and influence over all who approached him, which were mainly instrumental to his rapid rise. With great acuteness, he had a lively imagination; and though never for an instant forgetful of any end he may have had in view, there was a frankness and *naïveté* about his conversation, peculiarly agreeable. His observations and remarks were given ordinarily in short, terse, incoherent phrases, or in the shape of interrogatories; * but they were such as re-

* When the Adventurer in the Punjab appeared before Runjeet, seeking service, the following discourse took place, which affords a good idea of the style of his interrogatories: "I was asked what I knew, what I could do, and what I wanted—all in a breath. My reply was to the effect that I could do any thing, was ignorant

mained fixed in the recollection of the person to whom they were addressed, as uncommon, and displaying an original thinker. His eagerness for information and instruction was unbounded. He had great power of dissimulation, and, under the greatest frankness of manner, and even familiarity, in his intercourse, could veil subtle designs, and even treachery. In action he always shewed himself personally brave and collected, but his plans betrayed no boldness or adventurous hazard. Address and cunning, nay, even corruption, have always been preferred by him, as instruments of success, to any dash of enterprise, calculated to excite admiration or inspire awe. Mr. Moorcroft* relates an anecdote of Runjeet, mentioned by himself, which illustrates this part of his character:—"He told me that when Lord Lake entered the Punjab, in pursuit of Holkar, he felt a

ignorant of nothing, and having heard the fame of the king, was come from a far country to offer my services. 'Can you build a fort? Can you cure a long-standing disease? Can you cast a gun? Can you shoe a horse? Can you mend my watch, which has stopped?'"—Vol. i. p. 20.

* Travels, vol. i. p. 102.

strong desire to see the European general and his officers. His courtiers endeavoured to dissuade him, affirming that the very sight would be unlucky; but he was determined to gratify himself, and for that purpose disguised himself as a common trooper, and accompanied by a party of his soldiers, repaired to the British camp. They went to Mr. Metcalfe's tent, and sent word that some Sikhs had come out of curiosity to see the Sahibs, and begged he would indulge them. Mr. Metcalfe complied, but soon distinguished Runjeet Singh amongst his visitors." His fertility in expedients was wonderful, and he was never at a loss for a resource in the greatest difficulties; but many of his actions evinced caprice, and even instability of purpose, for the motive of them cannot be traced or imagined. His uniform conduct and career through life prove him to have been selfish, sensual, and licentious: not regardful of the ties of affection, blood, or friendship, in the pursuit of ambition or pleasure; and greedy in a profligate degree, plundering and reducing to misery, without the slightest remorse, widows, orphans, and families possessing claims to consideration and respect; at the same time, he almost invariably provided for the families of his conquered enemies. In his youth he was lavish in his gifts to favourites, and there was liberality in his general dealings; but as age came over him, his desire of accumulation degenerated into avarice and the desire of hoarding, which became the ruling passions, and he was approached, even by his confidential officers and those in favour, with more apprehension of robbery and exaction from themselves, than of hope to add to their acquisitions through his indulgence. His temper was in youth excellent, and always under command; but latterly, the irritability of an impaired constitution frequently overpowered him, and he has been known to break out into fits of passion, and to descend to the use of personal violence towards the objects of his rage; but there was no ferocity in his disposition, and he never punished a criminal with death, even under circumstances of aggravated offence.

Humanity, indeed, or rather a tenderness for life, in spite of some acts of harshness, was a trait in the character of Runjeet Singh: there is no instance of his having wantonly imbrued his hands in blood. "Never, perhaps," observes Baron Hügel—no partial witness—"was so large an empire founded by one man with so little criminality; and when we consider the country and the uncivilized people with whom he has had to deal, his mild and prudent government must be regarded with feelings of astonishment." Cunning and conciliation were his two great implements of diplomacy, whilst his consummate prudence, his great knowledge of mankind in general, and of Asiatics in particular, his energy and perseverance, enabled him to employ those implements with invariable success. When he is taxed with want of faith, it must be remembered that he was the only eastern prince whom the British Government never could accuse of a breach of his engagements.

His sensual indulgences were, as before remarked, the vices of his country; neither his own uncultivated mind, nor the society of those about him, offered any temptation to more refined gratifications. Hunting, in which he took great delight from his earliest years, was, perhaps, the most innocent of his recreations, and in these excursions, Runjeet realized the gorgeous descriptions given of the hunting expeditions of Asiatic monarchs. He was accompanied, as a soldier-king, by a camp, with elephants, troops, and cannon, and every luxury was provided that could charm the eye, captivate the ear, or pamper the grosser senses. At his court, troops of Cashmerian nautch-girls of the rarest beauty, "very fair, with expressive countenances, and large and lovely eyes,"* were constantly in attendance to enact their voluptuous dances. Amongst other caprices of Runjeet, he formed a band of Amazons, consisting of about 150 of the most beautiful girls of Cashmere, Persia, and the Punjab, who were magnificently dressed, armed with bows and arrows, and frequently appeared on horseback, mounted *en cavalier*, for the amusement of the Maharaja.

His passion for horses, which amounted almost to insanity, has been already mentioned. He was not singular in this passion,

* The Hon. W. Osborne.

for every Sikh keeps, if he can, a horse and a brood mare. Runjeet was fond of exhibiting his stud, and Mr. Moorcroft, an excellent judge of this animal, speaks of one as beautifully made. The efforts of Runjeet to secure the famous horse Lylee have been recorded.* This animal was seen by Lieut. Barr's party in the beginning of 1839 (when the horse was old), and it disappointed their expectations. It was "a speckled grey, overloaded with fat, filthily dirty, and its heels, for want of paring and exercise, were so high, that it limped along with much difficulty."† A Dakhini, for which the Maharaja had given about 1,000*l*., in their opinion, far exceeded Lylee in beauty. His horses were continually in Runjeet's thoughts, and almost constantly in his sight, covered (even the dray-horses) with jewels and rich caparisons. He was never weary of talking of them, or of caressing them.

Runjeet took great delight in military parade and display, and spent nearly half of every day in reviews, examining equipments, or in some way studying to promote the

* Vol. ii. p. 88. † Journal, p. 152.

efficiency of the different branches of his army.

Upon the subject of religion, it has been reported that Runjeet was indifferent; but this is an error. Although no bigot, and active in restraining the fanaticism of the Akalis and other zealots, he was scrupulous in the performance of all the prescribed ceremonies and observances of the Sikh faith, and for a certain number of hours every day he had the *Grant'h* read before him by gurus. He was liberal in alms to Fakirs and men of reputed sanctity, not excluding Bramins, for whom he had a reverence. He was popular on this account with his Hindu subjects, as well as for his severity towards the Mahomedans. He was, indeed, superstitious in the extreme, readily conceiving fancies in respect to his destiny and fortunes, and never failing to consult astrologers before entering upon any important undertaking. The usual mode of divination was by placing between the leaves of the *Grant'h* two slips of paper, on one of which was written the object of his wishes, and on the other the reverse; these papers were selected by a guru, without being looked at, and the question was decided by the paper first taken. He was by no means averse to the Christian creed. In 1830, he expressed a desire that an English missionary should call upon him in private, and explain to him the doctrines of our faith, and he was so interested in the subject, that he requested to be furnished with a copy of the Scriptures.* At a later period, he sought an interview with the Rev. Mr. Lourie, whom he consulted upon a project he had formed for establishing a system of education in his dominions, and urged the reverend gentleman to superintend it. The institutionary discipline of a young Khalsa Sikh is very compendious: when he can bend a bow, wield a sabre, and mount a horse, his instruction is completed.

With respect to the policy and internal government of Runjeet Singh, the most remarkable feature is, the entire absence of any thing like system or principle in his management. His career throughout was

* Communication from Archdeacon Corrie to the Calcutta Bible Association.—Asiatic Journal, N. S. vol. viii. p. 34.

that of an encroaching usurper, and seizer of all within his reach; but what he so possessed himself of, he subjected to no systematic administration. The whole was committed to farmers, with full power to deal with the lives and properties of the producing classes of the population, Runjeet trusting to his own military means for the control of these farmers, and for the exaction from them of any extra gains he might learn that they had made. Nevertheless, his extortions were directed chiefly against the old Sikh families, and his own state officers: merchants and traders were protected, and the duties and taxes were not for the most part immoderate. He however shewed a disposition to become a dealer in some articles, as in shawls, salt, &c., and all that he touched became of course monopoly, or in some other shape the source of exaction and corrupt gain.

Major Lawrence has given a brief sketch of Runjeet's revenue system (still in existence), which is too characteristic of that ruler not to be accurate. Two-fifths of the produce was the proportion nominally taken by the sirkar (state); at this rate, on an estimate of the average proceeds of a certain term of years, the whole country was farmed out in larger or smaller portions. The estimate might be too much or too little; but the farmer must realize the amount, and his own profits too, without collecting more than two-fifths, or his exactions were sure to reach the sovereign's ear, and a proportionate disallowance was made in his accounts. Should the farmer fail to realize the amount specified by the government, he was punished by imprisonment, or degradation; or forgiven, and allowed another chance elsewhere, with the balance written against his name, according to his interest at court, or the opinion entertained of his ability. Mr. Moorcroft mentions a new principle of rating the annual collections adopted by Mazar Mal, formerly Runjeet's chief financial minister. This was by a rough analysis of the soil. A given quantity of earth was put into a fine muslin sieve and washed with water till all the mould was carried through, and nothing but the sand was left, and according to its proportion to the whole, a deduction was made from the assessment. The general character of the soil of the Punjab, composed of mould and sand, renders this mode of appreciating its assessment more correct than might be supposed.

It cannot be said that Runjeet Singh gave to the Punjab any constitution, or fixed form of government. There is no law, written or oral, and no regular courts of justice have been anywhere established. The civil government and the power of life and death, in the provinces, is in the hands of the sirdars, jagirdars, and renters. The revenue-farmer is judge, magistrate, and often custom-master, within his jurisdiction. The personal character of each individual, therefore, is the standard by which justice is measured: some districts are tolerably administered; some oppressed. The adawlut, or nominal court of justice, is a rich source of revenue, fine being the punishment usually awarded. In civil cases the prisoner is mulcted one-fourth of the amount at issue, and it is common for both parties to endeavour to purchase a decision. Under such a system, the poor man has little chance; the vagabond thief, urged to plunder by necessity, loses his nose or ears (mutilation being the ordinary punishment for crimes); but the wealthy robber and dextrous ruffian are unmolested. From the customs alone a vast sum enters the state treasury; the trader, however, has not only to pay the regulated tolls, but the exactions of the subordinate officers. Every pass and ferry is guarded, and rules and rates are laughed at. Runjeet, whilst he overthrew the old political institutions of the Sikhs, substituted none in their stead. If he had any theory of government, it was a desire to reduce all the people of the Punjab to the same social level. He treated the chiefs of all his subjected states strictly as jagirdars, and obliged all to furnish quotas of troops for his most distant and dangerous expeditions, thus saving the khas troops of the state. The Gurumata, or old council of the Sikhs, has, with every other institution adapted to the state of things which existed before the establishment of his supremacy, been entirely discontinued. The last council of the kind was held when Holkar fled into the Punjab, and the British armies followed in pursuit, and it was a question what part the Sikhs, as a nation, should take in the juncture. Runjeet Singh, though the most influential chief, pretended not then to any supremacy of dominion, and the question was one which, as it concerned the whole body of the Sikhs, required that all should have a voice in determining. At present the government appears to be a pure despotism, the standing army, ever ready for active service, and eager to be employed where plunder and exaction are the objects, forming the whole machinery of administration. By it alone the treasury is filled, and control exercised over state officers, powerful subjects, and, indeed, over every class of the population. The personal influence and verbal orders of the head of the state form again the exclusive hold upon the discipline and affections of the troops. Thus the whole power and authority centres in the single individual placed at the head of affairs.

Runjeet, unfortunately, had not either the opportunity or the inclination to avail himself, in his civil administration, of European intelligence and practical knowledge, from which he derived so much advantage in his military affairs. The only foreigner he employed in a superior civil capacity was Mr. or Dr. Harlan, an American, a man of ability and enterprise, who was placed over the district of Goojrat, but soon lost the favour of his employer.*

The territorial possessions of Runjeet Singh, prior to the treaty with Shah Shuja, comprised the entire fork of the Punjab, as bounded by the Indus and Sutluj, the two extreme rivers. He held besides Cashmere, and the entire hill country to the Snowy range, and even Ladakh beyond the Himalaya; for though many of the rajas of this tract still remained in their possessions, they

* Major Lawrence (Adv. in Punjab, vol. i. p. 46), who does justice to the talents and abilities of Dr. Harlan, says he was a man of strong passions, and seems to have taken little pains to restrain them. It appears from a Lahore Ukhbar of 1832, that a complaint was made to Runjeet that Harlan had defrauded him in the settlement of the Goojrat district. He was accordingly summoned to Lahore with his accounts. He was afterwards dismissed, and immediately went to Dost Mahomed Khan, and was not ashamed to boast that he had brought down the Dost upon his former master.

had been reduced to the character of subjects, paying tribute equal to their utmost means, and contributing men to the armies of Lahore whenever called upon. Besides this extensive territory, Runjeet Singh had about 45 talooks entire, or in share with others, on the British side of the Sutluj; and westward of the Indus, he held Khyrabad, Akona, and Peshawur; Dera-Ghazi-Khan, which was farmed to the Nuwab of Bahawulpoor, and Dera-Ismael-Khan, assigned to Hafiz Ahmed Khan of Munkera, as before related. He also levied tributes from the Balooch chiefs of Tonk and Sagur to the southward.

Captain Murray estimated that the amount of land revenue and tributes, annually levied from the whole of these possessions, was ....*Rs.*	1,24,03,900
Besides which, the customs of the Punjab yielded	19,00,600
An item, called *Mohurana*, being a fee on every paper submitted for the seal of Runjeet Singh	5,77,000
Making a total Khalsa revenue of	1,48,81,500

The same officer estimated that there remained, still appropriated in jagirs, or held by old Sikh families and establishments, without paying any thing to the Khalsa, territory yielding 1,09,28,000

Thus making the entire resources of the country under the dominion of Runjeet, *Rs.* 2,58,09,500

This total is not very wide of the revenue set down in the books of the Mogul government as the produce of the Lahore Sooba, and, considering that Cashmere and some territory south of the Sutluj is included, the correspondence of amount is in favour of the correctness of the estimate, for the province cannot be so productive under the Sikhs, as it was in the peaceable times of the Mogul dominion.

By the treaties existing at his death, Runjeet Singh was confirmed in possession of all the territories bounded north and north-east by the portions of the Hindoo Kosh and Tibet mountains lying between the Otmaunkail mountains and the Sutluj; south-west by the Otmaunkail, Khybur, and Soliman ranges, the latter approaching the Indus in the vicinity of Mittunkote; and south-east by the river Sutluj from the Tibet mountains to its junction with the Indus; and by the

Indus from Mittunkote to Omerkote. The northern and eastern frontier may be estimated at 170 leagues; the north-west and western at 190 leagues; the south-eastern at 200 leagues; and the area of the territory included within these boundaries, at 14,000 square leagues.

Runjeet Singh had for many years been hoarding treasure, and the fort of Govindgurh, built by him, and kept always in excellent repair, was the principal place for its deposit. Captain Murray, speaking from the best information he could collect, which, however, was necessarily very imperfect, estimated the value of the property accumulated by Runjeet in cash, jewels, horses, and elephants, to have been not less than ten crores of rupees, or the same number of millions of pounds sterling. By some the estimate is carried much higher, but such computations, being for the most part conjectural, err generally on the side of excess.

The military force of the Lahore state, in 1832, is set down by the same officer, and his authority is the safest to follow on the point, as follows:

1st. The available regular troops.		
Cavalry disciplined by M. Allard, and the special troops mounted on horses of the state, the Gorchur, and Ghorchur Khas	Men. 12,811	
Infantry, disciplined battalions, Nujeebs, and troops, more or less drilled under the eye of the Maharaja	14,941	
Total regular troops, horse and foot		27,752
Garrison corps, including the troops employed in Cashmere,—Cavalry...	3,000	
Infantry, variously armed and equipped	23,950	26,950
Contingents of sirdars, consisting in the plains, principally of cavalry, but in the hills of foot soldiers		27,312
Total troops, horse and foot		82,014

The artillery of Runjeet Singh consisted of 376 guns and 370 swivels, mounted on the backs of camels, or on light carriages adapted to their size. For these, there was no corps of artillery regimented and organized, as is the custom in European armies, but there was a darogha, at the head of a large establishment. Several of the corps of cavalry, and all the battalions of infantry, had guns attached to them, the gunners of which were borne on the strength of the respective corps. The *jinsee*, or heavy train only, is distinct from the rest of the army.

The above accumulation of resources and of force had grown up and been produced entirely by the care and exertions of the Maharaja. His father left him nothing but a body of Sikh cavalry, little superior to that of his neighbours, who have all now been reduced to the condition of subjects. Runjeet Singh, in the formation especially of his military force, evinced the same inquiring activity, the same attention to minutiæ and perseverance in watching the execution of his plans, which characterized the first Peter of Russia. The want of a generalizing mind, to refer things to fixed principles, and to lead to the formation or adoption of systems, and a deficiency of the intelligence resulting from education, or from habitual converse with men of high cultivation, have been the main defects of his character, and are the causes of Runjeet Singh's government being based on no solid forms and institutions. But where were such to be found amongst an association of Sikh banditti, formed from the outcasts of society, and from the dregs in particular of the agricultural class, men all in the most desperate circumstances, and driven by want to adopt the life of robbers? All that was educated and refined had disappeared from the Punjab before Runjeet Singh was born. The natural effect, however, of the union of authority in his person has been, to create a court, where, in the course of time, science and refinement might be produced, or collected from the countries around, as the habits of peace and luxury supersede the perpetual activity of war and military expeditions.

And let not those, who are disposed to give to Runjeet Singh the credit due to him as founder of a kingdom and dynasty, take exception at the circumscribed limit of his dominion, as lowering his merit in comparison with others. The circumstances of his position, with the British Government on one side,—fresh risen to a majesty of power, that it would have been madness for him to think of encountering, and with the prejudiced and fanatic Musulman population of Afghanistan upon every other frontier, have been barriers against extension, which it was impossible to overcome, and effectually forbade the hope of carrying the Sikh dominion beyond its present limits. The gain that has already been made upon the latter, and the manner in which the brave and bigoted Mahomedans have, in many instances, been reconciled to the sway of a hated, and even despised sect, are amongst the most creditable features of the policy and career of Runjeet Singh.

Towards the British Government his conduct has been marked with equal sagacity. Careful not to offend to the point leading to actual rupture, he contrived to make his gain of the juncture, at the very moment when the British Government stepped forward to confine his dominion to the Sutluj, and to wrest from his grasp the valuable tract between that river and the Jumna, which was all held by Sikhs, and regarded by him, therefore, as his legitimate and certain prey. When the ill-will and suspicion, engendered by this interference, had subsided, and he felt assured that the interposing government had no desire to push its conquests, or further to interfere with his ambitious views, he cultivated its friendship, and desired to exhibit himself to the world as united to it by close relations.

It is remarkable that Mr. Forster, the traveller, writing in 1783, just after the birth of Runjeet, should have formed so accurate a prognostic of the destiny of the Sikh nation. "We may see," he observes, "some ambitious chief, led on by his genius and success, absorbing the power of his associates, display, from the ruins of their commonwealth, the standard of monarchy."

CHAPTER XX.

REIGN OF KHURUK SINGH.

A.D. 1839 AND 1840.

IT was believed by many persons well acquainted with Indian politics, that an authority so recently formed, and so ill-cemented, as that which had been created by Runjeet Singh, and maintained by his peculiar talents and personal influence, would dissolve into fragments at his death. This expectation was strengthened by the knowledge that his successor was weak, almost imbecile, and utterly incapable of controlling the elements of disorder which the removal of the firm hand of Runjeet would release from confinement. But not only had that powerful hand, in the space of forty years, impressed a shape and form upon the government, which made the parts cohere, but the relations maintained by the late Maharaja with the neighbouring state of British India provided a bulwark which would have enabled a successor of moderate talents to complete what Runjeet had left imperfect, and by directing his attention, no longer required in the field of conquest and aggression, to measures of internal improvement, to establish his authority upon a durable basis.

Fortunately for the Sikhs, the British agents in that quarter hitherto, Captain Ross and Captain Murray, had been men of ability, and at this critical juncture, the British political agent for Sikh affairs was Mr. George Russell Clerk, a gentleman possessing not only talents and energy, but practical good sense, and though of unflinching firmness, gentle, conciliating, and winning in his manners. He was just the person, says a very competent authority,* to manage the rude and boisterous Sikhs: prepared to yield, even to defend, their legitimate claims; to deny, firmly but gracefully, their false pretensions. Always on the alert, not listening to second-hand intelligence, but seeing every thing with his own eyes, he kept the Sikh authorities to

* Calcutta Review, No. II. p. 477.

their engagements, by shewing that, whilst we respected their just rights, we could enforce a due regard to ours.

The successor of Runjeet Singh possessed another advantage in the able minister who had been appointed to the vizeerat, in fact placed at the head of the government, namely, Raja Dhean Singh, supposing that his views did not reach beyond the station of minister, and aspire to the throne itself.

The Jummoo brothers, Rajas Golab Singh,* Dhean Singh, and Soochet Singh, who have exercised an important influence upon the politics of the Punjab, belonged to a respectable Rajpoot family (of the Dogur tribe), in the Lower Himalaya, which had fallen into obscurity. The three brothers were originally meeans, squires or dependants, of the Raja of Jummoo, and were introduced to the notice of Runjeet in the following manner. Dhean,† who was a private sowar (or lancer), having killed a

* Now (1846) the only survivor.

† According to Von Orlich (Punjab, vol. i. p. 173) and other authorities; but Lawrence (Adv. in Punjab, vol. i. p. 33) says it was the eldest brother, Golab.

man in a feud, fled from the vengeance of the victim's friends to the Sikh camp in the plains. Whilst Runjeet Singh was reviewing his troops, he observed, by the side of his elephant, a common lancer breaking-in a vicious horse. The beauty of the young man (then about twenty-five), as well as his skill and bold carriage, struck him, and the replies made to his questions confirmed his good opinion. Runjeet took Dhean into his household, made him first porter to the palace, then deohrewala (lord of the privy chamber, or chamberlain), and ultimately prime minister, in which capacity he amassed enormous wealth, became master of a large mountainous country in Little Tibet, and on the borders of Cashmere, studded with hill forts, maintaining an army of 25,000 men, and a fine artillery. He has been described as a fine-looking man, and though slightly lame, of a noble presence, rather above the usual height of natives, with a quick and intelligent eye, lofty handsome forehead, and aquiline features. Modest and unassuming in his speech and deportment, polite and affable in his manners, he nevertheless cherished a deep and rancorous hatred towards Europeans. He not only acquired Runjeet's confidence, but possessed great influence over the Sikh nation. At the durbar, he stood, or sat upon the ground, behind his master, whilst others, though his inferiors, occupied chairs. He was active, able, and intelligent, and supposed to be an adept in duplicity and dissimulation.

When Dhean had gained a firm footing at the court of Lahore, he introduced his brothers there. Golab, the eldest, had quitted the service of the Raja of Rajaoree and Jummoo, and entered the service of the Raja of Kishtewar. Runjeet was at this time (1819) preparing an expedition against the former, and he gave the command of it to Golab, who was completely successful; he took possession of the country and made the raja prisoner. By artifice and fraud, he made himself master of Kishtewar and of the person of the prince he had lately served, and carried him to Lahore, where he caused him to be poisoned. For these services, Golab was rewarded with the principality of Jummoo, in jagir, where he immediately began to extend his conquests on all sides, between Cashmere and Attock, nominally for the Sikh ruler, but really on his own behalf, and came to be considered, after Runjeet, the greatest lord in the Punjab. The character of this personage has been portrayed in very dark colours, as a cruel tyrant, whose ambition threatened to absorb all the independent rajaships in the hills, and under whose oppressions and extortions the people groaned.* He is accused of massacring his prisoners, and even flaying men alive and stuffing their skins with grass, to be exhibited as examples to others. Major Lawrence states that he is reported to have put to death no fewer than 12,000 persons. He had the management of all the family territories, under a compact with his brothers. He is indefatigable in business, and possesses much information. M. Jacquemont,† who visited him in his hill principality in 1831, described Golab as about forty, very hand-

* Burnes, Bokhara, vol. ii. p. 284. Vigne, As. Journ. vol. xxvi. p. 201. Lawrence, Adv. in Punjab, vol. ii. p. 75.

† Letters from India, vol. ii. p. 2.

some, a lion in courage, but with the plainest, mildest, and most elegant manners. Major Lawrence says, Golab's history would itself fill a volume.*

Soochet, the youngest brother, although he shared the favour of Runjeet, acquired jagirs, and was wealthy and powerful, did not raise himself to the same eminence as his brothers, and was not much trusted.

From the year 1827, these three persons engrossed the entire favour of Runjeet; yet, according to Burnes, Golab was the only one of them who could read, the other two being ignorant of the first rudiments of education. Major Lawrence asserts, that it was by ministering to Runjeet's debaucheries that Dhean first obtained his favour, and he retained it by the basest subserviency.

Khuruk Singh ascended the throne quietly. Some whispers were circulated respecting a design to substitute Heera Singh, the son of Dhean Singh; but this project seems inconsistent with the part acted by Dhean. Some movements were made by the Koonwur Sher Singh, or by his partisans; but, without en-

* Adv. in Punjab, *ut ante.*

couragement from the British Government, he had no prospect of success. A deputation, consisting of Mr. Clerk and Captain Osborne (military secretary to the Governor-General), proceeded to Lahore, in July, 1839, to compliment the new Maharaja on his accession. Sher Singh hastened to make his peace with his brother, and, by the intercession of Raja Dhean Singh, was favourably received.

Meanwhile, the expedition beyond the Indus had realized the utmost expectations of the projectors; Shah Shuja, by the aid of the British forces, had recovered his two capitals of Candahar and Cabul, with the fortress of Ghuzni; Dost Mahomed Khan was a prisoner, and the various chiefs of Afghanistan appeared to acquiesce in the Shah's authority. The British detachment, under Colonel Wade, destined to co-operate with the Sikh force at Peshawur, and that of Prince Timur, the son of Shah Shuja, passed the Sutluj, with the ready permission of the Sikh authorities, in February, traversed the Punjab, crossed the Indus at Attock in March, and arrived at Peshawur on the 27th of that month. The allied forces were composed of heterogeneous elements. The British troops (native) did not amount to 400; the Shahzadeh's levy consisted of about 3,500 men, Ghoorkas, Nujeebs (volunteers), Poorbeas (Hindustanis), &c. The Sikh auxiliaries amounted to 6,000, all Musulmans, conformably to the treaty. General Ventura (who had returned from a visit to Europe) was appointed to command this force; he arrived at Peshawur on the 11th April, being followed on the 26th by Prince Nou Nehal Singh. Although it is acknowledged that Runjeet, as far as his health allowed him to attend to public business, endeavoured to fulfil the engagements he had entered into by the treaty, the dislike of the Sikh army, officers and men, to co-operate with the British, was scarcely concealed.* They allowed our troops and Prince Timur's levies to enter the Khybur pass, in July, unassisted —expecting, or hoping, they would be defeated; but were mortified to find they forced that terrific defile, taking the fort of Ali Musjid, whence they reached Jelallabad on the

* Barr, March to Peshawur in 1839, p. 319.

17th August, and arrived at Cabul, which they found in the occupation of the British army, on the 2nd September. The campaign being over, our auxiliary forces quitted that city in the beginning of October, being followed by the army of the Indus, which on the 1st January, 1840, ceased to exist.

Intelligence of the death of Runjeet reached Peshawur on the 2nd July, in the midst of these operations; but Prince Nou Nehal Singh remained at that city, from whence he despatched General Ventura to Lahore.

A cordial understanding was not likely to subsist long between a weak, almost idiotic, prince, like Khuruk Singh, surrounded by artful and ambitious men, and the great minister, clothed with all the executive functions of the government, who was intent upon engrossing the whole power of the state. Towards the end of October, 1839, the Maharaja gave great offence to Dhean Singh, by taking into his councils and favour a low-born minion, of handsome person, named Cheyt Singh, bold, forward, and intriguing, who, if he had been content with the command of wealth and patronage, might have secured a longer reign over his feeble master. But Cheyt Singh, without a single qualification for the offiee, aimed at the post of minister, and the power attained by the Jummoo brothers had provoked, even amongst Runjeet's family, a sufficient number of enemies to render it a matter of little difficulty to raise a party against them.

Amongst the most confidential counsellors of Runjeet, next to the Jummoo brothers and the Fakir Uzeez-ud-deen, were the Bhaes (or brothers) Ram Singh* and Govind Ram, and Misr† Beni Ram. The latter had been Runjeet's treasurer, in which office he was continued by Khuruk Singh, and all three had many relations and connections in various departments of the government. These persons entered into the league formed to destroy the Jummoo Rajas, and they made daily accessions to the conspiracy amongst the army, having, it is said, gained over some of the regiments. The vigilance of Dhean

* Ram Singh alone took the *pahal*, and became a Sikh.

† The title of a particular class of Bramins.

Singh did not slumber. Aware that Nou Nehal Singh, then a spirited youth of twenty, was the idol of the army, he despatched intelligence of the intrigues to him, at Peshawur, urging the necessity of his presence to protect his own interests. Nou Nehal, though he feared and hated the Jummoo family, saw the prudence of availing himself of their influence to overthrow the upstart, Cheyt Singh. On the night of the 8th October, a large body of Golab Singh's hill troops occupied the citadel, with artillery, the matches burning, and surrounded the palace. Before daylight, Prince Nou Nehal Singh, accompanied by the three rajas, Golab, Dhean, and Soochet, their personal adherents and armed men, entered the palace, and penetrated, without causing alarm, towards the sleeping apartments of the Maharaja. In the outer area they were challenged by two orderlies, who were instantly cut down. Finding that the Maharaja and his minion were asleep in an upper room, the party proceeded thither, but were stopped by a company of soldiers, and a soobadar, who refused to let them pass; but the men, observing Prince Nou Nehal

Singh, declared they could not disobey him, and fell into his train. The altercation disturbed Khuruk Singh and his favourite, who concealed themselves in dark corners of adjoining rooms. Cheyt Singh was first discovered, and immediately cut to pieces; shortly after, the Maharaja was found, almost naked, cowering under some furniture. He begged in abject terms for life, and was assured that no violence was meditated against him. He was, however, placed under restraint; the guards were changed, and in the morning it was announced that Cheyt Singh, having been detected in a plot to sell the country to the Feringees (English), had been put to death by the Maharaja's orders. At the Dussera, a few days after, the whole party moved to Amritsur. The only other conspirator who appears to have been punished was Benee Ram, who was thrown into prison, upon the plea that he had refused to shew the heir-apparent the treasury.

From this time Khuruk Singh was not suffered to take any share in the administration of public affairs. He was present at the durbars, clothed with the insignia of royalty, but sat like a statue, and was really kept in strict, though not close, confinement; Nou Nehal Singh being the virtual sovereign. Some authorities say, that Khuruk gradually pined away under the effect of some slow, but subtle poison, which must have been administered by the orders, or with the connivance, of his son.

With the change of rulers, a change of councils took place at the court of Lahore. However hostile might be the feelings of the minister towards the English, he was convinced that sound policy forbade a rupture with the British Government, and therefore he strictly adhered to the obligations contracted with it by the late ruler. Nou Nehal Singh, entertaining the same sentiments regarding the alliance, had not prudence to veil them. An anti-English feeling pervaded all the departments of the administration; emissaries were discovered in various quarters exciting a prejudice against our countrymen; questions were raised upon the treaty respecting the adjustment of boundaries between the Sikh and Cabul dominions in the Peshawur territory and the Derajats; the maintenance of 5,000 Mahomedan troops by the Sikhs at Peshawur and the tolls upon the Indus and Sutluj were likewise matters of dispute, and even whether a passage should be granted to our troops to and from Afghanistan was a question debated with great excitement. Upon one occasion, it is reported, the prince, in open durbar, before all the sirdars, drew his sword, and declared that he was ready to use it for the destruction of the encroaching influence of the English. Meanwhile, it was said that warlike preparations were going on at Lahore; that the arsenals were being filled and cannon made upon a new principle, with percussion-locks.

It demanded all the powers and patience of Mr. Clerk to deal with dispositions so hostile; but at length the counsels of the anti-British party were overruled in the durbar, and all the points in dispute were conceded by the Sikh court.

Dhean Singh was not content with the present state of things. He found that Nou Nehal Singh had all the energy and talents of his grandfather, though with less tact and caution, and that his own influence was decreasing daily. Ram Singh and Govind Ram, with Jemadar Khooshal Singh,* formed the prince's privy council, and not only took the control of public affairs out of the hands of the minister, but treated him with personal disrespect.

Meanwhile, the health of Khuruk Singh continued to decline, and on the 5th November he expired, at the age of thirty-eight. He was not only of weak intellect, but an ill-looking man, in a court remarkable for the number of handsome persons, and his manners were awkward and repulsive.

Upon this occasion, another scene of self-immolation took place. On the day following

* Khooshal Singh was a Hindu, native of Saharunpur, in the British territory; he was a man of low birth, and, according to Burnes, cook to a private soldier. Being a fine, handsome young fellow, he won the base favour of Runjeet, who made him one of the hundred picked soldiers appointed to be his night guard. He turned Sikh, and for fifteen years held the command of the door-way, which was a post of influence as well as confidence. He was called jemadar, or lieutenant, as being second only to Runjeet. As a commander, he was harsh and tyrannical. Major Lawrence describes him as, in his time, a coarse, vulgar-looking man.

his death, the body of the deceased Maharaja was burned, and with it the Rani Issur, sister of Sirdar Mungul Singh, and three of her female attendants. No motive, but a slavish obedience to a tyrannical superstition, can be assigned for this act, Khuruk Singh's character being one which could have inspired neither affection nor respect.

The demise of the sovereign, which had been long expected, caused no other sensation than joy, since the event transferred the authority of the state, in all its plenitude, to the hands of a prince, who was popular amongst all classes, especially the military, and whose reign, it was anticipated, would shed an additional lustre upon the Sikh nation. This prospect, however, was disappointed by an occurrence which, if it were not well authenticated, might be supposed to be invented by the dispensers of poetical justice, as a punishment for the unnatural conduct of Prince Nou Nehal Singh towards his father, or be ascribed to the deep and artful contrivance of the Jummoo family. Upon the conclusion of the funeral rites, the new Maharaja and his court, including all the members of the Jummoo family, except Raja Golab Singh, were proceeding to the Ravi to bathe, when, in passing through one of the covered gateways of the city, the crush of elephants shook the structure, and caused one of the beams, of immense weight, to fall; it struck Nou Nehal Singh on the head, and Oodum Singh, son of Golab Singh (who was on the prince's elephant), on the loins. The latter died immediately; the prince lingered in an insensible state till night, when he expired.

Nou Nehal,* who was the only son of Khuruk Singh, did not yet number twenty years.† He was a young man of very promising talents, brave, high-spirited, active, with great firmness of character, and many of the better qualities of his grandfather, but rash and self-willed. In his moral habits he was an example to that corrupt court, being sober and comparatively temperate amidst the scenes of debauchery which surrounded him. His person and manners were

* This name signifies 'new stem,' or 'stock.'

† See p. 59. The official notification by the Indian Government makes his age twenty-two.

agreeable, and his countenance was intelligent, though not handsome.

During these transactions the Sikh arms were not idle. A strong force was sent by order of Nou Nehal Singh (in opposition to the advice of the minister) against the hill state of Mundi, in the Alpine Punjab, under the command of General Ventura and Lena Singh, Majethia. The raja of this state was a tributary of Lahore, and paid six lakhs of rupees to the Sikh treasury. The tribute being in arrear, the army was sent nominally to enforce its payment, but really to seize the territory. The raja discharged a portion of the debt, and gave security for the payment of the remainder, promising future punctuality; nevertheless, General Ventura took possession of the whole country, and of the raja's person, employing, for the latter object, a species of stratagem, so often resorted to by Runjeet Singh as to become a part of his policy. When the raja supposed that every thing was settled, he was invited to visit the general, in order to receive a khelat, or dress of honour, and upon his arrival, the tent was surrounded by a regiment of infantry, and the person of the raja secured. The success of this expedition enabled the general to extend the Sikh authority over other hill states in Kulu, Sukyt, and as far as the mountains which skirt the western course of the Sutluj. The events at Lahore, however, put a stop to these conquests. General Ventura was received with all the respect due to a conqueror, bringing the trophies of 200 forts, belonging to various hill chiefs, on his arrival at the capital, in December, 1840.

Towards the north and west, Raja Golab Singh had been for some years pushing his usurpations as far as the valley of Cashmere, and even beyond it. He had seized upon Little Tibet, invaded Ladakh, and taken Leh, the capital, placing upon the gudi a minion of his own. The capture of Little Tibet and of its sovereign is said to have been accomplished in the same treacherous manner as that which was so successful at Mundi. Zorawur Singh, one of the generals of Golab, invited Ahmed Shah, the raja (or gylfo), to visit him, when he was seized and put in chains. This Sikh general, who had gained a victory over the rightful raja of Little Tibet, in 1835, at Syru, near Zanskar, continued his conquests up to the very confines of the Chinese empire, which roused the jealousy of its very jealous authorities, and a severe conflict took place between the Sikh and Chinese forces, in which Zorawur Singh fell: but this event belongs to a later period of Sikh history.

CHAPTER XXI.

REIGN OF SHER SINGH.

A.D. 1840 TO 1842.

THE event which had created a vacancy of the throne was so sudden and unforeseen, that all parties were unprepared, and the succession did not so clearly belong, by right of primogeniture, to the next son of Runjeet, as to preclude all other claims. The circumstances of his birth* threw a doubt upon the legitimacy of Sher Singh, who had never been distinctly acknowledged by his reputed father, and was spoken of as the son of a *thoka*, or carpenter. The qualities of his character did not unfit him to wield the Sikh sceptre, and Dhean Singh, the minister, whose will inclined the balance, determined to embrace his interests. He accordingly concealed the death of Nou Nehal Singh,

* See vol. i. p. 281.

giving out that his injury was slight, and excluding all but his partisans from access to the prince whilst he lived. In the meanwhile, he despatched messengers to his brother Golab, and to Sher Singh, who was then at his district of Butala, about seventy miles from Lahore, urging him to lose no time in coming to the capital. Upon the arrival of Sher Singh, the death of Nou Nehal was announced; the sirdars were convened, and it was resolved that Sher Singh should be placed at the head of the government, as regent, it being suggested that the widow of the late Maharaja was pregnant. He was accordingly proclaimed sovereign of the Punjab on the 7th November.

During the few days occupied in the funeral ceremonies of the late Maharaja (in which his two wives, in the bloom of youth and beauty, were burnt with the corpse), when Sikh etiquette requires an entire abstinence from public business, a formidable opposition to the pretensions of Sher Singh was matured. Chund Kowr, the mother of Nou Nehal Singh, availed herself of the rule of succession recognized by the Manjee Sikhs,* whereby a widow has, in default of male offspring, a title prior to that of a brother, and claimed the throne in her own right. She was the first wife of Khuruk Singh, and at this time about forty-four years of age; her person was still pleasing, although rather corpulent. Being a woman of much energy, and little principle or compunction, as well as of dissolute manners, she took advantage of the period of twelve days' suspension of business to form a strong party, of which Ajeet Singh, Sindawala, her paramour, was the head. Before that period had expired, Uttur Singh, the head of the Sindawala family, the nearest to the throne after the direct descendants of Runjeet, arrived at Lahore, as well as Golab Singh, who, for some mysterious reason, took a different side from his brother Dhean. Even Dhean's son, Heera Singh, the favourite minion of Runjeet, and who performed so conspicuous a part in the drama afterwards enacted at this court, chose the cause of Chund

* Vol. i. p. 147.

Kowr, which was also embraced by the army. Dhean Singh now relinquished the attempt to maintain Sher Singh upon the throne, and the latter resigned his pretensions, being the first to present his nuzzur, of 101 pieces of gold coin, to Chund Kowr, who, with the consent of the sirdars, was on the 30th November proclaimed Rani.

The conduct of the Jummoo brothers in this affair is difficult of explanation. Most authorities agree in attributing the different parts taken by them,—Dhean and Soochet linking themselves apparently with the interest of Sher Singh, and Golab and Heera with the Rani,—to some deep-laid scheme of subtle policy. It may, perhaps, be traced to a motive which, in troubled times, impelled different members of one family in England to join opposite political parties, namely, a desire to preserve the family estates.

Had the Rani been a woman of prudence and decency, and had her council been men of ability and principle, she might have retained her position at the head of the government, in spite of the repugnance of a martial people like the Sikhs to be ruled by a woman.* But she regarded the supreme authority as a means of indulging her passions and vices; the licentiousness which was tolerated in Runjeet Singh was scandalous, even at Lahore, in a female; and, moreover, she forgot how much she owed to the army (which had, perhaps, placed her upon the throne), having not only omitted to distribute gifts amongst them, but curtailed their privileges. She did not appear in public, and her council consisted of men who were not popular. Khooshal Singh was hated by the troops; Ram Singh and Govind Ram were unacquainted with military matters, and these were her chief advisers, in addition to Golab Singh, whose sincerity and fidelity were equivocal. The Rani and her advisers were opposed to the restoration of Raja Dhean Singh to his former authority, though he still held the post of prime minister, and it was ordered by the council that hence-

* When this objection was suggested to Chund Kowr, it is said, she replied, "England is ruled by a queen; why should it be a disgrace to the Punjab to be governed by a rani?"

forward all decrees were to be signed with the Rani's own hand.

Discontent soon spread throughout the country; insurrections broke out in various parts, and the army at Lahore began to manifest that spirit of turbulence which led subsequently to such fearful consequences. Sher Singh was not an inattentive spectator of a state of things which portended a revolution. With a view of averting this calamity, or to secure the throne upon any terms, he proposed to marry Chund Kowr, his brother's widow, according to the Sikh rite of *Kurawa*, or *Chadur-dula*.* The Rani, though she had no design thus to part with power, affected to receive the proposal favourably, and invited Sher Singh to an interview, treacherously making arrangements to waylay and murder him. This plot was disclosed (it is said by Dhean Singh) to Sher Singh, who retired to Butala.

The majority of the sirdars now became convinced that the welfare of the nation required the removal of the Rani, and the restoration of Sher Singh to the throne.

* See vol. i. p. 147.

Dhean Singh and his brother Soochet, on pretence of a hunting-party in the hills, left Lahore, and in an interview with Sher Singh, advised him to march to the capital, declaring that the troops there were ready to join him, and that General Ventura would afford his aid. This declaration was confirmed by the arrival of secret agents from the army, pledging the troops to support his claims, on condition that he gave them a certain amount of donatives, which was specified in a written agreement.

The day of the Bussunt festival (10th January), when the Sikh troops at Lahore would be paraded, was fixed upon as that of the proclamation of Sher Singh, who set out from Butala, with about 500 men, on the 8th January, and marching with expedition, arrived with his little band before Lahore on the 10th. Rumours of an intended outbreak had reached the ears of the Rani's party, and Golab Singh occupied the Summun-boorj, or citadel of Lahore, with his personal troops, about 3,000 men, placing the city gates in charge of Sikhs who were sworn to be faithful to the Rani. Money and liberal promises were dispensed to the troops and even the people. Upon the arrival of Sher Singh in the vicinity of Lahore, General Ventura immediately went to him,* with 6,000 men and twenty-one pieces of artillery. Nearly at the same moment, Dhean Singh galloped up, having preceded a body of 15,000 hill-men, whom he was leading from his estates.

The rani had shut herself up in the Hazaree Bagh, or palace, with Uttur Singh, Ajeet Singh, Lena Singh, and others of her party; but they had no confidence. The troops in the city were not to be depended upon, and part of Golab's hill troops were occupied in watching the Sikh garrison. However, the gates of the city were closed, and the walls mounted with cannon, which repeatedly fired at the assailants; but in the night of the 14th, the latter gained an entrance into the city, where Sher Singh was welcomed with acclamations.

The citadel was defended with great obstinacy. An assault, after the gate and part of the wall had been breached, by a storming

* It is said that the general did not join Sher Singh, having taken an oath of fidelity to the rani.

party of Akalis and others, headed by Jowala Singh, was repulsed, and the party almost destroyed. The conflict raged till the evening of the 17th January, the assailants suffering more than the garrison, being completely without shelter. The loss of the besiegers, it is said, amounted to 2,000 men. The exasperated soldiers vowed revenge against Golab's party; at length Dhean Singh and Soochet Singh, having procured a promise of pardon for Golab Singh and Heera Singh, by the intervention of General Ventura, a parley was entered into, and the citadel surrendered; but it required great efforts, and all the influence of General Ventura, to prevent the massacre of the brave garrison, which marched out secretly at night, a Sikh priest being sent as a hostage for their safety.

The Sikh soldiers, baulked of their revenge upon the garrison of the citadel, seem to have wreaked their fury upon the city. The enormities of which they were guilty, it is said, almost baffle belief. Property was plundered and wantonly destroyed; merchants and shopkeepers were tortured; under the pretext of seeking for obnoxious commanders and moonshees, every species of violence and cruelty was perpetrated. "Had the city been taken by storm, it would not, probably, have suffered more."* General Court, who, like M. Ventura, however favourable he might have been to the cause of Sher Singh, scorned to violate his oath, was an object of peculiar hatred to the Sikh troops; his house was pillaged, and he was obliged, in order to save his life, to seek refuge in the British territory, whither he was followed by the Sindawala sirdar, Uttur Singh. Khooshal Singh was generously protected by Sher Singh at the risk of his own life; others escaped by being carried out of the city in tubs and baskets. Golab Singh and Heera Singh retired with their troops to the right bank of the Ravi.

Meanwhile, Chund Kowr, though a prisoner, experienced no other violence; she was allowed to occupy apartments in the fort, with Tek Chund, her treasurer, and, as reported, one of her paramours, and an ample allowance was made to her. Previous to the

* Calcutta Review, No. II. p. 488.

fall of the citadel, she had despatched Ajeet Singh to Mr. Clerk, then at Umbala (towards whom, upon her accession, she held very high language), and afterwards to Mr. Metcalfe, the resident at Delhi, proposing to make over six annas in the rupee of the revenues of the Punjab (namely, one-half) to the British Government, if it would support her with its troops against Sher Singh, whom she described as the son of a low man, then living at Aminabad. Ajeet afterwards proceeded to Calcutta, but he was refused an audience by Lord Auckland. It is scarcely necessary to say that the proposition with which he was charged was never for a moment entertained. In fact, upon the death of Nou Nehal, Mr. Clerk had sent a message of congratulation to Sher Singh.

The deposed Rani remained in this state of restraint for more than a year, treated with outward respect, but closely watched; during this time the Sindawala sirdars in the British territory, in conjunction with the Rani's partisans at Lahore, carried on intrigues for her restoration, secretly levying troops, even corrupting some of the Khalsa regiments, and it is not improbable that, had she lived much longer, a counter-revolution would have been essayed. But her life was brought to a sudden close in a mysterious manner. Whilst Sher Singh was absent from Lahore, the ex-Rani was one morning, in June, 1842, found in her apartment with her skull fractured, occasioned, it was discovered, by four of her slave-girls having beaten her with their slippers,—an instrument of severe correction commonly employed in India,—in which state she lingered for three days, and then expired. The punishment of the criminals, who lost their hands, ears, and noses, and were exiled beyond the Ravi, did not extinguish the suspicion that the deed was done in obedience to orders, as an easy mode of removing a dangerous person whose life could not be openly taken.*

Sher Singh was again proclaimed on the

* According to a Lahore Ukhbar of September 6, 1843, Sher Singh incautiously acknowledged that he was the author of the Rani's death. Having been informed, shortly before his own assassination, that Ajeet Singh was conspiring against him, he declared that, if he found this to be true, he would put him to death, "as he had done with Chund Kowr."

27th January, 1841. The services rendered, and the risks encountered, by Raja Dhean, made his restoration to office almost a debt of justice, and from that moment he became the virtual ruler of the state. It is said that Sher Singh manifested his deference towards Dhean Singh so far as not only to make no order in the slightest matter without his approbation, but to rise and fold his hands, —a mark of respect from an inferior to a superior,—in the presence of his minister. His brother Golab, and his son Heera, were invited to court; the latter was soon after appointed commander-in-chief of the army, whilst all offices at court and in the provinces were filled with Dhean's creatures, so that the power and influence of the Jummoo family were now almost unlimited. The chiefs of the Zenana party, the enemies of this family, were punished by the sequestration of their jagirs; that of Khooshal Singh, being contiguous to Dhean's, was, of course, added to the minister's overgrown possessions, and the jagirs of the Sindawala sirdars were confiscated to the Khalsa. Every attempt made to divide the favour of the Maharaja with the minister brought punishment, if not ruin, upon the aspirant. Some were sent on distant employments, others were banished, and Jowala Singh, who had headed the storming party at the Summun-boorj, and was a personal friend of Sher Singh, endeavouring to make head against the minister's monopoly of influence, was thrown into prison upon a charge of treason, and starved to death.

But whilst the minister was thus intrenching his authority, and the Maharaja, a good-natured sensualist, was solacing himself with an unrestrained indulgence in every species of intemperance, a spirit was growing up in the army, which, like the demon in Eastern fiction, threatened to devour the magician who had raised it. The troops in the provinces,—at Peshawur, Multan, Cashmere, and Mundi,—imitated the licentious example of those at the capital, and the year 1841 is described as a year of terror throughout the Punjab. The manner in which these eruptions of turbulence and rapacity were met at those places is characteristic of the various individuals who had to deal with them. General Avitabili, at Peshawur, when the mutinous battalions demanded the gratuities which had been given to their fellows at Lahore, paid them all they demanded, and discharged them, giving secret information to the neighbouring peasantry—Mahomedans in faith and robbers by profession—that the retiring soldiers were rebels, who had plenty of money. The hint was acted upon; the Sikhs were attacked by the Afghans, and though they made a vigorous resistance, were glad to disgorge their extortions, and return to the service. At Multan, Dewan Sawun Mull, the able governor of that province, in like manner, complied with all the demands of his rebellious troops, and allowed them to depart to their homes, despatching, at the same time, bodies of trusty soldiers, who took from the Sikhs (travelling in small parties) the money they had received. At Cashmere, the governor, Mean Singh, a man of great firmness, refused to comply with the impudent demands of his Sikh soldiers, upon which they murdered him in open durbar, an act which brought upon them speedy and appropriate punishment. Golab Singh, being in the neighbourhood, promptly moved upon Cashmere; the mutineers made a desperate resistance, and were destroyed almost to a man. At Mundi, the mutineers seem to have been uncontrolled, the general, Ventura, being absent, and several Europeans suffered. Mr. Foulkes, an English adventurer, a young man of much promise, a colonel in the Sikh service, was attacked in his tent, cut down, and cast, while yet alive, upon a burning pile.* A French officer, Colonel Mouton, was saved by the heroism of his wife, who threw herself between him and his assassins, and called upon them to

* Colonel Foulkes is well spoken of by Mr. Vigne (Travels in Kashmir, vol. i. p. 130) and Lieut. Barr (Journal, p. 75). The former states that he distinguished himself at the siege of a virgin fortress, called Ambota, taken from the Mundi raja by General Ventura. The troops under his command being in a state of mutiny, he was advised not to interfere, but to depart. He refused, however, with proper spirit, to leave his post. In the night he was awakened by the cries of his orderly, who called to him to fly; but the soldiers rushed into the tent, cut him down, and a pile being heaped up and set fire to, he was cast upon it and burnt before life was extinct. Some of these miscreants were punished at the instigation of Mr. Clerk.

kill her, a sight which touched the feelings of even those savages, and diverted them from the crime. In this state of things, General Ventura, and all the European officers who could leave the service, retired from the Punjab.

The disorganized condition of the army produced a corresponding effect upon the internal state of the country. Bands of robbers roamed about; old feuds revived; boundary disputes were decided by the sword; assassination stalked in the open day, and every vestige, even of the imperfect system of law which had hitherto preserved order and tranquillity, was rapidly disappearing.

The abilities and energies of Dhean Singh, great as they were, could not subdue these manifold evils. The most urgent was the condition of the army, and he endeavoured to rid himself of the more turbulent of the troops by discharging them with gratuities, and replacing them by hill-men. But whilst these raw levies deteriorated the character of the army, the discharged soldiers augmented the plundering bands which desolated the provinces. Some of the disbanded troops crossed the Sutluj, and occasioned great disorders in the British territory.

The minister, moreover, was not altogether without opposition at the durbar, where a party still maintained its ground, consisting of men who, though bitter enemies of the Jummoo family, were too cautious and prudent to come in open collision with its power. The heads of this party were Futteh Singh Man, an old, brave sirdar; Sham Singh, Atarewala; and Lena Singh, Majethia. The influence of their advice upon the mind of the Maharaja was sometimes visible to the minister, who, in order to remove it, would leave Lahore, apparently in disgust, and go to hunt, or pay a visit to his hill estates; he soon found that his absence was intolerable, and that he was soothed, and courted back to manage the difficult functions of the government, and keep in subjection the unruly soldiery, who would surround the palace, and even offer direct affronts to the Maharaja himself.

During this eventful year, various events occurred of minor importance. In July, 1841, the widow of Nou Nehal Singh was delivered of a still-born son, which relieved Sher Singh from one source of apprehension. In the month of April, the Maharaja had a narrow escape from drowning. Having embarked on the Ravi, upon an excursion of pleasure, with Dhean Singh, and other persons of rank, the boat, being overladen, went down in deep water. The elephants, which attended the party on the banks, were driven into the water, and all the persons were saved except Umur Singh, Aloowala. In the previous month, Tek Chund, the treasurer of the Rani, Kowr Chund, was murdered in her apartment, the lady being wounded in the vain endeavour to preserve the life of her favourite. The object of the assassins being to force Tek Chund to reveal the place where certain treasure was supposed to be concealed, it must be presumed that they were authorized by persons in authority.

At the close of the year, the calamitous outbreak at Cabul occurred, taking every one by surprise, fulfilling, however, the sagacious prognostications of Runjeet Singh. The critical situation in which our troops in that country were placed, and the difficulty of relieving them, rendered the friendly co-operation of the Sikh Government a matter of vast importance. It must be allowed that, as far as the government itself was concerned, there was little reason to complain, though its orders, being intrusted to unwilling agents, were inefficiently executed.

No sooner was the intelligence received at Lahore, than the strongest assurances were given to Mr. Clerk, that all the obligations contracted by the Sikh Government, under the tripartite treaty, should be punctually fulfilled. In conformity with this engagement, strong reinforcements were sent off to Peshawur, under the command of Raja Golab Singh, who was accompanied by Pertab Singh, the Maharaja's son. Disaffection and insubordination had, however, spread throughout the army, and impaired the authority of its commanders. Brigadier Wild, who was ordered to enter the Khyber Pass in the beginning of 1842, and occupy the fort of Ali Musjid, had no guns, and sought the loan of a few, with some troops, from General Avitabili, at Peshawur, who acknowledged that he had received orders from the Maharaja to co-operate with the British forces. But he confessed, at the same time, that his men were so mutinous that they would not obey his orders. "The Sikh soldiers," Brigadier Wild wrote, on the 8th January, 1842, "are in a disorganized and insubordinate state; the men, as well as their chiefs, are decidedly averse to contribute in any way to the success of our arms. General Avitabili told me that he ordered, to-day, two battalions, which it was intended should co-operate with us, to move out to Jumrood, from their lines at Peshawur, and they flatly refused, giving him to understand that they intended to return to Lahore. In the next place, he also ordered three guns to be taken to Jumrood; but as these were in progress, the soldiers seized on one of them, and let only the other two proceed."* The commandants of the corps alleged that they had received secret instructions not to move. Captain Mackeson had a conference with the commandants, and at length prevailed upon them to promise to co-operate with Brigadier

* Papers relating to Mil. Operations in Afghanistan, 1843, p. 93.

Wild in entering the pass and occupying Ali Musjid; and four Sikh battalions, with artillery, were appointed to advance with him. Within a few hours of the time fixed for the operations, the Sikhs abandoned the Brigadier, who, in the attempt to force the defile as far as Ali Musjid, was repulsed by the Khyburis and Afreedis, and forced to retreat to Jumrood with a heavy loss.

The negotiations with the Lahore durbar respecting these matters were placed by the Indian Government, with almost discretionary powers, in the hands of Mr. Clerk, whose personal influence with the durbar, the Sikh chiefs, and even the population, was great, and who was enabled to establish an intimate intercourse directly with the Maharaja and the minister; by his means every effort was employed to overcome the obstacles to a hearty co-operation with our forces on the part of the Sikh troops. Mr. Clerk wrote from Amritsur, on the 6th March, 1842, that he had held a conference with the Maharaja upon this subject; that the durbar had urged the necessity of caution in advancing, and that, when General Pollock had been reinforced by General McCaskill's brigade, Golab Singh had been ordered to co-operate; and it does not appear in any case that there was backwardness on the part of the Sikh commanders. "The chiefs," observes General Pollock, "are, as far as I have observed, courteous, and perhaps well-disposed towards us; but the bearing of the soldiery, one and all, is insolent, and they scruple not to express their wish that we may meet with reverses: they are a disorganized rabble."*

Upon the occasion of the advance of General Pollock's army into the Khybur, the Sikhs (a portion of Golab Singh's army) redeemed their character, by forcing the Jubhagi entrance, with a loss equal to that of the British troops. An agreement was made with Golab Singh that he should hold the pass as far as Ali Musjid.

The most friendly intercourse continued to be maintained by Mr. Clerk with the Lahore durbar, and in June, 1842, the Maharaja proceeded in person to the westward, to lend the weight of his own presence and influence to the endeavours made for

* Papers, *ut ante.*

restoring order and discipline in the Sikh army at Peshawur.

Several reasons are assigned by Mr. Clerk, which should moderate our indignation at the conduct of the Sikh army. A very strong impression seems to have prevailed amongst them, and even their commanders, that we had taken possession of Cabulistan on our own account, and intended to occupy Peshawur, which was a dependency of the Durani empire; and with reference to their refusal to provide carriage-cattle to the British commissariat (of which General Pollock heavily complained), Mr. Clerk ascribed it to "a religious and an invincible repugnance to consign their bullocks to a kine-killing army." So far from the British Government meditating acquisitions of Sikh territory, Lord Ellenborough authorized Mr. Clerk to inform the Lahore Government, that if it should be desirous of adding to its dominion the territory lying between the right bank of the Indus, the Sufeed Koh, and the Himalaya, the British Government would not object to that object being effected, and would facilitate it by placing Jelalabad (which the

Maharaja desired to possess) in the hands of the Sikhs.* The latter proposal was accepted by the Lahore durbar, and General Pollock was accordingly directed, upon his retirement from Cabul, to give up Jelalabad to the Sikh troops in its existing state.

In June, 1842, a Sikh force, of 5,000 men, advanced through the Khybur Pass, and took up a position near Jelalabad; a circumstance which, considering the state of the troops, was viewed by our commanders with some uneasiness. Moreover, the feverish state of the Lahore durbar, in the month of August, excited apprehensions in the mind of Lord Ellenborough, who determined to assemble an army of reserve, which, whilst it would facilitate the operations of our armies in Cabul, would "strengthen the existing government of Lahore." The Governor-General referred, at the same time, to the recent murder of Chund Kowr, the evident suspicions of Raja Golab Singh, the jealousies and uneasiness of the Maharaja, "and his occasional indiscretion in making known his feelings, together with the conversations

* Papers *ut ante*, p. 292.

in the durbar,* which exhibit generally, on the part of the chiefs, doubts of the continuance of our power, and suspicions of our intentions, if we should retain it."†

From the reports of these conversations, which appeared in the Lahore Ukhbars at this time, it is manifest that Sher Singh evinced much impatience, if not disgust, at the turmoils of his court, and at the state of subjection in which he was retained by the Jummoo family, and some hasty expressions fell from him, which denoted that, in his opinion, ease, security, and personal freedom would not have been purchased too dearly by a transfer of his sovereignty to the British Government. It would seem that Dhean Singh apprehended such a step, and to prevent it, redoubled his vigilance, watching all the motions of the Maharaja, who was virtually a captive. Either the minister, or his son Heera Singh, or one of their confederates, was in proximity to him day and night. Whether at the durbar, or in his private

* These conversations are published in the Ukhbars, being taken down by news-writers in attendance.

† Letter to Secret Committee, 6th August, 1842.

apartments, reviewing his troops or hunting, the prince was never unattended by one of these spies upon his motions, whose respectful demeanour gave him no ostensible ground of complaint.

The Governor-General of British India (Lord Ellenborough) having removed from Calcutta towards the Sutluj, in order to be near the scene of operations whilst our troops were retiring from Afghanistan, a communication was made from his lordship to the Lahore durbar by Mr. Clerk, on the 7th September, expressing a desire to meet the Maharaja, "to discuss some weighty political matters." This proposal was altogether inconsistent with the views of the minister, and accordingly it was at first declined for the present, upon the ground that, as the Sikh troops were absent on foreign service, the Maharaja could not appear properly attended. The point, however, was urged by the Governor-General, and at a special durbar on the 9th December, Mr. Clerk had an interview with Sher Singh, which lasted an hour and a half. After his departure, the question was discussed, when, though the sirdars were averse to it, the Maharaja declared himself in favour of the interview, and a letter was accordingly sent to Mr. Clerk, stating that his highness was ready to conform to the wishes of the Governor-General. Dhean Singh endeavoured to alarm the prince's fears, observing that the English had 60,000 men then assembled at Ferozepore (including the troops returned from beyond the Indus), and "it did not become his highness to pay a visit to the Governor-General in a foreign country, surrounded by such a force." Sher Singh seems to have been at first struck with this suggestion. He had, however, gone too far to recede, and a deputation was sent to Ferozepore, where Lord Ellenborough was then residing, and soon after Raja Dhean Singh was directed to accompany Pertab Singh (the son of the Maharaja), with 5,000 men, to carry the compliments of Sher Singh to his lordship. This mission was received with much honour, and a return mission, with Mr. Secretary (now Sir T.) Maddock at the head, proceeded to Lahore, where it arrived on the 6th January, 1843.

The reception of this mission was in every respect most friendly. Mr. Maddock, with a numerous suite,* was introduced the next day to the Maharaja, at a full durbar. They were conducted into the palace-garden, the paths being spread with shawl-carpets, lined on either side by the body-guard, in splendid dresses. Passing through these, they were conducted to a platform, forty feet long by twenty broad, entirely covered with shawl-carpets, sumeenas, or canopies, supported by silver poles, being stretched over it. Here the durbar was held. Mr. Maddock was received, on alighting from his elephant, by Pertab Singh, then a fine boy, ten years of age, and on ascending the flight of steps, he was met by the Maharaja, and the persons composing the party (twenty-seven in number), after being introduced, were conducted to chairs, which extended in a row from the right of the Maharaja, who seated himself in a gold chair. With the exception of some of the principal persons of the court, most of the sirdars and ministers squatted down on his left hand. At this preliminary dur-

* Including Lord Altamont and Captain Von Orlich.

bar, nothing but introductions took place. The following day, another durbar was held, at which the presents were exhibited. On the 9th they were entertained by the Maharaja in the palace. Entering the Summunboorj, they were received by Sher Singh, who, after they had sat for a few minutes, took Mr. Maddock's hand, and conducted him and the party into an open court, illuminated on all sides. In the centre was a tank of water, on the surface of which floated a golden peacock, made of coloured lamps, and various water-fowls, whilst a fountain played at each corner. On one side of the square was a promenade; on another, were shawl canopies on silver poles, beneath which carpets were spread and chairs arranged; on a third side was the *Shish Mahal*, or Hall of Mirrors, being entirely lined, ceiling and walls, with looking-glasses. Between the reservoir and the Hall of Mirrors, tables were arranged, with viands and liquors, including excellent champagne, sherry, and other European wines. Whilst these liquors were passing round, and the nautch-girls were dancing, the Maharaja ordered his stud of fat, richly-caparisoned horses, as well as his jewels, to be exhibited to his visitors, and he unclasped from his arm the celebrated koh-i-noor, which had been rescued from Jugernat. On the following day the Maharaja reviewed, in company with Mr. Maddock, the troops at the capital, amounting to 60,000 men, the line extending to between eight and nine miles.

The projected interview between the Maharaja and the Governor-General did not take place; upon the close of this year a sanguinary revolution changed the whole face of affairs at the court of Lahore.

Before entering upon this painful narrative, it may be proper to notice some incidents in Sikh history less important, but not without interest.

In January, 1843, Dost Mahomed Khan, released from his confinement by the untoward events in Afghanistan, in his progress towards Cabul through the Punjab, could do no less than pay a visit to the Maharaja at Lahore. Had his choice been perfectly free, he would probably have avoided an interview which, for many reasons, must have been mortifying. Despoiled of all the attributes of rank and dignity, indebted to the clemency of his conquerors for his liberation, he presented himself before the chiefs of a nation which hated him and was hated by him, and had been a party to his humiliation. But the Ameer experienced generous treatment at the hands of Sher Singh, who received him on the 21st January, in full durbar, with all the honour due to a royal visitor. Dost Mahomed Khan remained at the court for more than a month, during which time much negotiation was observed between him and the Sikh ministers, and some treaty or compact was executed by the Ameer, the effect of which did not transpire, beyond a statement in one of the Ukhbars, that the latter had consented to pay tribute to Lahore for some territory to be ceded to him. In May, Mr. Clerk visited Lahore, to be present at the marriage ceremony of Prince Pertab Singh, the eldest son of the Maharaja, and heir-apparent. At the same time, General Avitabili resigned the governorship of Peshawur, in consequence of his health, and came to Lahore to obtain leave to visit Europe. The government of Peshawur, civil and military, was committed to Tej Singh.

The Maharaja, about this time, paid a visit to the estates of Golab Singh at Jummoo, in connection with which some incidents had recently happened, but the narrative requires to be taken up from an earlier period.

Reference has already been made to the military operations and conquests of the Sikhs in Tibet, which appear to have been carried on upon a larger scale than was supposed at the period when they took place.

Tibet is commonly distributed into three great provinces, namely, Upper Tibet, or Bootan; Middle Tibet, or Ladakh; and Little Tibet, or Bulti. Middle Tibet, which immediately adjoins the territory of Cashmere, in the reign of Aurungzeb, was invaded by the Kalmaks, and the ruler of the country, unable to repel them, applied for aid to the Mogul governor of Cashmere, who granted it on condition that Ladakh became tributary to the Mogul empire. From that period, until the reign of Mahomed Shah, Ladakh paid, through Cashmere, a small annual tribute to the court of Delhi. On the invasion of Hindustan by Ahmed Shah Abdali, the tribute was transferred to the Durani government of Cabul, and was paid to their officers in Cashmere, until that province was invaded and subdued by the Sikhs. Runjeet Singh intimated his intention to enforce his claim upon Ladakh, as lord of Cashmere, and the raja (or khalun) was advised to ward off this claim, which he knew would eventually lead to the appropriation of the whole territory, by tendering his allegiance to the government of British India, as the legitimate representative of the dynasty of Timur. This step was delayed till the reception of a message from the court of Lahore, through the governor of Cashmere, inquiring why the tribute had not been paid as usual, and threatening a forcible levy, if it was not speedily despatched. At this critical juncture (1821), the late Mr. Moorcroft happened to be at Leh, the capital of the state of Ladakh, and the khalun requested him to be the medium of forwarding his tender of allegiance to the British Government, as his paramount sovereign. Mr. Moorcroft consented to do so, apprizing the Sikh ruler, at the same time, by letter, of what he had done, expostulating likewise with that chief on his unjustifiable demand of tribute. Mr. Moorcroft conceived that his motives justified this interposition, though he was clothed with no official character: on the one hand, he averted from an amiable and harmless people the oppressive weight of Sikh exaction and insolence; on the other, he secured for his country an influence over a state which, lying on the British frontier, offered a central mart for the extension of her commerce to Turkistan and China, and a strong outwork against an enemy from the north. His conduct was, however, wholly disapproved of, and he was severely censured by the Supreme Government at Calcutta, for taking unauthorizedly a part in political arrangements. The allegiance of Ladakh was declined, and Runjeet Singh was informed that Mr. Moorcroft had acted without the sanction of the British Government; consequently, the khalun of

Ladakh and his state were left at the mercy of the Sikh ruler.*

Runjeet, however, was not in a condition or humour to take advantage of his opportunity in this quarter, until the Jummoo raja, Golab Singh, had extended his authority in the hills, and acquired by his severities a reputation which became the terror of the country, and he was then authorized to enforce the demands of the Sikh court upon Ladakh. Golab placed an army under the command of Zorawur Singh, who gradually subjected the whole province, and, defeating the khalun in 1835, deposed him from his

* Moorcroft's Travels, vol. i. p. 420. Professor Wilson, in the preface to his edition of Mr. Moorcroft's Travels, observes: "The fear of giving offence to Runjeet Singh, no doubt, induced the Government to reprove Mr. Moorcroft, and to decline the proffered allegiance of Ladakh; but it is much to be regretted that any such needless apprehension should have persuaded them to relinquish so justifiable an opportunity of extending British influence. Runjeet had not the shadow of a right to claim Ladakh as his own. It was an independent principality, at liberty to seek protection where it chose, and the buckler of the British power might have been warrantably thrown over it, without injury to its own independence, or to the rights of its neighbours."

authority, and vested it in a person appointed by Golab Singh. Ladakh is now little better than a Sikh province, the Ladakhis being treated by their conquerors with insolence and cruelty.*

The occupation of Ladakh was only a step to further encroachments. When Sher Singh was governor of Cashmere, he endeavoured to make himself master of Little Tibet, which likewise adjoins the valley to the north. He advanced towards Iskardo, the capital, as far as Godyh, where a rapid torrent joins the T'hung Kurym stream at right angles, and forms with it and the surrounding mountains a barrier impassable by any native invader. Here he found a matchlock behind every rock on the opposite bank of a furious river. He attempted to gain his end by diplomacy, and the gylfo, Ahmed Shah, kept the Sikhs in play till the severe weather suddenly commenced, when

* Major Lawrence (Adv. in the Punjab, vol. i. p. 37) says, the first intimation Runjeet Singh received of the operations on the Ladakh frontier was the announcement of the occupation of Ladakh itself by Zorawur Singh.

they commenced a precipitate retreat. The cold chilled them, and in a snow-storm hundreds perished upon the plateau above Burzil.*

Golab Singh, however, having pushed his conquests to the edge of the valley of Cashmere, soon subjected Little Tibet, which is now tributary to the Sikhs, or to the Jummoo family.

On the eastern frontier of Ladakh lies the large province of Chan-tan, known to the Booteas as Hiundes, or Hemdes, the 'Region of Cold,' comprehending what has been called Upper Tibet. This country was formerly subject to independent princes, but their authority gradually merged in that of H'lassa (the name of the capital of Bootan), which is under the nominal authority of China, a Chinese governor residing in the city. By virtue of some ancient agreement, the wool of the shawl goat, of which this cold country is the chief resort, is sold exclusively to the people of Ladakh: hence probably arose some constructive claim on the part of the Sikhs. In the season of 1840,

* Vigne, Travels in Kashmir, vol. ii. p. 216.

Zorawur Singh, the commander of the Sikh army, marched from Leh, the capital of Ladakh, along the valley of the Sinh-ka-bab, or great eastern branch of the Indus, subjecting the places in his progress, passing the hills to Rodokh on the north, and pressing onward to Gartokh on the south-east, whence he appears to have reached the eastern shore of the celebrated Manasarowur lake. He encountered little or no opposition; the leaders of the Tibetan troops,—a few thousand rabble, unworthy of the name of soldiers,—were panic-stricken, and the inhabitants, armed and unarmed, fled in consternation before him. The deb, or chief, of Chan-tan having retreated with his forces, Zorawur Singh took possession, without resistance, of Tuklahah, a large commercial town situated in a fine valley, as extensive as that of Nepaul.

The advance of the Sikhs, thus unopposed, to the northern confines of the British provinces of Gurhwal and Kumaon, excited the attention of our authorities on the frontier, and some communications passed between them and the Sikh commander, who was extremely courteous, and professed a readiness to comply with all the wishes of our Government. The political agent at Simla (Mr. Erskine) was, however, informed that the Government had resolved not to interfere in the aggressive movements of the Sikhs. Subsequently, the British commissioner in Kumaon had a conference with Zorawur Singh at Tuklahah (a place never visited before by a European), which appeared to be a city inferior only to H'lassa. With the exception of sending (with the consent of the Lahore court) a British officer (Lieutenant Cunningham) to the Sikh camp in the hills, no interruption, therefore, of their career of conquest was offered by the British Government, and the court of Nepaul seems to have been either in collusion with the Sikhs, or to have partaken of the general panic inspired by their arms. Under these favourable circumstances, Zorawur Singh continued his acquisitions, and in September, 1841, he had subdued the whole of Kulu, and possessed himself of all the strongholds in the mountains, from the right bank of the Upper Sutluj to the innermost recesses of Tibet.

His career was stopped by the Chinese commander in Chan-tan, who marched from H'lassa against the Sikhs, with an army of 10,000 men, about one-fifth Ghoorkas, and the rest Tibetans and Tartars. An action was fought in December, 1841, or January, 1842, near Tuklahah, in which the Sikh army was entirely defeated, and Zorawur Singh was slain. The victors cut off the ears and head of the Sikh general, and sent them as trophies to H'lassa. His successor in the command entered into a treaty with the Chinese general, by which the Sikhs engaged to give up their arms, and to trust to his mercy. They had, probably, deserved little mercy, and they experienced none; they were not, indeed, massacred, but they were suffered to perish with cold and hunger, save a miserable remnant, consisting of about 100, who found their way, exhausted and frost-bitten, to the British hill station of Almorah.

After the defeat and fall of Zorawur Singh, the Chinese-Tibetan army proceeded to Gartokh, expelled most of the Sikh garrisons in that province, Dapa, and other forts, and advanced to the frontiers of Ladakh. Intelligence of these events reached Golab Singh whilst he was at Peshawur, in command of the army of co-operation. He immediately proceeded to Cashmere, to collect his forces and organize his plans for the defence of Ladakh, the people of which had risen in opposition to the Sikhs upon the approach of the Chinese-Tibetan army.

The departure of Golab Singh wrought a mischievous effect upon the troops at Peshawur, who broke out again into insubordination, occasioning much apprehension to the British commanders.*

* Papers relating to the Mil. Operations in Afghanistan, 1843, pp. 261, 267, 289.

CHAPTER XXII.

A.D. 1843 AND 1844.

THE tragical events which closed the reign of Sher Singh are still wrapped in mystery. The destruction of the chief agents; the rapid succession of revolutions, each of which almost obliterated the memory of the preceding; the dark and apparently inexplicable motives of some of the actors, and the imperfect and often contradictory reports of the native news-writers, upon which the historian is constrained to rely,* conspire to cast a cloud of obscurity over these transactions which will probably never be altogether dissipated.

It has been already related that, upon the overthrow of Chund Kowr's authority and the re-establishment of Sher Singh upon the throne, the sirdars of the Sindawala family

* These news-writers may, in ordinary times, be trusted as to facts, though not as to inferences.

(descended from a common ancestor with Runjeet Singh), who had embraced the Rani's party, fled across the Sutluj, except Lena Singh, Sindawala,* who was seized and imprisoned. Uttur Singh, the head of that family, and Ajeet Singh, the paramour of the late Rani, whilst refugees in the British territory, maintained constant intercourse with their party at the court, where a faction still remained hostile to the Jummoo family. The army was tainted with this spirit of discontent, infused and fed by the intrigues of the Sindawalas, which caused the Maharaja and his minister much uneasiness. Mr. Clerk, writing to the Indian Government, in May, 1842, said that the subject most occupying the mind of the Maharaja at that time was the position of the Sindawala chiefs, and that "there is nothing which his highness would at present feel so great an obligation as the restraining these chiefs from creating commotion in his army, and their renewing their allegiance on perfectly submissive terms to the throne." By the

* To be distinguished from Lena Singh, of the Majethia family.

intervention of the British Government, a reconciliation took place, and these chiefs were recalled, pardoned, and restored to their estates.

Uttur Singh is described* as a respectable man, well versed in Sikh politics, one of Runjeet's school, and therefore he drew around him the genuine Khalsas, who reverenced the name of the great Maharaja. In person he was middle-sized, of stout build, with a plain, unmarked countenance, and, like the old Sikh leaders, of simple and unostentatious manners. He, however, wanted some of the qualities, including tact and political firmness, essential to a leader in those peculiar times.† Lena Singh was tall,

* Calcutta Review, No. II. p. 495.

† The writer of the Review adds: "We happened to meet Uttur Singh as he was flying from a place near the hills, where he resided when Sher Singh was murdered. It was just at night-fall: he was bivouacking on a wide plain, in the midst of a small party of forty or fifty retainers, and though he had then reached the protected Sikh states, and was comparatively safe, we found him on the alert. He was up in an instant, and did not seem half-inclined to step out a few paces from his followers to talk to a single European. After a little conversation his suspicions fled, and he told

very dark, much addicted to strong liquors, but having the rare character of a speaker of the truth. Ajeet Singh, nephew of Uttur, was a fat, broad-faced man, of blunt speech, good manners, but corrupt morals.

Upon the restoration of these persons and their adherents to court, Sher Singh hoped to extinguish intrigue and to lead a quiet life; but he seems to have rendered more complicated the toils which surrounded him. Lena and Ajeet were observed to have acquired the favour and confidence of the Maharaja; they received likewise demonstrations of respect and attention from Raja Dhean Singh, the minister, who was at this time raised to the highest rank next to the throne.* In the early part of the year 1843, a visible alienation was observed in Sher Singh towards his minister, or rather towards the whole Jummoo family; attempts

told us very composedly the circumstances of the recent tragedy, and that then was the time for the British to seize Lahore—that it would be very easy with his help, —very difficult without."

* "This day, Raja Dhean Singh was invested by the Maharaja with the highest dignity in the state."—Lahore Ukhbar, December 18, 1842.

were made to lessen their influence, by removing their friends and dependants from office, which were filled by persons in whom the Maharaja's party could place confidence. Sher Singh, a man of easy temper, open-hearted and indolent, is not likely to have spontaneously entered upon so hazardous a scheme of policy, and to have given wanton umbrage to a man whose power was superior to his own; who had raised him to the throne, and could alone keep him there: it is evident that he must have been the passive agent of some insidious and secret advisers.

A conspiracy was formed against Sher Singh, which comprehended the Jummoo rajas, the Sindawala chiefs, and even the Fakir Uzeez-ud-deen, a party strong enough, with the army (under the command of Heera Singh), if their views had been perfectly concurrent, to have deposed the Maharaja without recourse to wholesale assassination; but it cannot be doubted that the elements of this conspiracy were discordant, and that the actors were conspiring against each other.

Raja Dhean Singh had had recourse to his customary mode of shewing his displeasure towards his master, by absenting himself from the court and paying a visit to his hill estates. The Maharaja, at the instigation of his indiscreet or treacherous advisers, commanded the raja to return; requiring him to explain his proceedings for the last five years, and to render his accounts, as well as the customary nuzzurana, or tributary presents, threatening, if he refused, to send General Ventura with a military force to fetch him. Golab Singh persuaded his brother to obey the mandate, and the raja accordingly appeared at the durbar at Amritsur, on the 9th July, 1843, when he was called upon to explain the reasons why he had proceeded to Jummoo. The answer of the proud minister cannot be better related than in the words of the news-writer.

"Raja Dhean Singh presented himself, and having embraced the feet of his highness, was asked why he had gone to Jummoo; to which the minister answered, that there were several reasons which had induced him to do so; first, that he was anxious to see Raja Golab Singh, who was ill; secondly, to be present at his nephew's marriage. He further begged to represent, that his highness's constant devotion to the chase and the bottle, during the greater part of the day, had a baneful effect upon the state, and reflected disgrace on the minister as well as the monarch; and with regard to the accounts and nuzzurana required of him, they were all forthcoming, and all he possessed was the Maharaja's. He took occasion at the same time to remark on the jealousy which many of the sirdars entertained towards him. The Maharaja replied, that he should be protected."

A speech like this, delivered in open durbar, by a minister to his sovereign, although not altogether repugnant to the manners of the Sikhs, must have satisfied any one that the prince's authority rested upon a very frail foundation. Intimations were said to have been given to Sher Singh that a conspiracy was forming against him; that his life was threatened, and the very day, the 15th September, 1843, was named as that on which some disastrous event would occur.

Although the Maharaja and Dhean Singh appeared to be outwardly upon good terms, yet there are sufficient indications that all cordiality had ceased, and that the former was intent upon humbling the minister and his family. With his habitual want of caution, the prince threw out hints that he designed to call Raja Golab Singh to court, in order that he might render an account of his proceedings.

Meanwhile, Sher Singh seems to have exerted himself with some energy. He frequently reviewed the troops, examining their discipline and appointments, punishing several commanders who had taken upon themselves to call out their regiments without orders; two of these officers had their tongues split, and were paraded through the camp. The congregation of the troops in the vicinity of the capital was a circumstance of suspicion; but it was supposed to be explained by the approach of the Dussera festival, which it was usual to celebrate with military spectacles. On the 7th August, Ram Chund reported that the army of the Khalsa was extending around Lahore for four kos in every direction, to which the Maharaja replied, that "it was well, as he was anxious to see the whole of his forces assembled at the Dussera."

An unauthorized and a most presumptuous step, taken by the Jummoo rajas and their party, might very reasonably have awakened the darkest suspicions in the breast of Sher Singh. Dhuleep Singh, a child of eight or nine years, who had been recognized by Runjeet Singh, towards the close of his life, as his son, with a full knowledge that he was not so, had been brought privately to Jummoo, and was now sent for by the minister to Lahore. On the 31st August, at a durbar, at which were present Dhean Singh, Soochet Singh, Heera Singh, Ajeet Singh, Lena Singh, and the Hakim Uzeez-ud-deen, the great minister informed the Maharaja that he had sent for Prince Dhuleep Singh, son of Runjeet Singh, from Jummoo, who had arrived at Lahore, and proposed that a salute should be fired upon the occasion. The Maharaja inquired why he had been brought, and desired that he might not be introduced to the durbar. The raja replied, that the boy's mother was sick, and had desired to see him. On the following day, the Maharaja directed a letter to be addressed to Golab Singh, at Jummoo, inquiring why he had sent Dhuleep Singh to Lahore, without acquainting the Maharaja; and ordered that some of his own attendants should replace those of Dhean Singh in the care of the person of Dhuleep; an arrangement which Dhean Singh opposed. At a durbar held on the 4th September, a letter was received from Golab Singh, stating that, as he was anxious to see his highness, he should shortly present himself. Private information was the same day given to Sher Singh, that Dhean Singh, Soochet Singh, Heera Singh, Lena Singh, and Ajeet Singh, had met secretly at the house of Dhuleep Singh's mother, and had been in consultation for three hours. A hurkara was appointed to watch and report the proceedings of these sirdars. The next day, after the durbar, at which General Ventura was present, the latter solicited a private audience of the Maharaja, at which he informed him, in distinct terms, that the five individuals before named had conspired against him; that it was for that end they had sent for Dhuleep Singh, and that Golab Singh was on his way from Jummoo to aid them; recommending him to use every precaution. Sher Singh replied, that he could not believe this of Dhean Singh, "as it was to him he owed his elevation." On the 6th the Maharaja sent for his own guru, Saheb Singh, and communicated to him the report of the conspiracy. The priest discredited it, observing that Ajeet was bound by blood to the Maharaja, and desired to know who had informed his highness. The Maharaja refused to tell, but remarked, that "if he found that Ajeet Singh was conspiring against him, he would certainly put him to death, as he had done with Rani Chund Kowr."

Golab Singh arrived at Lahore on the 8th September, and on the 9th presented himself at the durbar, when he was received most kindly by the Maharaja, and in return assured him that "he and his brothers were devotedly attached to his highness's person." The Maharaja said he should require an oath from him that he entertained no evil designs against him, from which Golab Singh excused himself for two or three days. Upon the same day, Prince Pertab Singh informed his father that he did not believe there was occasion to distrust any of the sirdars, except Ajeet Singh, who was not to be depended upon: orders were thereupon given to exclude Ajeet from the durbar during his highness's pleasure. On the 10th, a durbar was held, after dismissing which, the Maharaja took Golab Singh and Dhean Singh aside, and having assured them that he felt it was to their aid he owed his elevation, asked what they were meditating? They both placed their hands upon the Maharaja's head (a most solemn form of adjuration), and swore they were and would continue to be good servants; adding that, as far as Ajeet Singh and his troops were concerned, his highness need not fear them. On the 14th September, a durbar was held, when Dhean Singh suggested to the Maharaja that he ought to review Ajeet's troops and gain their good-will by bestowing honours and rewards upon the officers; and Sher Singh promised he would do so the next morning. On the same night, the Rani Issur Chund gave birth to a son; the Maharaja sent for a pundit to cast the infant's nativity, who reported that it was not favourable.*

On the 15th September the catastrophe took place. The accounts of this bloody transaction are so various and conflicting, that it is impossible to combine them into a consistent narrative.

The purwaneh addressed by the reigning Maharaja to his vakeel at Ferozepore, which, under ordinary circumstances, should be considered as containing the most authentic report of the facts, states, that Lena Singh and Ajeet Singh went, accompanied by Sikh and other troops, to announce the muster of their troops to the Maharaja, who was in the garden of the Shah Belawal, having gone

* The minute circumstances above detailed, which may throw some light upon the plot and upon the motives of the actors, are taken from the reports of the native news-writers at Lahore.

thither to enjoy the fresh air, and amuse himself on the river. The sirdars went to him in the garden, where he was sitting, and offered him a rifle, and while the Maharaja was examining it, Ajeet Singh drew a pistol and fired at him, wounding him in the face. The two sirdars then struck off the Maharaja's head. Several of his ministers and personal attendants fell at the same time, including Boodh Singh and Gunga Singh. After this, Lena Singh went, "accidentally," to the garden of Tej Singh, near that of the Shah Belawal, and there killed Pertab Singh, son of Sher Singh, who was celebrating the festival, and beheaded him. The conspirators then proceeded towards the city, and on the road met Raja Dhean Singh, who was alone. They informed him that a disturbance had taken place in the garden; that the Maharaja had been killed, and as it would be dangerous for him to go alone there, proposed that he should return with them to the city, and take measures for settling the succession. The raja complied, and on their way, when they had approached the Kureeani gate, Ajeet drew a pistol and fired at Dhean Singh, who exclaimed, "Oh, sirdar, what a foul deed!" and laid his hand upon his sword. The followers of Ajeet then fired at the raja, who fell from his horse.

The account given by the news-writers, though equally circumstantial, is totally different from the preceding. This report states, that Sher Singh set out on horseback towards the northern gate of Lahore, to review the troops of Ajeet, as he had promised. His *suwaree*, or *cortège*, no sooner approached the regiments (about twenty), than officers and men loudly abused him; whereupon Ajeet Singh came forward, and in an insolent tone, told him he was no son of Runjeet Singh, but a purchased slave, brought up by his supposed mother. Sher Singh, astonished and provoked at this address, turned round to look for the Rajas Golab Singh and Dhean Singh; but they were not to be seen. He then discharged an arrow at Ajeet, but missed him, and that sirdar drew a pistol and shot the Maharaja through the head, who fell, and was instantly beheaded by Ajeet. General Ventura, having been informed of this event, drew out his troops against those of Ajeet Singh; but the latter were so superior in numbers that he was obliged to retire, leaving 200 men on the field. He hurried to Pertab Singh, to inform him of what had happened. The prince ordered out his two regiments, and issuing from the city, met Ajeet at the head of his troops, and saw his father's head borne on a spear. The sirdar immediately attacked the prince, slew him with his own hand, and beheaded him.

Major Lawrence, who states that he has heard the transaction related by many people (Generals Avitabili and Court included) in as many different ways, gives the following as the most probable account. The Maharaja, having been warned of some calamity, sent his son out of the way to General Court, to see a gun cast. Sher Singh was inspecting a party of sowars, when Ajeet Singh stepped up, under pretence of shewing him a double-barreled gun (the prince being a great gun-fancier), and shot him dead. A scuffle ensued, in which Boodh Singh and others fell. Soon afterwards, Pertab Singh was met, returning from the foundry, and instantly despatched.*

The assassination of Dhean Singh is likewise variously related. It is, however, agreed that he was either stabbed or shot by Ajeet Singh, and it is suggested that this deed was prompted by the Bhae Goormukh Singh, a man of little ability but of great cunning, who affected a reputation for deep piety, which he made subservient to intrigue. This man bore a secret enmity to Dhean Singh, and when the assassin Ajeet told him he had killed the prince, declared that his life was not safe an hour unless he destroyed the minister.

By this act, the Sindawala party held themselves out to the world as the prime agents in this conspiracy,—coveting all the advantages and incurring all its odium and responsibility. Heera Singh, the son of Dhean Singh, with great decision and promptitude, accompanied by his uncle Soochet Singh and other sirdars, hastened to the nearest body of regular troops, harangued

* Calcutta Review, No. II. p. 499.

them with spirit and resolution, telling them that the murders perpetrated by the Sindawalas had made those sirdars masters of the state: he denounced their crimes, expatiated upon their treachery, and concluded a pathetic address by a proposition pregnant with eloquence—he offered them liberal gratuities, and promised to discharge all the arrears, and raise the pay one-half, of all who would follow him and revenge the murder of their sovereign, his son, and his minister. This appeal had its due effect; the troops demanded to be led against the assassins, declaring that they would not sit down to a meal until they had destroyed the faithless Sindawala sirdars. In the course of the day succeeding the assassination, 50,000 troops surrounded the citadel, in which Ajeet Singh, Lena Singh, and their adherents, had hastily thrown themselves, Uttur Singh having effected his escape. A heavy cannonade was opened upon the place, which continued during the night. The next day, repeated assaults were made, and repelled by the besieged, who, knowing that their lives were at stake, offered a desperate defence. Towards the evening, however, the citadel was carried by storm; Ajeet Singh and Lena Singh, with many of the garrison, to the number of 600, were put to the sword. The head of Ajeet was brought to Heera Singh, who ordered the body of his father's murderer to be cut in pieces, which were exposed upon the different gates of the city. His house was destroyed, and it was decreed that thenceforward his lands should be no longer ploughed with oxen, but with asses.

The effect of these sudden and rapid revolutions was to place the conduct of affairs in the hands of Heera Singh, a young man of twenty-three, who appears to have developed talents suited to the emergency, and for which he had not hitherto obtained credit. With the aid of his uncles, and the influence he derived from his position and popularity, when the boy Dhuleep Singh was proclaimed Maharaja, Heera Singh was nominated his vuzeer.

Whilst these tragedies were enacted, the city was in a state of uproar and disorder. The soldiers plundered at their will; murder was committed in the open day; all business was suspended, and those who were able to escape (including the French commanders of the Sikh army) rejoiced to fly from this scene of horrors.

The funeral ceremonies of the late Maharaja were performed with a respect which implied, or was intended to imply, that the individuals now in power were not accessary to his assassination. Sher Singh had three wives; but, though no suttees are mentioned as having dishonoured his pile, no less than eighteen women, wives and concubines of Dhean Singh, are reported to have burnt themselves with his corpse. A deputation was sent to the British authorities at Ferozepore, to obtain permission for the transport of the ashes of Sher Singh and Dhean Singh across the Sutluj to the Ganges at Hurdwar.

The character of Sher Singh exhibits no qualities which are calculated to inspire us with any extraordinary commiseration for his fate. He was a man of average ability, and of much courage; but a thorough sensualist. He was enamoured of European manners, which he affected so far as to rouse the jealousy of Runjeet, who was a strict Sikh. Unhappily, Sher Singh, like many other Eastern imitators of the customs and habits of Europe, copied those only in which imitation is least to be desired or commended. He had some knowledge of our language, in which he was desirous that his son should be instructed, and when the Rev. Mr. Wolff visited Cashmere, in October, 1833, Sher Singh, then its governor, desired to be furnished with a copy of our New Testament. It is now well understood that he was no son of Runjeet, who never acknowledged him (except by allowing him a chair in his presence), and his twin-brother, Tara Singh, was treated by that prince with uniform neglect, and lived unnoticed, except as a dissolute profligate in the common bazars, at Lahore. When governor of Cashmere, Sher's indolence left the management of affairs in the hands of Jemadar Khooshal Singh, whose exactions impoverished and depopulated that province, from whence Sher Singh was in consequence removed. He, however, gained some reputation by the successful expedition against the fanatic

Seyud Ahmed. He is described as a fine, manly-looking fellow by Captain Osborne. Other writers represent even his personal features less favourably. His countenance was not unpleasing when he smiled, but the eye expressed violence and imperiousness, and the lower part of the face indicated the vilest sensuality. His manners were often marked by unbecoming freedom.* Captain Osborne relates the following incident as occurring in 1838, at the durbar. Runjeet Singh, anxious that the deputation sent to receive the mission from the Governor-General should do credit to his court by the splendour of their appearance, ordered the persons who composed it to attend him previous to their setting out. After complimenting Soochet Singh upon his dress and jewels, he angrily demanded of Sher Singh why he was without his usual magnificent ornaments. The Koonwur, touching the hilt of his sword, replied, "I am a soldier, and this is the only jewel I value." The Maharaja, however, insisted upon knowing what had become of them, and at last ex-

* *Calcutta Star.*

torted the confession from Sher Singh, that they were in the royal treasury, having been presented by him to Runjeet, as a nuzzur, and accepted, some months before.

Pertab Singh, who was only twelve years of age when involved in the late massacre, was a very promising youth, full of spirit and energy. Sher Singh was extravagantly fond of him. Captain Osborne says, he was one of the most intelligent boys he ever met with. His person was good-looking, with singularly large and expressive eyes. His manners were easy, polished, and in the highest degree graceful and engaging.

Sher Singh left an infant son, named Shah Deo, who still survives.

CHAPTER XXIII.

REIGN OF DHULEEP SINGH.

A.D. 1843 TO 1845.

UNDER a minor sovereign, at a court where so many who might have been competitors or enemies had been swept away, the vuzeer, or minister, was the absolute ruler of the Punjab. The favour which had been bestowed upon Heera Singh by Runjeet, though acquired in a manner which, in any other country, would have rendered him infamous for ever,* gave him a strong hold upon the Sikh nation, who venerated the memory of their first ruler. His family connections and hereditary power placed him in the highest rank of the Punjabi nobility. The command of the army had established his relation with a body which had the power of disposing of the throne itself. The sympathy generally felt for the fate of his father

* Osborne, p. 76.

tended to strengthen the other ties of attachment to him, which were still further cemented by his personal qualities. Heera Singh was strikingly handsome, though somewhat effeminate in his appearance. Shrewd and intelligent, good-tempered, urbane, and entertaining, "he is certainly," says Captain Osborne, "one of the most amiable and popular persons at the court of Lahore."

With all these advantages, however, Heera Singh's position was one of great difficulty and peril. The convulsions which had brought him to the surface of power, and cast him upon his present eminence, had deranged all the machinery and functions of the government, whilst the army, upon which he was constrained to depend, was an unruly and insatiable monster, whose voracity, after exhausting every expedient, he found it in the end impossible to appease.

In conjunction with his uncles, Golab and Soochet, and Lena Singh, Majethia,* he

* Lena Singh, Majethia, the son of Desa Singh, one of Runjeet's companions, and who has been often confounded with his namesake of the Sindawala family (who was an ignorant drunkard), is a man of talents and respectability, designed probably, in more quiet times,

addressed letters to the provinces, retained the great officers in their posts, and, by soothing measures, endeavoured to tranquillize the minds of both chiefs and people. He caused the Bhae Goormukh Singh and Misr Benee Ram* to be imprisoned; they were placed in the custody of the governor of the Jalendra Doab, and have not since been heard of. The citadel was occupied by a strong garrison of Golab Singh's hillmen, and at length Heera began to feel

times, to act a conspicuous part in Sikh politics. He is not merely educated, but has a taste for the sciences, especially astronomy and mechanics. He was Runjeet's master of the ordnance, and exhibited much ingenuity in casting guns, shrapnel-shells, &c. He had always the reputation of integrity and rectitude of purpose, and is said to be the only really respectable man (according to European notions) amongst the Sikh sirdars. He is about forty-three years of age, of middle stature, inclined to corpulency; his features are good, though rather heavy. His manners are mild and pleasing, with none of the rudeness of the old sirdars. He seems to have taken no decided part in the early revolutions at Lahore, quietly recognizing the victor, and if he did not approve of his measures, absenting himself from the durbar.

* A well-informed writer in the *Calcutta Star* pronounced the Misr one of the ablest and honestest men in the Punjab.

his authority, which for some weeks was precarious, becoming more secure.

The whole history of Heera Singh's administration is little more than a narrative of his endeavours to keep the troops in subordination to him. Large sums were from time to time distributed amongst them, but their appetite grew from what it fed on. The officers lost their control over the men, and when expostulated with by the vuzeer, frankly declared their inability to manage them. Attempts were made to remove some of the most refractory from Lahore, and to introduce Hindustanis into the army; but the success of these attempts was limited: the great body of the troops remained in the vicinity of the capital. At the earnest entreaty of his nephew, Golab brought a large body of hill-men from Jummoo, who for a time overawed the Khalsas. Having endeavoured to conciliate the sirdars and to restore discipline amongst the soldiers, whom he threatened with punishment, the raja returned to his principality, having renewed the family compact with Heera Singh, and carrying off, with the connivance of his nephew, large sums of money from the treasury.

It was not long before a coolness appeared between the young minister and Soochet Singh, his uncle. Like all the Dogur family, Soochet was extremely handsome, of a noble and commanding figure, but was far inferior to his brothers in intellect. As a soldier, he was brave and chivalrous, but deficient in the qualities of a leader. Vain, conceited, and proud, he thought himself treated with less consideration by Heera Singh than he was entitled to claim, and had always cherished, on that account, a dislike of him. He was a dissolute man, and having lost the roof of his mouth by the use of violent medicines, he could not articulate, being almost, if not quite, dumb. This infirmity, which debarred him from acting a prominent part in state affairs, preyed upon his spirits and soured his temper. He began to absent himself from the durbar, and at length, all Golab's efforts to reconcile his brother and nephew failing, the former returned to his estates.

The first appearance of disunion in the

Dogur family was fomented by the Mae Chund, mother of Dhuleep Singh, a clever woman, and her brother, Jowahir Singh, an intriguing, dissipated man, destitute of talent or influence. The former complained that her son was secluded by Heera Singh; that she was not regent during his minority, and that the minister had rejected a proposal of marriage made to Dhuleep Singh by the Sirdar of Roopur on behalf of his daughter. Golab Singh in vain strove to pacify the Mae, who threatened to take her son from the gudi. On the 24th November, 1843, Jowahir Singh managed by stratagem to remove the young Maharaja from the harem, and carried him out of the city to the lines of the troops, to whom he represented that Heera Singh had laid a plot for the destruction of the young prince, and implored them to take him under their protection. The officers, doubting the truth of this story, separated the prince from his uncle, and privately communicated the occurrence to Heera, who proceeded to the camp, convinced the soldiers that the charge was false, re-conveyed the young Maharaja to the fort, and threw Jowahir Singh into irons.

This measure of justifiable severity exasperated the Mae, whose cause was espoused by Raja Soochet Singh, between whom and his nephew an open rupture took place. These incipient disorders occasioned apprehensions at the capital; many sirdars quitted the court, and General Ventura and the other European officers left the Sikh service. Large sums of money as well as jewels were removed from Lahore to the hills, and it was remarked that, at the installation of the young Maharaja, which took place on the 2nd February, 1844, the koh-i-noor diamond was not amongst the ornaments which adorned the person of the prince.

In this state of things, two other adopted sons of Runjeet, born in his zenana, named Kashmeera Singh and Peshora Singh, who had distant commands, but were weak young men, excited the suspicions of Heera Singh, and he contrived to have them placed in custody. The troops, however, demanded their liberation, and the minister was obliged to comply. Provoked by persecution, or encouraged by the favour shewn them by the army, they renounced allegiance to Dhuleep Singh, and in February took post with a few adherents at Sealkote, on the left bank of the Chenab. Their confidence was not without grounds, for when the vuzeer ordered some Khalsa regiments to march to Sealkote, their officers flatly refused, declaring that they would not fight against the sons of their old master, and a body of troops sent against the princes from Peshawur joined them.

At this juncture, Raja Soochet Singh, being informed that the army at Lahore was disaffected, and would gladly obey his orders, came down from Ramnuggur, with a small force, towards the capital. Heera, by dint of largesses and promises, prevailed upon the army not to desert him, and on the 27th March moved out with 20,000 men, cavalry, infantry, and artillery, against his uncle, who, with barely 600 followers, had occupied a fakir's dwelling, a few miles from Lahore. Soochet refused all terms, and rushing with characteristic impetuosity and rashness upon the Khalsa troops, fell, with Rae Kesree

Singh, an able and gallant officer, and many others, sword in hand. Heera Singh is said to have shed tears at the fate of his gallant uncle, which in no degree improved his situation.

This event caused the two princes to evacuate Sealkote; but they were now joined by a Sikh sodee, or priest, named Bhae Bheer Singh, who seems to have acquired some influence by his reputed sanctity. Their cause soon received an accession of strength in Uttur Singh, Sindawala, and Lena Singh, Majethia. The former, after the revolution of September, 1843, had fled across the Sutluj, and taken refuge first at Puteala, and then at Thanesur, Sikh states under British protection. Lena Singh, having received some disgust, quitted Lahore in April, 1844, and on pretence of a pilgrimage to Hurdwar, paid a visit to Uttur Singh, who seduced him from the prudent maxims which had hitherto guided his political conduct, and he consented to league with the princes. The junction of these sirdars gave some countenance to a false report that their enterprise was encouraged by the British

Government, which rather prejudiced than served their cause.

The Bhae and the two princes, at the head of about 6,000 men, marched from the upper part of the Bari doab down the right bank of the Beas, till they were joined by the malcontent sirdars, who crossed the Sutluj at Huree-ke-puttun. As soon as intelligence of this movement reached Heera Singh, though alarmed, he lost no time in taking measures to meet the danger. Convening the officers of the army at Lahore, he told them that Uttur Singh was coming to seize the Sikh kingdom, and give it up to the British; adding, that he was only a servant of the Khalsaji, and was ready to obey its orders; "but," he artfully added, "if Uttur Singh should succeed, and give up six annas in the rupee to the British, whence would the troops get their present high rate of pay?" He touched a chord which instantly responded; the soldiers declared, with enthusiasm, that they would march against Uttur Singh, and not spare even the guru.

Heera Singh, accordingly, moved from Lahore on the 5th May, at the head of twenty-four regiments of infantry, a large body of irregular cavalry, and 120 guns,—a force with which it was utterly hopeless to contend. On the evening of the 6th he came up with the enemy, who had fallen back to a strong position at the village of Nouringabad, about fifteen miles from the right bank of the Beas. On the morning of the 7th, the Khalsa troops advanced to attack the insurgents, who were drawn up in line. Previous to the engagement, Bheer Singh having waved his chudder, the signal was understood by the opposite party as an ensign of peace; whereupon an officer was sent by Heera Singh across a branch of the Beas, which separated the combatants, and being assured by the Bhae that he was disposed to come to terms, offered the following conditions, namely, that Uttur Singh should be given up; and that the Khalsa army should be allowed to pass the stream unmolested, and occupy the position of the insurgents. Uttur Singh hearing this, drew a pistol and shot the officer through the head. This was the signal for a fierce and sanguinary conflict. After a heavy cannonade (which was heard at the British station of Ferozepore), the Khalsa troops charged. Bheer Singh, who had been mortally wounded by a cannon ball, was cut to pieces; Uttur Singh, selling his life dearly, was likewise killed, and his head sent to Lahore. Kashmeera Singh also fell, refusing to surrender; Lena Singh fled, and crossing the Sutluj, ultimately found his way to Benares, where he still resides. Peshora Singh, who seems to have had some misgivings, deserted his own cause at the commencement of the battle. The wreck of the insurgent army, which had suffered severely in the cannonade, fled across the Beas, and many, including 200 women, wives of a Sikh corps which had deserted to the princes at Sealkote, were drowned in the river.

The Khalsa troops, in the excitement of victory, exasperated at the report that the British authorities had fomented this insurrection, determined to cross the Sutluj, and attack Ferozepore. The political agent at that place was informed, on the 9th May, that 20,000 Sikhs, with sixty guns, were on their march to the river, and that boats had been collected to convey them across during the night, at a ghat about ten miles north of Ferozepore. All the British troops at the station were accordingly collected to repel the aggression; but it appeared that Heera Singh, having been informed by his vakeel that the British authorities were wholly unconcerned in the expedition of Uttur Singh, had recalled the army to Lahore.

This success, which was celebrated with great rejoicings at that city, confirmed for a time the authority of Heera Singh, who, on the 28th June, was formally installed in the office of chief minister, in the presence of all the military and other authorities, under the title of "Raja Saheb." He took advantage of the anti-English temper of the army to dismiss the Europeans remaining in the Sikh service, on the ground that they made themselves acquainted with all that passed in the Lahore cabinet, and imparted the information to the English. He declared that "there was no faith to be found in Christians," and from this moment the young minister seems to have entertained very unfriendly feelings towards the British. In concert with his dewan, a Hindu, named Jella Pundit, a shrewd, clever man of business, he laboured to reform the army, granting their discharge to all Sikh soldiers who sought it; disbanding such regiments as could be so got rid of, and filling their places with Punjabi Mahomedans, Afghans, and Hindustanis.

But whilst the capital was restored to temporary quiet, the provinces were in a state of utter disorder. Anarchy, systematic plunder, and private assassination, were carried on without let or hindrance, in the absence of all legal restraints.

Meanwhile, symptoms of coolness, if not estrangement, appeared between the Raja Saheb and his powerful uncle, Golab Singh. The death of Soochet, of which Heera was the cause, seems to have sown the first seeds of this enmity, which was diligently fostered by the widow of Soochet Singh, a woman of restless disposition, who is said to have importuned the British authorities, as well as Dost Mahomed Khan of Cabul, for troops to revenge the death of her husband. Golab is represented at this time to have espoused the cause of Peshora Singh, whom he considered to have a preferable claim to that of the infant now upon the throne.

On the 20th September, Sawun Mull, the nazim, or governor, of Multan, for the Maharaja of the Sikhs, was assassinated. For a time Heera Singh bore the odium of this act, it being supposed that he desired the removal of a powerful officer, who designed to seize the sovereignty of that rich province. It appeared, however, that he was shot by a criminal whilst under examination before him. He was a man of great vigour and ability, and the prosperity of the province is mainly attributable to his administration. He was succeeded in the office by his son, Mulraj.

Towards the close of the year 1844, the Dussera having passed over quietly, the army being satisfied with the largesses they from time to time received, a reconciliation took place between Golab and his nephew; Meean Jowahir Singh, the brother of Heera, having visited Jummoo, and Meean Sohun Singh, eldest son of Golab (and adopted heir of Soochet), bringing a friendly message from his father. This adjustment, after both parties had armed for war, may be in part ascribed to the assemblage of a large body of British troops at this time within a few easy marches of the Sutluj.

An interval of about two months was passed in comparative quiet, but it was the repose which precedes a hurricane. On the 21st December another sanguinary revolution annihilated the few vestiges of regular government which remained at Lahore, and transferred the sovereign authority to a mutinous army.

The real causes of this convulsion are still but imperfectly known. It appears, however, that the fall of the Raja Saheb may be attributed to the agency of three parties,—the old Khalsa chiefs, who always entertained a dislike to the Dogur family; the mother and uncle of the young Maharaja, suspicious of designs against him, or actuated by a thirst for power; and the army, which could not obtain from an impoverished treasury the extravagant donations they demanded. Jowahir Singh, backed by his sister and by some of the officers of the army, desired a military command. The Raja Saheb was too wary to clothe so dangerous an enemy with power, but he gave him a jagir, requiring him to reside upon it. Jowahir Singh, however, proceeded to Amritsur, where he caballed against the minister, who summoned him to Lahore, and, upon his tardy arrival, determined, by the advice of Pundit Jella, not only to cut him off, and confine the Mae herself, but to dethrone Dhuleep Singh, and place the infant son of Sher Singh upon the gudi. He was not, however, aware of the full extent of his weakness and his danger. The *punchayets*, or deputies of five from each corps, — for the Sikh army made known its wishes, like Cromwell's, by the medium of agitators,—had formally renounced their allegiance to the Raja Saheb, and pledged themselves to acknowledge no authority but that of the Mae, and such minister as she should appoint. The Mae Chunda, on her part, declared that, unless Heera Singh retired from office, she would withdraw, with her son, from Lahore. On the 19th December, Heera Singh ordered that Jowahir Singh should be placed under restraint in his own house, and prepared to seize him, with a party of hill-men, of whom he had about 2,000 in the fort. This was no sooner known, than the army assembled, and the minister was compelled to abandon the scheme. Next morning, Heera Singh summoned the officers of the army, and told them that he had been placed in his high office by the will of the troops; that his authority was now disputed by the Mae and her party; that he did not covet power, and was ready, if the army desired it, to transfer his authority to any other hands they might deem fitter for its exercise, and to accept an inferior employment, if he could thereby render a service to the state. The officers required time to deliberate and consult with the troops, whom the Mae and her partisans had, in the meantime, secured by telling them that the minister's pecuniary resources were exhausted, and by promising them large rewards for removing a wicked minister, who oppressed the people and meditated the destruction of their sovereign. On the 21st, the troops assembled, when Jowahir Singh, by his own authority, carried the Maharaja from his apartments, placed him upon his state elephant, and proceeding to the parade, accompanied by most of the influential sirdars at Lahore, presented him to the soldiers.

Heera Singh, who had waited in his house the issue of the affair, now made preparations for flight to Jummoo. At dawn on the 22nd, he secretly quitted Lahore, with Jella Pundit, Sohun Singh (brother of Raja Golab), Lab Singh, and a few other adherents, joining about 600 sowars, with some elephants laden with treasure, without the walls, leaving the hill troops to defend his house. As soon as the flight of the minister became known, he was pursued by Jowahir Singh, at the head of a body of troops, who came up with the fugitives at a place called the Jemadar's Baoli (well), about thirteen miles from Lahore. Heera Singh prepared to face his pursuers; but now, for the first time, discovered that his own escort were traitors or cowards, who deserted him. He took shelter, with the small party who adhered to him in this desperate emergency, in a house, which was surrounded by the Khalsa troops, who fired it. The party was compelled to come forth; Heera offered to surrender, but was instantly cut down; Pundit Jella, who had rendered himself very obnoxious, Sohun Singh, Lab Singh, and the minister's secretary, Dewan Chund, shared the same fate. The heads of the principals were brought to Lahore, and after being paraded through the city, were stuck upon the gates.

Jowahir Singh, on his return to Lahore, proceeded to the house of Heera Singh, which, with its treasure, amounting to 50,000*l*., was given up without resistance by the guard, who even entered the service of the state. The measures of the conspirators seem to have been so well taken, that this revolution was attended by little or no bloodshed at the capital, and riot and disorder were in a great measure prevented, by excluding, as much as possible, the troops from the city.

"Thus fell," says a chronicler of these events,* "a personage who, whatever estimate may have been formed of him prior to

* The Asiatic Journal, 3rd Series, vol. iv. p. 551.

his elevation to power, exhibited after it qualities which, in less intractable circumstances, might have secured to him a long tenure of authority. How far his acts may have been the result of his own prudence and judgment, or how far they may have been dictated by stern necessity, could only be determined by time and experience. His fall seems to have been brought about by causes independent of his own merits or demerits, arising from that total disorganization of the state which every one foresaw would follow the death of Runjeet Singh."

The number of suttees consequent upon this revolution was no less than twenty-four; namely, two widows and ten slaves of Heera Singh; two widows and five slaves of Sohun Singh; a widow and two slaves of Lab Singh; the widow of Pundit Jella, and the widow (only fourteen) of Dewan Chund.

CHAPTER XXIV.

A.D. 1845 AND 1846.

THE subversion of the Raja Saheb's power, which, resting upon no solid foundation, had fallen to pieces by a slight touch, was accomplished with far more facility than the erection of a new fabric of government, for which no adequate provision seems to have been made. The avenue to the vuzeerat was open to Jowahir Singh, and the Mae (or Rani) Chunda proposed that her brother should be nominated minister; but the troops rejected the proposal, and, with a strange inconsistency or perversity, caused letters to be written to Lena Sing, Majethia, then at Benares, and to Peshora Singh, residing at Ferozepore, both of whom they had made exiles, inviting the former to accept the post of minister, and the latter that of commander-in-chief of the army. The prince, the least qualified person of the two for the post tendered to him, eagerly embraced the offer, and arrived at Lahore on the 1st January, 1845. He was well received by the troops, and upon his appearance at the durbar, he unbuckled his sword and placed it at the feet of the Maharaja. But this token of submissiveness did not disarm the jealousy of the Rani Chunda and her brother, who had sufficient influence to baulk his ambition, and he was honourably exiled, with a jagir of 4,000*l.* per annum, in the neighbourhood of Sealkote. The prince, it is said, secretly sounded the troops, who at first manifested an inclination to uphold his pretensions; but finding that he had nothing to give them, whilst the Rani was prodigal of jewels and bracelets, they recommended "patience" to the prince, who proceeded to his estate. Lena Singh, with less ambition or more discretion, declined the glittering bait, and, notwithstanding urgent messages, remained in his secure retreat at Benares.

Meanwhile, the evils of a dissolution of authority were not slow to appear. On the 23rd December, a grand durbar was held, at which the sirdars congratulated each other upon the emancipation of the state from the oppressions of the Dogur family, and issued their summons to Golab Singh to appear at Lahore and account for the treasures he had abstracted during the rule of Dhean Singh and Heera Singh. The recal of the European officers was likewise ordered, with a view of commencing military operations against the potent Raja of Jummoo. But these demonstrations were altogether futile in the existing state of the troops, who acted as if they were the real depositaries of the sovereign power, and absolved from all responsibility, abusing, beating, imprisoning, and expelling their officers, and maltreating all who shewed the slightest inclination to contravene their will. In one of their excesses, Jowahir Singh brought the young Maharaja before them, and endeavoured to soothe them, and by reasoning and admonition restore them to subordination; but they paid no mark of respect to the prince, and told the sirdar that he had better retire, adding, that they were determined to have only those whom they pleased to rule and lead them.

Jowahir Singh seems very soon to have fallen into complete disgrace with the army, who threatened to banish him from the city.

All military operations were now undertaken by the sole direction of the army authorities, namely, the punchayets, or regimental committees; and these operations were dictated by a desire for plunder rather than by a regard for state policy, or the safety of the country. Meean Jowahir Singh, the younger brother of Heera Singh, upon the first news of the late revolution, hastened to Jesrowta, the capital of the family possessions in the hills, where their valuables were deposited, a large portion of which he removed to the fortress of his uncle at Jummoo. The army despatched a force under Sham Singh, Atareewala, to get possession of Jesrowta, which was accomplished by the usual treachery, the troops offering to place the Meean in the office of vuzeer, upon condition that he paid down a certain sum, and engaged to raise their pay. Young Jowahir believing this offer to be as sincere as it was characteristic, fell into the snare, and admitted a party of the troops into the fort; but, soon discovering his error, he fled to Jummoo. The army plundered the place, as well as all the villages subject to the Dogur family in the neighbourhood, the zemindars and inhabitants flocking to Jummoo to implore the protection of Golab Singh.

The details of the administration were at this time carried on (subject to the wishes of the army) by the Rani Chunda, Jowahir Singh, and Bhae Ram Singh, the guardian of the Maharaja, a man of character and energy. The Rani was a person of some accomplishments for a Sikh lady, being skilful in the use of her pen, whereby, it is supposed, she was able to arrange and combine the means of Heera Singh's overthrow; but, belonging to no high family (being the daughter of a respectable zemindar), she possessed no family influence. She presided in person in the council, within a *purdah* (curtain), outside of which sat the boy Maharaja. Her brother was a man of no talents, uneducated, and addicted to low dissipation. The Rani's party was strengthened by the recal of the Sindawala chiefs, who had been banished after the revolution of September, 1843, and who returned to Lahore on the 30th January, where they were received with great distinction.

The state of the country was such as might be expected where government was in abeyance, or, what is worse, in the hands of an ignorant, bloodthirsty, rapacious, and insubordinate army. The capital was a scene of turbulence and disorder; the Sikh chiefs, in their feudal castles, ruled as petty sovereigns; the Alpine Punjab, from Rajaoree to Attock, and the Sind-sagur Doab to Mittunkote, were in a ferment. Sheikh Golam Mohi-ud-deen, the governor of Cashmere, a bold, crafty, time-serving Mahomedan, was making arrangements for renouncing his allegiance, having opened a negotiation with some British authorities; and Multan was in the hands of the family of Sawun Mull.

From this period the history of the Punjab is little more than a foul chronicle of the extravagancies of its mutinous army, the follies and crimes of the individuals who, for selfish purposes, sought by vile arts to propitiate its favour, and their gross and shameless debaucheries.

The hope of plunder impelled the military rulers to send a force of about 9,000 men, in February, against Golab Singh, who, removing the greater part of his treasure to an impregnable fortress, intrenched himself at Jummoo, and waited the attack at the head of a considerable force. Upon the arrival of the Khalsa troops near his capital, the raja resorted to craft, in which he was an adept. He negotiated at the same time with Lal Singh, the commander of the Sikh army, and directly with the troops themselves, through the agency of his son, Meean Punnea, who consented to pay down to the soldiers five lakhs, and to transmit, at some future time, fifty lakhs to the treasury. A party of Khalsa troops, accordingly, proceeded to Jummoo, and brought away the money; but, on their return, they were set upon by a detachment of hill-men, who re-took the treasure, and put nearly all the party to the sword. The Khalsa troops, exasperated at this successful act of treachery, but more at the loss of the money, attacked the raja, but were repulsed by him with considerable loss, and shortly after, he fell unexpectedly upon the Khalsa camp, and killed about 2,000, including several sirdars and officers of distinction.

This intelligence caused much alarm at Lahore, and the Rani, finding that Golab Singh's strength had been underrated, was anxious for an accommodation. Her fears were augmented by the news that Golab had succeeded in corrupting the Khalsa troops opposed to him, a great proportion of whom had joined his army, which, numbering 17,000 men, was following, with hasty marches, the few corps that had remained faithful. On the 6th April, Golab arrived with his army on the north bank of the Ravi, where he was joined by some of the discontented troops from Lahore, and a considerable body of men belonging to the widow of Soochet Singh. It was now manifest that this movement of the hill raja had been preconcerted with the leaders of the army and some of the chiefs at Lahore, for Golab Singh, after some decent hesitation, accepted an invitation to enter the city, where he was received with great honour. Jowahir Singh, whose enmity towards the Dogur raja was known, was not admitted to the durbar, when Golab was present, till he had laid aside his arms. Upon that occasion the politic raja offered his first mark of respect to the Rani, laying his head upon the ground before her purdah, and then he made his reverence to the Maharaja. After this, the Rani took Golab's hand and that of her brother, and, joining them, made both swear to renounce their mutual enmity. The vuzeerat was now offered to Golab, which he prudently declined, but accepted the command of the army; a nominal office, the troops acknowledging no authority, and dictating their own orders.

In the month of May, these contentions were suspended by a dreadful visitation of the cholera morbus, which first appeared at Lahore on the 5th, and in the course of the month swept off from 500 to 700 victims each day. On the 26th May, 2,000 matchlocks, and a vast number of golden bracelets, belonging to soldiers who had died of this disease, were brought into the treasury. Before the pestilence began to abate, in

June, not fewer than 22,000 persons had perished. Consternation seized the troops as well as the citizens; all business was at an end; the city was almost deserted; the villages and towns (including Amritsur) were thronged with fugitives, who spread the plague far and wide in the provinces. Frightful as have been the devastations of this mysterious scourge in other places, it has, perhaps, nowhere made greater havoc of human life than in the Punjab.

Before the disease had reached an alarming height, the Rani succeeded, after long and angry discussions with the troops, in obtaining, or rather purchasing, their consent to the nomination of her brother to the vuzeerat for four years, when the minority of the Maharaja would expire; and Jowahir Singh, accordingly, with the concurrence of Golab Singh, on the 14th May, was formally installed in an office which he was destined to hold but for four months.

The cholera had scarcely ceased its ravages before the court and army relapsed into their former extravagances. Authentic details have been furnished by the British agent* of the debauchery which prevailed amongst the rulers of Lahore in the months of June, July, and August, 1845, and they are almost without a parallel.

On the 5th June, the punchayets proceeded in a body to the palace to remonstrate against Jowahir Singh's continuance in the government, reproaching that sirdar to his face with drunkenness and incapacity. They went to the Rani, and insisted upon seeing her, requiring the dismissal of her brother from the vuzeerat and the substitution of Dewan Deena Nath, Bhugut Ram, or Lal Singh, or the three conjointly. The Rani was divided between her family regard for her brother, and her illicit attachment to Lal Singh, her favourite paramour; she at length effected a reconciliation between the two, cementing the tie by a present to each of a handsome slave-girl, sent from the Mundi chief. Soon after this, Jowahir Singh and Lal Singh were seeking to assassinate each other. The vuzeer was often so drunk, having caroused

* Papers laid before Parliament relating to the campaign on the Sutluj, 1846.

all night with his favourites and women, that he could not hold a durbar. The Rani herself, besides her unbridled profligacy with her paramours, indulged in similar excesses, and in August her mental faculties became seriously impaired by these indulgences; she had lost all her vivacity and sunk almost into a state of stupor, from which she could be roused only by the stimulus of strong drink. Men of low origin, horse-jockeys, palace peons, and menial servants, were admitted to the vuzeer's society and confidence. On the 2nd August, when a letter from the Governor-General waited for an answer, none could be sent, Jowahir Singh, the Rani, and even the young Maharaja, being all drunk. The next day, again, there was no durbar, Jowahir Singh and the members of the council being intoxicated; they would attend to no business, but sent for dancing-girls, and Jowahir, emulating the worst examples at ancient Rome, dressed himself as a dancing-girl and danced with them.

Such a state of things at the capital invited insurrection in the provinces; Peshora Singh accordingly raised the standard of revolt, and his progress alarmed the Rani and her dissolute council. Some battalions were prevailed upon to march against the prince, but, instead of resisting, they went over to him. In June, he surprised a party conveying six lakhs of government treasure, which he seized. Troops were sent to Sealkote to compel him to disgorge the booty, but, either through cowardice or treachery, they were defeated with considerable loss. In the same month, the prince got possession, by stratagem, of the fort of Attock, and three battalions of Khalsa troops marched ostensibly to recover the place in August, but they joined the standard of Peshora Singh. A stratagem was now resorted to, which succeeded with this weak prince. By the contrivance of the vuzeer, he was invited to Lahore, with a secret assurance that the leading sirdars were resolved to place him upon the gudi, and that the army was in his interest. The general, Chuttur Singh, Atareewala, after much hesitation, entered into this plot, and it is supposed (but the fact is not yet placed beyond doubt) that the Koonwur Peshora Singh was by his means put to death on his way from Attock to Lahore. When this news reached the army it sealed the fate of the vuzeer.

The discerning eye of Golab Singh seems to have perceived premonitory symptoms of another revolution, and with his characteristic discretion he removed from the scene of danger, alleging a desire to pay a short visit to his estates. This was at the end of August. In the succeeding month, the army proceeded deliberately to make a change in the machinery of the government, and the coolness and regularity of their motions prove how complete was the supremacy they had established.

It appears from the most authentic report* we yet have of this transaction, that, about the middle of September, the army assembled in a camp in the plain of Mujan Meer, on the south-east side of Lahore, establishing strict discipline towards the city and the neighbourhood. The punchayets held nightly meetings, and in the morning issued the orders determined upon, under the designation belonging to the Sikh sect

* From Major Broadfoot's agents. Papers *ut ante.*

before the reign of Runjeet Singh, namely, Khalsaji-ka Punt'h. They sent letters bearing their seal, inscribed merely with the name of the deity, to all local officers, military leaders, and members of the durbar, requiring their obedience or their presence, and in short assumed the executive functions of the government. They issued their commands to the Rani to repair to the camp, with her son, and to deliver up her brother and the murderers of Peshora Singh, if he was really dead, intimating that disobedience would entail upon her their punishment. The Rani endeavoured to negotiate with the troops, but found them inexorable. Jowahir Singh vainly hoped to hold the fort with the new levies and the artillery, commanded by his minions and partisans, but he soon found that these troops were ready to obey the orders of the Khalsa Punt'h. On the 19th September, the Rani and the vuzeer despatched the dewan Deena Nath, the fakir Noor-ud-deen, and Uttur Singh, Kaleewala, to prevail upon the troops to return to their allegiance, suggesting fears of an invasion by the English; and it appears that when the vuzeer first learned the irritation of the army at the news of Peshora Singh's death, he endeavoured to divert their indignation from him by measures calculated to precipitate a collision with the British troops, which, however, was prevented by the more prudent members of the durbar. The troops immediately made those deputies prisoners, or rather hostages, releasing the fakir, whom they sent to warn the Rani that the following day was the last allowed to her for compliance with their commands. They at the same time, by written orders under seal of the Punt'h, required the troops in the fort to take care that no one escaped, and posted guards at each gate of the city for the like purpose. The vuzeer corrupted the troops at the fort, who connived at his evasion in the night of the 20th; but he was stopped by the troops at the gate, and obliged to return in despair.

In the afternoon of the 21st it was announced that four battalions had marched from the camp towards the city, to destroy all persons remaining in the fort, the garrison of which had joined the troops at Mujan

Meer. Immediate compliance with the behest of the army offered now the only chance of safety. Accordingly, the Rani, in a palanquin well protected, followed by the Maharaja on a state elephant, with Jowahir Singh in the same houda, attended by the members of the durbar who had not already gone to Mujan Meer, left the fort, and were met without the walls of the city by the four battalions, which turned back, and escorted the procession in silence to the camp, which they did not reach until it was dark. The Rani, her son, and their immediate attendants, were conducted to their tents by the troops. The mahout (driver) of the Maharaja's elephant was ordered to make the animal kneel, and upon his hesitating, a shot, which wounded him in the side, enforced instant compliance. The young Maharaja was taken from the houda, and carried to his mother's tent by some soldiers. The elephant was then made to rise, with Jowahir Singh in the houda, at whom a volley was immediately fired, the effects of which he seems to have escaped. He attempted to parley, pleading for his life, which he had hoped to purchase by the money and bracelets he had brought; but the soldiers knew that the booty was already theirs, and a second volley hurled him to the ground, where he was cut to pieces. Two of his low associates, Bhyar Chuttur, a door-keeper, and Ruttun Singh, a horse-jockey, with some common sowars, who had been much consulted by the vuzeer on affairs of state, were also put to death. The other members of the durbar of his party were either slain, imprisoned, or fugitives. The Rani and her son were detained in the camp during the night, but were allowed to return to the fort, along with the hostages, in the morning. On passing the spot where her brother's corpse lay hacked and mutilated, she burst into loud lamentations, and was permitted to remove it for cremation. Four wives of Jowahir Singh consented to burn upon the funeral pile of their profligate and brutalized husband, and the barbarous rapacity of the soldiers was exhibited in robbing these wretched victims of their jewels and ornaments. The suttees, whose blessings and curses are deemed alike prophetic, bestowed their benedictions upon the Rani and her party, and their heaviest maledictions upon the Sikh Punt'h, solemnly declaring, before the pile, that, during the present year, the independence of the Sikh nation would cease, the sect be annihilated, the country made desolate, and the wives of the Khalsa troops become widows: a prophecy which made a deep impression upon the superstitious multitude.

After the Dussera (in October), the Rani was declared regent of the state, but all affairs were carried on under the real control of the army punchayets, by whom the precarious and perilous office of the vuzeerat was actually put up to auction. Raja Lal Singh (who, during the late outbreak, had been imprisoned by the troops on the charge of having dishonoured the Rani, "the Mother of all Sikhs," and afterwards released) offered, it is said, fifteen rupees per man; whilst some other competitor tendered eighteen rupees. The troops were most disposed to place the vuzeerat in the hands of Raja Golab Singh, if he would increase their pay and make a liberal donation, and a member of the Jummoo family, named Purthee Singh, who had been deep in the court intrigues, was popular amongst them. Tej Singh, the governor of Peshawur (a nephew of Khooshal Singh), arrived at Lahore, and commenced intrigues on his own account. He was offered the vuzeerat, on the usual terms, which he declined. The Rani, who found the administration burthensome without the aid of some one to share the labour and responsibility, resorted to the expedient (suggested, it is said, by the priests at Amritsur) of deciding the choice in the manner adopted by Runjeet Singh to determine difficult questions, namely, by lot or divination. Five slips of paper were accordingly prepared, two of them blank, and the others bearing the names of Golab Singh, Tej Singh, and Lal Singh. The young Maharaja drew the lot, which fell (by accident or contrivance) upon Lal Singh. But the troops, whose avarice was proof against even superstition, refused to recognize him, and the Rani was unable, out of an exhausted treasury, to bribe them to compliance.

This profligate but able woman seems to

have been roused by the exigency of her circumstances to act with energy and spirit. She laid aside to a great extent her debaucheries, appearing frequently in public, and continued to carry on the government in her own name as regent, consulting alternately Dewan Deena Nath, and Bhae Ram Singh, with her paramour Lal Singh. Her difficulty lay principally with the troops, who, from her inability to feed their rapacity, were on the point of proclaiming the infant son of Sher Singh. In order to turn the thoughts of those turbulent and mercenary men in another direction, the Rani and her party appear to have originated the proposal of a campaign across the Sutluj, which promised them a rich harvest of plunder. The grounds alleged by the Lahore durbar for this sudden determination were four: first, our military preparations; secondly, our non-compliance with a demand for the restitution of certain moneys (amounting to about eighteen lakhs), said to have been deposited by the late Soochet Singh in the treasury at Forozepore; thirdly, the non-restitution, by the Raja of Nabba, of the village of Mowran, which had escheated to him, the escheat having been confirmed by us; and lastly, the refusal of a claim for the free passage of the Sikh troops into the Khalsa possessions on the British side of the Sutluj.

The events of this brief compaign will form the subject of the next and concluding chapter.

CHAPTER XXV.

CAMPAIGN OF THE SUTLUJ.

THE views and intentions of the general Government of British India, during the whole progress of the transactions before recorded, were of the most forbearing and pacific character. So early as the month of June, 1845, Sir Henry Hardinge declared* that no efforts should be spared to maintain a Sikh government in the Punjab as long as possible, and that, "as a means of averting risk and of carrying our policy more securely into effect," he proposed in October to proceed to the Upper Provinces. In September, and again in the early part of October,† the Governor-General repeated his determination to "maintain a pacific course of policy." The forbearance of our

* Minute, 16th June, 1845.

† Letters to Secret Committee, 6th September and 1st October.

Government, in spite of many provocations, was carried to an unusual extent, and advice and warnings were repeatedly conveyed to the Lahore Government, in the plainest language, even at the risk of giving offence. Precautions were indeed taken, in such a manner as could not justly give umbrage to that government, to provide against the possibility of our being taken unprepared by its army, which had cast off all subordination to legitimate authority; but the Governor-General, down to the beginning of December, continued to be of opinion (with the Commander-in-Chief and the political agent) that the Sikh army would not cross the Sutluj.

Meanwhile, the momentous question of peace or war seems to have engrossed for some time the deliberations of the punchayets, who at length, on the night of the 17th November, called upon their leaders, Tej Singh and Lal Singh, to advance to the Sutluj, pledging themselves to be faithful and obey their orders. This resolution was approved by the durbar. Money was drawn from the sacred depositories at Govind Ghur, and after a solemn meeting of the deputations and the commanders at Runjeet Singh's tomb, the Sikh army, consisting of 60,000 men and 200 cannon, were put in motion towards the British frontier.

Much reliance seems to have been placed upon the efforts made by emissaries to corrupt our sepoys. Sir Henry Hardinge says,* "I have every reason to believe that endeavours have been systematically made, on a very extensive scale, to tamper with our native army; promises of promotion and reward have been liberally made, and their religious prejudices forcibly appealed to." This was the foundation of a vaunt uttered by Lal Singh, that he would bring over the whole army of the English to the Sikhs, and take Ferozepore without fighting. There was also ground for believing that active intrigues had for some time past been employed to induce the chiefs of our protected Sikh territories to rise in arms against the British power as soon as a Sikh army should cross the Sutluj.

The Sikh troops moved on the 24th No-

* Letter to Secret Committee, 2nd December, 1845.

vember, in several divisions; on the 28th, one division had reached Behrana, the others marching in parallel routes; and on the 8th December the whole force had assembled on the banks of the Sutluj (fifty-three miles from Lahore), extending from opposite to Ferozepore, in masses, as far as Huree-ke-ghat. Upon the 11th, 12th, and 13th, the Sikh troops, parties of whom had previously crossed the Sutluj, and carried off some camels, passed the river in large bodies, with guns, on a bridge of boats, about ten miles above Ferozepore.

The Governor-General, in conformity with his determination, set off for the Upper Provinces in October, and in consequence of the reports he received from his agent (Major Broadfoot), he left Delhi on the 19th November, and arrived on the 26th at Kurnaul, where he had an interview with the Commander-in-Chief (Sir Hugh Gough), who, with Major Broadfoot, had come for that purpose from Umbala. Sir Henry reached this place on the 2nd December, and remained there till the 6th, making arrangements for the now inevitable campaign. On his route from Umbala to Ferozepore, he visited Lodiana on the 11th, inspecting the troops, which were required, as at other stations, to hold themselves in readiness to move at the shortest notice. Besides his anxiety to give no possible ground of complaint to the Sikh Government, our frontier was too long to be defended on all points by any force we could move, and our two posts on the frontier, Ferozepore and Lodiana, were strong enough to be maintained until relieved: at the former was a regiment of Europeans, seven regiments of native infantry, two regiments of native cavalry, and twenty-four field guns, exclusive of heavy ordnance, under Major-General Littler; at Lodiana, were one European regiment, five regiments of native infantry, one regiment of native cavalry, and two troops of horse artillery. Even after he was informed that the Sikh army had marched in hostile array towards the Sutluj, Sir Henry declared that he would not consider this as a cause justifying hostilities, unless the frontier was actually violated. "The Lahore Government," he observed, "had as good a right to reinforce their bank of the

Sutluj as we to reinforce our posts on that river." Up to the 8th December, no forward movement was, therefore, made from Umbala or Meerut, though the forces in the rear of the latter place were ordered up. The Sikh commanders consequently possessed great advantages in commencing operations.

When the Governor-General heard, on the 8th December, that preparations were making by the Lahore Government upon a large scale for artillery and munitions of war, he directed the Commander-in-Chief to bring up the force from Umbala, Meerut, and other stations in the rear, and considered it no longer prudent to delay the forward movement of the troops, and the whole of the forces destined to move up to the Sutluj were in full march on the 12th. Upon his visit to Lodiana, Sir Henry had inspected the fort and cantonments, and it appeared to him most advisable that the whole of the force at that station (5,000 men and twelve guns) should be marched up with the Umbala force (7,500 men, and thirty-six guns); restricting the defence of Lodiana to the fort, which could be securely garrisoned by the more infirm soldiers, the risk of leaving the town and cantonments to be plundered being less than that of not insuring the strength and sufficiency of the force which might separately be brought into action with the whole of the Sikh army. The joint forces, under Brigadier Wheeler, by a rapid march upon Busseean, where the roads leading from Umbala and Kurnaul meet, formed the advanced column of the army, and secured the supplies at that place.

On the 13th December, the Governor-General received information that the enemy had crossed the Sutluj, when he issued a Proclamation* declaring the views and objects of our Government.

This document sets forth that the British Government had ever been on terms of friendship with that of the Punjab, and had faithfully observed the treaty of amity and concord concluded with Maharaja Runjeet Singh in 1809; that since the death of Sher Singh, the disorganized state of the Lahore Government had made it incumbent on that of British India to adopt precautionary mea-

* Appendix, No. I.

sures for the protection of our frontier, which were fully explained to the durbar; that, notwithstanding this condition of the Lahore councils during the last two years, and many most unfriendly proceedings, the British Government had shewn the utmost forbearance, desirous only of seeing a strong government re-established in the Punjab, able to control its army, and protect its subjects; that the Sikh troops had recently marched from Lahore towards the British frontier, by orders of the durbar, to invade the British territory, and no reply was given to repeated demands of the British agent for explanation; that the Sikh army had now, without a shadow of provocation, invaded the British territories, and the Governor-General must, therefore, take measures for protecting the British provinces, and for punishing the violators of treaties and the disturbers of the public peace. The document then declares the possessions of Maharaja Dhuleep Singh on the left, or British, bank of the Sutluj confiscated, and annexed to the British territories.

On the 18th the British forces were concentrated at Moodkee, twenty miles from Ferozepore, with the exception of two European and two native regiments, expected on the following day; the Umbala force having marched 150 miles in six days.

The Sikh corps, which had crossed the Sutluj, after investing Ferozepore on one side, took up an intrenched position at the village of Ferozeshuhur, about ten miles in advance of Ferozepore, and about the same distance from the village of Moodkee. In this camp they had placed 108 pieces of cannon, some of large calibre, with an army exceeding 50,000 men, for the purpose of intercepting the approach of the British force moving up from Umbala to the relief of Ferozepore. On the 18th, the day they had arrived, the British troops, in a state of great exhaustion, were engaged in cooking their meals, when information was received that the Sikh army was in full march to surprise their camp. Sir Hugh Gough pushed forward with the horse artillery and cavalry, directing the infantry and field batteries to follow, and found the enemy in position about two miles off, with from

15,000 to 20,000 infantry, the same number of cavalry, and 40 guns. The country was a dead flat, covered with jungle dotted with sandy hillocks, behind which the enemy screened their infantry and artillery; and whilst our battalions formed into line, opened a very severe cannonade. Our artillery seemed to paralyze theirs, and a flank movement of some of our cavalry turned the left of the Sikhs, and sweeping along the rear of their infantry and guns, silenced the latter for a time, and put their numerous cavalry to flight. The infantry, under Major-Generals Sir H. Smith, Gilbert, and Sir John M'Caskill, then advanced, and attacked in echellon of lines the enemy's infantry, almost invisible amongst the wood and in the approaching darkness. The resistance of the Sikhs was determined; and their line, from superiority of numbers, far outflanked ours; but their whole force was driven from position to position with great slaughter (our infantry using the bayonet), and the loss of seventeen pieces of artillery. Night prevented a pursuit, and the British force bivouacked upon the field for some hours before it returned to its encampment, having no enemy before it. This victory was dearly purchased, Major-General Sir Robert Sale and Major-General Sir John M'Caskill being amongst the killed.

The army halted on the 19th and 20th to refresh the men, and on the 21st, having been joined by the two European regiments and some guns, the Commander-in-Chief, leaving the baggage, wounded, and captured guns at Moodkee, protected by two regiments of native infantry, marched early in the morning against the enemy, who was posted in great force, with a most formidable artillery, four miles on the road to Ferozeshuhur, having been, since the action of the 18th, incessantly employed in intrenching his position. Instead of advancing to the direct attack of these formidable works, our force manœuvred to the right, out of cannon-shot. A communication had been made during the preceding night with Sir John Littler, at Ferozepore, informing him of the intended line of march, and desiring him to move out with such a part of his force as would not endanger their safety or that of the post; and he accordingly left Ferozepore with 5,000 men, two regiments of cavalry, and twenty-one field-guns. The junction of the two forces being effected, Sir Hugh Gough, with the concurrence of the Governor-General, who was present and served as second in command, made arrangements for an attack of the enemy's position. The British force consisted of 16,700 men, and 69 guns, chiefly horse-artillery; the Sikhs, who were commanded in chief by Tej Singh, numbered from 48,000 to 60,000 men, with 108 cannon, of heavy calibre, in fixed batteries.

The enemy's intrenched camp was a parallelogram, about a mile long and half a mile broad, including within its area the strong village of Ferozeshuhur; the shorter sides looking towards the Sutluj and Moodkee, the longer towards Ferozepore and the open country. The attack was directed against the last-named face, the ground in front of which was covered with low jungle. Sir H. Gough conducted the right wing; Sir H. Hardinge the left. The divisions having deployed into line, the artillery in the centre, a heavy cannonade, well directed, was opened by the enemy, which our less numerous and lighter artillery could not silence. In the face of a storm of shot and shells, our infantry advanced, and carried these formidable intrenchments, throwing themselves upon the guns, and wresting them from the enemy. But when the batteries were partially within their grasp, our soldiers had to face such a fire of musketry from the Sikh infantry arrayed behind their guns, that, in spite of heroic efforts, a portion only of the intrenchments could be carried. Night came on whilst the conflict was everywhere raging. Although the division of Sir H. Smith, forming the second line, was brought up, and captured another point of the position, and some of the most formidable batteries were taken by the 3rd light dragoons, yet the enemy remained in possession of a considerable portion of the great quadrangle, whilst our troops, intermingled with the enemy's, kept possession of the remainder, and finally bivouacked upon it, exhausted by their exertions, reduced in numbers, and suffering extremely from thirst.

In this state of things, the night wore away, the enemy continuing to harass our troops by the fire of artillery wherever their position could be discovered. At daylight of the 22nd, our infantry formed line, supported by horse artillery on both flanks, whilst a fire was opened from our centre by such heavy guns as remained effective. A masked battery played with great effect upon this point, dismounting our pieces and blowing up our tumbrils. At this moment, the two commanders (Sir H. Gough and Sir H. Hardinge) placed themselves at the head of their respective wings; the line advanced, unchecked by the enemy's fire; drove the Sikhs rapidly out of the village of Ferozeshuhur and their encampment; then, changing front to its left on its centre, continued to sweep the camp, bearing down all opposition, and dislodged the enemy from his whole position. The line then halted, as on a day of manœuvre, being masters of the field, of seventy-three pieces of cannon, and the standards of the Khalsa army.

The toils and glories of the victors were, however, not yet over. In the course of two hours, Tej Singh (who had commanded in this great battle) brought up from the vicinity of Ferozepore fresh battalions and a large field of artillery, supported by 30,000 Ghorepurras, hitherto encamped near the river, with which he made three several attempts to retake the position, which were repelled by our exhausted troops, our artillery, the ammunition having been expended, being unable to fire a single shot. The Sikhs suffered greatly, their camp being the scene of a most terrible carnage. Our loss was very severe, Brigadier Wallace (who succeeded Major-General McCaskill), and Major Broadfoot, the political agent, being amongst the killed. The captured camp was found to be protected by charged mines, by the successive springing of which many officers and men were destroyed. Sir H. Hardinge's general staff were all disabled, with the single exception of his son, Captain Hardinge.

The result of the battle of Ferozeshuhur, which is considered to be the severest ever fought in India, and one of the most honourable to the British arms in that country, was, that the Sikhs, disheartened by the loss of nearly all their artillery, retired in confusion upon the fords of the Sutluj.

Tej Singh, the commander of the Sikh forces, came to the British camp and had an interview with the Governor-General, who refused to enter into any negotiations until the British troops should be under the walls of Lahore.

On the 31st December, the Governor-General issued a Proclamation,* which, after stating that the Lahore government had, without provocation, or any declaration of hostilities, and notwithstanding a treaty of amity and alliance, invaded the British territory by a large Sikh army, which had been driven across the Sutluj with the loss of ninety pieces of artillery, it had become necessary for the British Government to take measures for punishing this aggression and for preventing similar acts of treachery. It called upon all natives of Hindustan, who had taken service under the Lahore government, to place themselves under the orders of the British Government, on pain of for-

* Appendix, No. II.

feiting all claim to British protection, and being treated as traitors to their country and enemies of the British Government.

The enemy made a further effort upon the Upper Sutluj. Pressed for supplies upon his own bank of the river, he strove to draw them from the jagir estates on the southern bank. At Dhermkote, about forty miles to the westward of Lodiana, where there was a depôt of grain, the Sikhs had a small garrison of mercenaries, and on the 18th January Major-General Sir H. Smith was sent against this place, with a single brigade of his division, and a light field battery. He easily effected its reduction; but whilst he was yet in march, the Commander-in-Chief received information that Runjoor Singh, Majethia (brother of Lena Singh), had crossed the Sutluj at Philor, the route to Lodiana, at the head of a numerous force, and established himself in position at Baran Hara, between the old and new courses of the Sutluj; not only threatening Lodiana, but indicating a determination to intersect the line of our communications at Basseean and Rajkote.

Major-General Smith was upon this directed to advance with his brigade and Brigadier Cureton's cavalry from Dhermkote, by Jugraon, towards Lodiana, and his second brigade under Brigadier Wheeler, moved on to support him. The combinations became now very delicate and important, it being necessary to guard the whole frontier from Roopur down to Mundote. Upon the Major-General advancing from Jugraon, Runjoor Singh, relying on the superiority of his force, endeavoured to intercept his progress, by marching in a line parallel to him and opening a furious cannonade. Sir H. Smith continued, however, to advance, and when the Sikh general, bending round one wing of his army, enveloped his flank, extricated himself by retiring with great steadiness and regularity, and effected his communication with Lodiana, but not without severe loss. Sir H. Smith was now strengthened by the force under Brigadier Godby at Lodiana, consisting of three native regiments, whilst reinforcements were gradually coming up, including the 53rd regiment of foot: but, on the other hand, his manœuvres had thrown him out of communication with Brigadier Wheeler, and a portion of his baggage had fallen into the hands of the enemy. The Sikh general had strongly intrenched himself at Budhowal; but threatened on either flank by General Smith and Brigadier Wheeler, he decamped in the night of the 22nd, and moved down towards the ford of Tulwun (being cut off from that of Philor), the British troops occupying his abandoned position at Budhowal. Having been joined by Brigadier Wheeler on the 26th, as well as by the 53rd regiment and the Shekhawuttee brigade, Sir H. Smith prepared to attack the sirdar on his new ground, where he was also strongly intrenched; but Runjoor Singh having been reinforced on the 27th, from the right bank of the river, with 4,000 regular troops (Avitabili's), twelve pieces of artillery, and a large body of cavalry, advanced towards Jugraon, apparently with the view of intercepting our communications by that route. Sir H. Smith marched at daylight on the 28th. Having proceeded about six miles, the enemy was observed in motion, directly opposite the front of the

British army, on a ridge, of which the village of Aliwal was the centre. His left appeared still to occupy its ground in the circular intrenchment he had formed (his flanks resting on the river); his right was brought forward and occupied the ridge. The general directed the necessary movements, which were performed with the celerity and precision of the most correct field-day. Upon the line advancing in order of battle, the enemy opened a fierce cannonade. The British line was halted for a few moments, though under fire, till the brigades on the right were brought up, when a rapid charge was made and the village was carried. The line again advanced, European and native troops contending for the front, and the battle became general. The British cavalry on the right drove the enemy's upon their infantry, and his left flank was forced back, and some guns taken. While these operations were going forward on the right, the British left was pressing the Ayeen troops, called Avitabili's. Being well driven back on his left centre, the enemy endeavoured to hold his right, to cover the passage of the river, and he strongly occupied the village of Bhoondi, but this was carried by the bayonet. Repeated charges were made upon the flying infantry, and upon the bodies that attempted to make a stand, and the destruction was very great. Our troops kept advancing with the most perfect order to the common focus—the passage of the river. The Sikhs, completely hemmed in, were precipitating themselves in disordered masses into the ford and boats, in the utmost confusion and consternation; and the wreck of their army appeared upon the opposite high bank of the river, flying in every direction. Every gun the enemy had (fifty-seven in number) fell into the hands of the victors, or was spiked or sunk in the river; all his baggage, ammunition, and stores were abandoned. The Sikhs fought with much resolution, maintaining frequent rencontres with our cavalry hand to hand. In one charge of infantry upon the 16th Lancers, they threw away their muskets, and came on with their swords and targets against the lance. Our loss, though comparatively small, was severe.

The immediate result of the victory of Aliwal was the evacuation by the Sikh garrisons of all the forts hitherto occupied on the British side of the Sutluj, and the submission of the whole of the territory on the left bank of that river to the British Government.

Though defeated on the Upper Sutluj, and disheartened by the spectacle of the numerous corpses that floated from thence to the bridge of boats at Sobraon, the enemy continued to hold his position on the right bank, and the formidable *tête de pont* and intrenchments on the left bank of the river, in front of the main body of our army. These works had been repeatedly reconnoitred, and observation, with the reports of spies, led to the conclusion that they held not fewer than 30,000 of the best Khalsa troops, with seventy pieces of cannon, united by a good bridge to a reserve on the opposite bank, where the enemy had a considerable camp and some artillery, commanding and flanking his field-works on the British side.

The Commander-in-Chief was not in a state to attack this intrenched position until the troops under Major-General Sir H.

Smith should have rejoined his camp, and the siege-train and ammunition should have arrived from Delhi. The first portion of the siege-train reached the camp on the 7th and 8th February; and on the latter day, the brigades which had been detached from the main army, for the operations in the neighbourhood of Lodiana, rejoined it. On the 10th, the Commander-in-Chief resolved (with the approbation of the Governor-General) to undertake the arduous task of attacking these strong works. The British troops took possession, without opposition, of two forts, at Kodeewala and the Little Sobraon. The battering and field artillery was then put in position in an extended semicircle, embracing within its fire the works of the Sikhs. On the margin of the Sutluj, on the British left, two brigades of Major-General Dick's division, under his command, stood ready to commence the assault against the enemy's extreme right. In reserve was another brigade, to move forward from the intrenched village of Kodeewala. In the centre, Major-General Gilbert's division was deployed for support or attack, its right resting on and in the village of the Little Sobraon. Major-General Sir H. Smith's division was formed near the village of Guttah, with its right towards the Sutluj. Brigadier Cureton's cavalry threatened the ford at Huree, and the enemy's horse under Raja Lal Singh, on the opposite bank. The rest of the cavalry, under Major-General Sir J. Thackwell, was held in reserve.

Our batteries opened shortly after day-break, but, though spirited and well directed, their fire could not silence that of seventy pieces behind well-constructed batteries of earth, plank, and fascines, or dislodge troops covered by redoubts or epaulments, or within a triple line of trenches. At nine o'clock, Brigadier Stacey's brigade (belonging to General Dick's division), supported by artillery, moved to the attack; but so hot was the fire, that it seemed for some moments impossible that the intrenchments could be won under it. Perseverance, however, triumphed, and the army had the satisfaction of seeing Brigadier Stacey's troops driving the Sikhs in confusion before them within the area of their encampment. As it was soon found that the weight of the whole force within the Sikh camp was likely to be thrown upon the two brigades that had passed its trenches, it became necessary to convert into close attacks the demonstrations of the centre and right, and the battle raged with inconceivable fury from right to left. The Sikhs, even when, at particular points, their intrenchments were mastered with the bayonet, strove to regain them by the fiercest conflict, sword in hand; nor was it until the cavalry of the left had moved forward and ridden through the openings of the intrenchments made by our sappers, in single file, and reformed as they passed them, and the 3rd Dragoons had on this day, as at Ferozeshuhur, galloped over and cut down the defenders of batteries and field-works, and until the full weight of three divisions of infantry, with every field artillery gun which could be sent to their aid, had been cast into the scale, that victory finally declared for the British. The fire of the Sikhs first slackened and then nearly ceased, and the victors then, pressing them on every side, precipitated them in masses over the bridge, and into the Sutluj, which a sudden rise of seven inches had rendered hardly fordable. In their efforts to reach the right bank, through the deepened water, they suffered from our horse artillery a terrible carnage. Hundreds fell under this cannonade; hundreds upon hundreds were drowned in attempting the perilous passage. "Their awful slaughter, confusion, and dismay," observes Sir H. Gough, "were such as would have excited compassion in the hearts of their generous conquerors, if the Khalsa troops had not, in the early part of the action, sullied their gallantry by slaughtering and barbarously mangling every wounded soldier whom, in the vicissitudes of attack, the fortune of war left at their mercy."

The victory of Sobraon placed in the hands of the British 67 more pieces of cannon, upwards of 200 camel-swivels, numerous standards and munitions of war. Our loss was severe, including Major-General Dick, who was mortally wounded. The loss of the Sikhs was immense, not fewer than 8,000 being killed, wounded, or drowned.

Amongst the slain were Sham Singh, Atareewala, and five or six other sirdars; and amongst the wounded, Tej Singh, who commanded in chief.

The British army now prepared to pass the Sutluj. During the night of the 10th, on which the victory was achieved, the advanced brigades of the British army were thrown across the river. Early on the 12th the bridge was completed, and on the 13th the whole force (excepting the heavy train and the division left to bring in the wounded and the captured guns) was encamped in the Punjab, at Kasoor (sixteen miles from the bank of the river, and thirty-two miles from Lahore), where the Governor-General joined the camp of the Commander-in-Chief on the morning of the 14th. On the same day, he issued a Proclamation,* declaring that the occupation of the Punjab by the British forces would not be relinquished until ample atonement should have been made for the infraction of the treaty, and the unprovoked invasion of the British provinces, including full indemnity for all expenses incurred dur-

* Appendix, No. III.

ing the war, and such arrangements for the future government of the Lahore territories as would give perfect security against similar acts of perfidy and aggression; that no extension of territory was desired by the Government of India, though the measures necessary for providing indemnity and security would involve the retention by it of a portion of the Lahore territories, the extent of which would be determined by the conduct of the durbar, and by considerations for the protection of the British frontier; that the Government of India would, under any circumstances, annex to the British provinces the districts, hill and plain, situated between the Sutluj and Beas, the revenues being appropriated as a part of the indemnity required from the Lahore state; that although the conduct of the durbar had been such as to justify the most severe and extreme measures of retribution, the Governor-General, nevertheless, was still willing that an opportunity should be afforded to the durbar and the chiefs to submit to the British Government, and by a return to good faith and the observance of prudent counsels, enable the

Governor-General to organize a Sikh rule in the person of a descendant of its founder, the late Runjeet Singh, the faithful ally of the British power. TheProclamation, therefore, called upon the Sikh chiefs to act in concert with the Governor-General for carrying into effect such arrangements as would maintain a Sikh government at Lahore, capable of controlling its army and protecting its subjects, and based upon principles that would provide for the future tranquillity of the Sikh states, secure the British frontier against aggression, and prove to the whole world the moderation and justice of the paramount power of India. The document concludes with declaring that, if this opportunity of rescuing the Sikh nation from military anarchy and misrule were neglected, and hostilities renewed, the Indian Government would make such other arrangements for the future government of the Punjab as the interests and security of the British power might render just and expedient.

When the news of the victory at Sobraon reached Lahore, the Rani and durbar urged Raja Golab Singh to proceed immediately to the British camp, to beg pardon in the name of the Sikh Government, and endeavour to negotiate some arrangement. Before he undertook this mission, the raja stipulated that the durbar, the chief officers, and the punchayets of the army should sign a solemn declaration that they would abide by such terms as he might obtain from the British Government. This was immediately acceded to, and on the 15th Raja Golab Singh, Dewan Deena Nath, and Fakir Noor-ud-deen arrived in the Governor-General's camp* at Kasoor, with full credentials, empowered to agree, in the name of the Maharaja and the government, to such terms as the Governor-General might dictate. Sir H. Hardinge received the raja (who was accompanied by the Barukzye chief, Sooltan Mahomed Khan, and several of the most influential sirdars) in durbar, as the representative of an offending government, omitting the forms observed on the occasion of friendly meet-

* By some accident, the raja did not arrive till four hours after the time he had fixed by a previous message; a circumstance which increased the coldness of his reception.

ings, and refusing the proffered nuzzurs and complimentary offerings. He briefly explained to the raja and his colleagues the serious nature of the offence and the unwarrantable conduct of the chiefs and army; observing that he recognized the wisdom, prudence, and good feeling evinced by the raja, in having kept himself separate from the unjustifiable hostilities of the Sikhs, and was prepared to mark his sense of that conduct, and he referred the chiefs to Mr. Currie, the chief secretary to Government, and Major Lawrence, the agent to the Governor-General, that they might learn from them the principles and details of adjustment which he had determined to offer for their immediate acceptance.

The chiefs remained the greater part of the night in conference with Mr. Currie and Major Lawrence, and, before they separated, a paper was signed by them, conceding all the demands. These were, the surrender, in full sovereignty, of the territory, hill and plain, lying between the Sutluj and Beas rivers; the payment of one crore and a half of rupees, as indemnity for the expenses of the war; the disbandment of the present Sikh army, and its re-organization under the system and regulations with regard to pay which existed in the time of Runjeet Singh; the arrangement for limiting the extent of the force which might be henceforth employed to be determined on in communication with the British Government; the surrender of all the guns that had been pointed against us; the entire regulation and control of both banks of the river Sutluj, to be ceded to us, and such other arrangements for settling the future boundaries of the Sikh state, and the organization of its administration, as might be determined on at Lahore. It was further arranged that the Maharaja, with Bhae Ram Singh, and the other chiefs remaining at Lahore, should forthwith repair to the camp of the Governor-General, and place themselves in his hands, and that they should accompany his camp to Lahore.

It was determined that the Maharaja should meet the Governor-General at Lulleana (eleven miles in advance of Kasoor, and nearly mid-way between the Sutluj and Lahore) on the 18th; but before the arrival of the camp at Lulleana, the Governor-General learned that the Maharaja, with Bhae Ram Singh and other chiefs, had hastened from Lahore, and that his highness was ready at once to wait upon him. Sir Henry considered it right to abide by the first arrangement, and declared he would receive his highness, on the day appointed, at Lulleana. Accordingly, on the afternoon of the 18th February, the Maharaja, attended by Raja Golab Singh, Dewan Deena Nath, Fakir Noor-ud-deen, Bhae Ram Singh, and ten or twelve other chiefs, had an interview with the Governor-General in his durbar-tent, the Commander-in-Chief and staff being present. The usual salute to the Maharaja was omitted, and the other customary ceremonies on his arrival at the tent were curtailed, Sir Henry causing it to be explained that, until submission had been distinctly tendered by the Maharaja in person, he could not be recognized and received as a friendly prince. Submission was accordingly tendered by the minister and chiefs who accompanied the Maharaja, and the pardon and clemency of the

British Government were requested, on such conditions as Sir Henry should dictate, in the most explicit terms. Sir Henry stated that the conditions having been distinctly made known to the minister, Raja Golab Singh, and the chiefs accredited with him, it was unnecessary to discuss them in that place, and in the presence of the young Maharaja, who was of too tender an age to take part in such matters, and that, as all the requirements of the British Government had been acquiesced in, and their fulfilment promised in the name of the Maharaja and durbar, he should consider himself justified in treating the young Maharaja from that moment as a prince restored to the friendship of the British Government, which extended its clemency to a prince, the descendant of one who had for so many years been the faithful ally and friend of the British Government, as the representative of the Sikh nation, selected by the chiefs and the people to be their ruler, on the condition that all the terms imposed by the British Government, and previously explained to his highness's ministers and chiefs, should be faithfully executed.

After some remarks regarding the character of the late Maharaja Runjeet Singh, and a hope expressed that the young prince would follow the footsteps of his father, and that such relations should henceforward exist between the two states as would tend to the benefit of both, the Governor-General broke up the durbar. On his taking leave, the customary presents were made to the Maharaja; and, on his retiring from the tent, the usual salute was fired.

In the course of discussion, the minister asked if the young Maharaja should now return to the Rani at Lahore, or remain at the British camp; intimating that it was for Sir Henry to dispose of the young chief as he pleased, and as he might consider best for his highness's interests. Sir Henry replied, that he thought it advisable that his highness's camp should accompany his, and that he should himself conduct him to his capital.

The inhabitants of Lahore and Amritsur being in great alarm at the approach of the British army, apprehending that those cities might be sacked and plundered, the Governor-General issued a Proclamation* to the chiefs, merchants, traders, ryuts, and other inhabitants, informing them of the result of the interview with the Maharaja, and assuring them of protection, in person and property, if the durbar acted in good faith, and no further hostile opposition was offered by the army.

Meanwhile, the remains of the Sikh army (from 14,000 to 20,000 horse and foot, with about thirty-five guns), under Tej Singh and Raja Lal Singh, on retiring from Sobraon, had encamped at Raeban, about eighteen miles east of Lahore. They had been positively ordered by Raja Golab Singh to remain stationary; and the Mahomedan and Nujeeb battalions, in the interest of the minister, had been placed in the citadel and at the gates of Lahore, with strict orders to permit no armed Sikh soldier to enter the town.

On the morning of the 20th, the British army appeared in sight of Lahore, and about noon pitched its tents on the plain of Mujan Meer, under the walls of the Sikh capital,

* Appendix, No. IV.

without opposition. On the same afternoon, the Maharaja was escorted to his palace in the citadel. The escort consisted of two regiments of European cavalry, two regiments of native cavalry, one regiment of irregular horse, and two troops of horse artillery, all under the command of Brigadier Cureton. The secretary of the government (Mr. Currie) took charge of his highness and suite, accompanied by the political agent (Major Lawrence), the Governor-General's private secretary (Mr. C. Hardinge), and various other functionaries. About three-quarters of a mile from the Maharaja's camp, it was met by Raja Golab Singh and some of the chiefs. On reaching his highness's camp, the troops of the escort drew up, and the Maharaja, with Bhae Ram Singh on the same elephant, came forward from his tent, accompanied by several chiefs; and after the customary compliments, the procession, headed by the Maharaja and Mr. Currie on their elephants, side by side, moved round the walls of the city to the gate of the citadel, when the escort drew up in front of the gateway, and Mr. Currie, attended by the officers of the escort, and Raja Golab Singh and the other chiefs, took the Maharaja into the interior of the citadel, and to the inner door of the palace. Mr. Currie then observed to his highness and the chiefs, that, by order of the Governor-General, he had thus brought the Maharaja, conducted by the British army, to his palace, which he had left for the purpose of tendering submission to the British Government, and for placing himself, his capital, and his country, at the mercy of the Governor-General, and requesting pardon for the insult that had been offered; and that the Governor-General had thus restored him to his palace, as a mark of the favour which he desired to shew to the descendant of the late Maharaja Runjeet Singh. A salute of twenty-one guns was then fired by the horse artillery. The escort then took leave of the Maharaja at the gate of his palace, and returning to the outside of the city, continuing its progress round Lahore, returned to the camp, situated opposite the south-east end of the city face, the citadel being immediately within the city walls at the north-west angle, so that it made the entire circuit of Lahore.*

* Lahore, once an imperial city, rival of Delhi, has fallen from its former magnificence; judging from its ruins, which are scattered over a large extent, Lahore is not one-tenth the size it was. It is surrounded by a strong and handsome brick wall, thirty-five feet high, with circular towers and angular bastions, inclosing some new ground, forming a sweep of about seven miles. The wall throughout the greater part of its extent is fronted by a fausse-braye, and a deep ditch, with a counterscarp of twenty feet. There are twelve gates, each having a double entrance. The fort or citadel is at the N.W. angle of the city. The interior of Lahore presents a strange confusion of majestic buildings, intermixed with ruins, rubbish, and wretched huts. Close to the palace are mounds of dirt, crumbled mud walls, and heaps of stone. The houses are two or three stories high, built of brick, with flat roofs, and generally ornamented with carved wooden balconies: they have a mean appearance, and look gloomy, being inclosed with dead walls. The streets are very narrow, dirty, and, in wet weather, a perfect slough; the main street is only thirteen feet wide and very filthy: they are crowded with people, showily dressed in silks of every colour. Very strong moveable awnings project over the shops and nearly occupy the entire breadth of the narrow crooked roadway. Stuffs hung out to dry, carts with oxen, horsemen, camels, elephants make a motley scene, whilst on the finely-carved balconies the wealthy banyans, with painted faces and red turbans, present

On the morning of the 22nd, Sir Hugh Gough conducted a brigade of British troops into the city, which took formal possession of the Badshahi Musjid,* and the Hazari Bagh,† forming a part of the palace, and

their low obeisances, or some of the dark beauties of the place salute the passer-by with "Salaam, Maharaja!" The population has been variously estimated at from 80,000 to 120,000.

* The Badshahi Musjid (or Mosque), built by Aurungzebe, is a magnificent edifice, massive, simple, and of beautiful proportions. It is constructed of red free-stone, inlaid with white marble, the mosque itself being surmounted by three large marble domes, crowned with gilt spires. The principal gateway leads into a court 580 feet square. The lofty minarets, 150 feet high, at the angles, elegantly proportioned, are described as "complete works of art."—Barr, p. 96.

† The Hazari Bagh, formerly the residence of the Mogul emperors, consists of three large quadrangles; the first, 500 paces long, is surrounded by vaulted buildings, now used as magazines. The western side is occupied by the Badshahi Musjid. This quadrangle leads to the garden court, likewise surrounded by vaulted open halls, with a pavilion of white marble in the centre. A ponderous gate admits to the third quadrangle, or citadel, which is surrounded by numerous buildings, among which is the winter-palace of the Maharaja, on its northern side, with a winding staircase rising above the highest platform.—Von Orlich, vol. i. p. 213.

the gateway of the citadel of Lahore. The remaining part of the citadel was the residence of the Maharaja and of the families of the late Runjeet Singh: no troops were, therefore, posted within the precincts of the palace gate.

On the 8th March, a conference was held between Mr. Currie and Major Lawrence, on the one part, and Bhae Ram Singh, Raja Lal Singh, Sirdar Tej Singh, Dewan Deena Nath, and Fakir Noor-ud-deen, on the other, at the tent of the Governor-General's agent, for the purpose of signing the treaty. The minister and chiefs produced, on the part of the Maharaja, a letter addressed to Major Lawrence, acknowledging the consideration, kindness, and generosity which had been evinced by the Governor-General towards the Lahore state, and expressing a desire that, as the government was endeavouring to arrange its affairs, and it was necessary that effectual measures should be taken to prevent the recurrence of any disturbances, some British regiments, with artillery and officers, should remain at Lahore for a few months, for the protection of the state. It was observed in reply that, from the wording of the letter, it was not evident that the retention of a British force at Lahore was sincerely and urgently desired by the government, and the nature of the disturbances to be provided against were not specifically described; and as the British Government desired to exercise no interference with the government of Lahore after the treaty of peace was concluded, if for any special reason its assistance and intervention were desired by the durbar, the fact and causes should have been more distinctly stated. A formal *khureeta*, or official communication,* bearing the seal of the Maharaja, was thereupon sent to the Governor-General, urging the request in more distinct and explicit terms, and the Governor-General determined that a British force should, under certain conditions, to be entered in a separate engagement, occupy Lahore for a limited time. The treaty was then signed by the commissioners, and the meeting broke up.

On the following afternoon, the treaty was ratified by the Governor-General, in his

* Appendix, No. V.

state-tent, in the presence of the Maharaja and the Sikh chiefs, and of the Commander-in-Chief and staff, the Governor of Scinde (Sir Charles Napier) and staff, the generals of division, the brigadiers, the head of each department, and all officers commanding corps, with one native officer from every British regiment.

The young Maharaja, attended by the minister, Lal Singh, Raja Golab Singh, Sirdar Tej Singh, and about thirty other sirdars and civil officers being present, the treaty of peace was ratified and exchanged, and the Governor-General then addressed the chiefs, his address being translated, sentence by sentence, by Mr. Currie. In this address, Sir Henry repeated his desire that peace and friendship might always subsist between the two governments, and that a Sikh government might be re-established, that could control its army, protect its subjects, and respect the rights of its neighbours. He recommended the policy of Runjeet Singh towards the British Government as the model for their future imitation ; and enforced " wisdom in council, and good faith in fulfilling engagements." He declared, that the British Government had no objects of aggrandizement by hostilities, and did not desire to interfere in their internal affairs; that he had reluctantly consented, at the earnest solicitation of the durbar, to leave a British force in garrison at Lahore, until the Sikh army was reorganized according to the treaty, but in no case should it remain longer than the end of this year. If, he observed, the friendly assistance now afforded by the British Government were wisely followed up by honest exertions, the state might prosper, and his co-operation should not be wanting; but if they neglected this opportunity, no aid on the part of the British Government could save the state.

At the close of this address, the sirdars expressed in warm terms their gratitude to the Governor-General, and their resolution to follow the advice his Excellency had given them.

By this treaty,* the Maharaja renounces all claim to, or connection with, the territories to the south of the Sutluj, and cedes to

* Appendix, No. VI.

the East-India Company the whole doab between the Beas and Sutluj. His Highness being unable to pay, or give security for the eventual payment of, a crore and a half of rupees (about £1,500,000), as indemnification of the expenses of the war, he cedes to the Company, as an equivalent for one crore, his possessions in the hill countries between the Beas and the Indus, including the provinces of Cashmere and Hazara, engaging to pay the remaining fifty lacs on or before the ratification of the treaty. He engages to disband the mutinous troops, and to reorganize the regular or Ayeen regiments of infantry, upon the system, and according to the regulations as to pay, observed in the time of Runjeet Singh. The regular army of Lahore is not to exceed 20,000 infantry and 12,000 cavalry, and the guns, thirty-six in number, which had been pointed against the British troops on the right bank of the Sutluj, are to be surrendered. The control of the rivers Beas and Sutluj, with the Ghara and Punjnud, to the confluence with the Indus at Mittunkote, and from

Mittunkote to the borders of Baloochistan, is, with respect to tolls, to rest with the British Government. Free passage is allowed to the British troops through the Lahore territories, and no European or American is to be employed by the Lahore government without the sanction of the British. In consideration of his services, Raja Golab Singh is to be recognized as an independent sovereign in the territories which the British may make over to him. All changes in the frontiers of the Lahore state are prohibited, and all its disputes are to be referred to the British Government, which is not to interfere in its internal administration.

On the 10th March, the Governor-General paid a state visit to the Maharaja in his palace, when Dewan Deena Nath, by direction of the minister and assembled chiefs, read an address expressing the gratitude they felt for the generosity, kindness, and mercy of the Governor-General, in maintaining the government, for his excellent advice given to the sirdars the day before, and for leaving a garrison of British troops in Lahore, in compliance with their solicitations.

The following day, articles of agreement* were concluded between the British Government and the Lahore durbar, with reference to the retention of the British garrison at Lahore; and on the 16th March, a treaty† was concluded at Amritsur, between the British Government and "Maharaja" Golab Singh, by which the former made over to him all the hilly country situated to the eastward of the Indus and westward of the Ravi, including Chumba, and excluding Lahoul, being part of the territory ceded by the Lahore state to the British Government; Maharaja Golab Singh stipulating to pay to the British Government seventy-five lakhs of rupees, and to acknowledge its supremacy, in token of which he engages to present annually to it one horse, twelve shawl goats, and three pairs of Cashmere shawls.

The kingdom of the Punjab has, therefore, ceased to exist, and has now become the state of Lahore.

Thus terminated a contest which, in its origin, incidents, and consequences, has few parallels in the military annals of any nation.

* Appendix, No. VII. † Ibid. No. VIII.

Sudden and unprovoked, it was brought to a rapid and glorious close by one short and brilliant campaign, in which the enemy, possessing all the advantages of opportunity, numbers, and discipline, directed by skill and backed by desperate resolution, was overwhelmed, and a powerful kingdom was laid prostrate at the feet of its conquerors, whose forbearance, when all was in their power, suffered them to exact "nothing more from the vanquished than was necessary for the maintenance of peace and security against violence and rapine."*

* Form of Prayer and Thanksgiving for the Victories in India, for Sunday, 12th April, 1846.

APPENDIX.

No. I.

Proclamation by the Right Hon. the Governor-General of India.

The British Government has ever been on terms of friendship with that of the Punjab.

In the year 1809 a treaty of amity and concord was concluded between the British Government and the late Maharaja Runjeet Singh, the conditions of which have always been faithfully observed by the British Government, and were scrupulously fulfilled by the late Maharaja.

The same friendly relations have been maintained with the successors of Maharaja Runjeet Singh by the British Government up to the present time.

Since the death of the late Maharaja Sher Singh, the disorganized state of the Lahore government has made it incumbent on the Governor-General in Council to adopt precautionary measures for the protection of the British frontier; the nature of these measures, and the cause of their adoption, were at the time fully explained to the Lahore durbar.

Notwithstanding the disorganized state of the Lahore government during the last two years, and many most unfriendly proceedings on the part of the durbar, the Governor-General in Council has continued to evince his desire to maintain the relations of amity and concord which had so long existed between the two states, for the mutual interests and happiness of both. He has shewn on every occasion the utmost forbearance, from consideration to the helpless state of the infant Maharaja Dhuleep Singh, whom the British Government had recognized as the successor to the late Maharaja Sher Singh.

The Governor-General in Council sincerely desired to see a strong Sikh government re-established in the Punjab, able to control its army and to protect its subjects. He had not, up to the present moment, abandoned the hope of seeing that important object effected by the patriotic efforts of the Sikhs and people of that country.

The Sikh army recently marched from Lahore towards the British frontier, as it was alleged, by the orders of the durbar, for the purpose of invading the British territory.

The Governor-General's agent, by direction of the Governor-General, demanded an explanation of this movement, and no reply being returned within a reasonable time, the demand was repeated. The Governor-General, unwilling to believe in the hostile intentions of the Sikh government, to which no provocation had been given, refrained from taking any measures which might have a tendency to embarrass the government of the Maharaja, or to induce collision between the two states.

When no reply was given to the repeated demand for explanation, and while active military preparations were continued at Lahore, the Governor-General considered it necessary to order the advance of troops towards the frontier, to reinforce the frontier posts.

The Sikh army has now, without a shadow of provocation, invaded the British territories.

The Governor-General must, therefore, take measures for effectually protecting the British provinces, for vindicating the authority of the British Government, and for punishing the violators of treaties and the disturbers of the public peace.

The Governor-General hereby declares the possessions of Maharaja Dhuleep Singh on the left or British banks of the Sutluj confiscated and annexed to the British territories.

The Governor-General will respect the existing rights of all jaghirdars, zemindars, and tenants in the said possessions, who, by the course they now pursue, evince their fidelity to the British Government.

The Governor-General hereby calls upon all the chiefs and sirdars in the protected territories to co-operate cordially with the British Government for the punishment of the common enemy, and for the maintenance of order in these states. Those of the chiefs who shew alacrity and fidelity in the discharge of this duty which they owe to the protecting power, will find their interests promoted thereby, and those who take a contrary course will be treated as enemies to the British Government, and will be punished accordingly.

The inhabitants of all the territories on the left bank of the Sutluj are hereby directed to abide peaceably in their respective villages, where they will receive efficient protection by the British Government. All parties of men found in armed bands, who can give no satisfactory account of their proceedings, will be treated as disturbers of the public peace.

All subjects of the British Government, and those who possess estates on both sides the river Sutluj, who, by their faithful adherence to the British Government, may be liable to sustain loss, shall be indemnified and secured in all their just rights and privileges.

On the other hand, all subjects of the British Government who shall continue in the service of the Lahore state, and who disobey this proclamation by not immediately returning to their allegiance, will be liable to have their property on this side the Sutluj confiscated, and declared to be aliens and enemies of the British Government.

By order of the Right Hon. the Governor-General of India.

F. CURRIE,
Secretary to the Government of India
with the Governor-General.

Camp, Lushkuree Khan-ke-Serai,
Dec. 13, 1845.

No. II.

Proclamation by the Right Hon. the Governor-General of India.

Foreign Department, Ferozepore,
Dec. 31, 1845.

The Lahore government has, without provocation, or any declaration of hostilities, and notwithstanding the existence of a treaty of amity and alliance, made war upon the British Government. A large Sikh army has invaded the British territories, which has been repulsed and driven across the Sutluj with the loss of ninety-one pieces of their artillery, now in our possession. It becomes necessary, therefore, for the British Government to take measures for punishing this unprovoked aggression, and for preventing in future similar acts of treachery by the government and army of the Punjab. The British Government considers it right now to call upon all natives and inhabitants of Hindostan who have taken service under the Lahore government, to quit that service, and place themselves under the orders of the Governor-General of India. As long as relations of amity existed between the two states, there was no objection to the natives of the one territory taking service with the government of the other; but now that the Lahore state has become the avowed enemy of the Government of Hindostan, it is incumbent on all natives of Hindostan, whose homes and families are under British protection, to quit the service of the common enemy, and join that of the Government of their own country. All persons of the above description are, therefore, hereby called upon to repair to the British side of the Sutluj and to report themselves to the British authorities; their interests will in all cases be respected; they will, if fit for the military service, be taken into that of the British Government, with all the advantages of pay and allowances enjoyed by British soldiers.

All natives of Hindostan who, after the promulgation

of this proclamation, continue in the service of the enemy, will be considered to have forfeited all claim to British protection, and will be treated as traitors to their country and enemies of the British Government.

By order of the Right Hon. the Governor-General of India.

F. CURRIE,
Secretary to the Government of India
with the Governor-General.

No. III.

Proclamation by the Right Hon. the Governor-General of India.

Foreign Department, Kussoor,
Feb. 14, 1846.

The Sikh army has been expelled from the left bank of the river Sutluj, having been defeated in every action, with the loss of more than 220 pieces of field artillery.

The British army has crossed the Sutluj, and entered the Punjab.

The Governor-General announces by this proclamation that this measure has been adopted by the Government of India, in accordance with the intentions expressed in the proclamation of the 13th of December last, as having been forced upon the Governor-General, for the purpose of "effectually protecting the British provinces, for vindicating the authority of the British Government, and for punishing the violators of treaties and the disturbers of the public peace."

These operations will be steadily persevered in and vigorously prosecuted, until the objects proposed to be accomplished are fully attained. The occupation of the Punjab by the British forces will not be relinquished until ample atonement for the insult offered to the British Government by the infraction of the treaty of 1809 A.D., and by the unprovoked invasion of the British provinces, shall have been exacted. These objects will include full indemnity for all expenses incurred during the war, and such arrangements for the future government of the Lahore territories as will give perfect security to the British Government against similar acts of perfidy and aggression.

Military operations against the government and army of the Lahore state have not been undertaken by the Government of India from any desire of territorial aggrandizement. The Governor-General, as already announced in the proclamation of the 13th of December, "sincerely desired to see a strong Sikh government re-established in the Punjab, able to control its army and to protect its subjects." The sincerity of these professions is proved by the fact that no preparations for hostilities had been made when the Lahore government suddenly, and without a pretext of complaint, invaded the British territories. The unprovoked aggression has compelled the British Government to have recourse to arms, and to organize the means of offensive warfare, and whatever may now befal the Lahore state, the consequences can alone be attributed to the misconduct of that government and its army.

No extension of territory was desired by the Government of India; the measures necessary for providing indemnity for the past and security for the future will, however, involve the retention by the British Government of a portion of the country hitherto under the government of the Lahore state. The extent of territory which it may be deemed advisable to hold will be determined by the conduct of the durbar, and by considerations for the security of the British frontier. The Government of India will, under any circumstances, annex to the British provinces the districts, hill and plain, situated between the rivers Sutluj and Beas, the revenues thereof being appropriated as a part of the indemnity required from the Lahore state.

The Government of India has frequently declared that it did not desire to subvert the Sikh government in the Punjab; and although the conduct of the durbar has been such as to justify the most severe and extreme measures of retribution (the infliction of which may yet be required by sound policy, if the recent acts of violence be not amply atoned for, and immediate submission tendered), nevertheless the Governor-General is still willing that an opportunity should be given to the durbar and to the chiefs to submit themselves to the authority of the British Government, and by a return to good faith, and the observance of prudent counsels, enable the Governor-General to organize a Sikh government in the person of a descendant of its founder, the late Maharaja Runjeet Singh, the faithful ally of the British power.

The Governor-General, at this moment of a most complete and decisive victory, cannot give a stronger proof of the forbearance and moderation of the British Government than by making this declaration of his intentions, the terms and mode of the arrangement remaining for further adjustment.

The Governor-General, therefore, calls upon all those chiefs who are well-wishers of the descendants of Runjeet Singh, and especially such chiefs as have not participated in the hostile proceedings against the British power, to act in concert with him for carrying into effect such arrangements as shall maintain a Sikh government at Lahore, capable of controlling its army and protecting its subjects, and based upon principles that shall provide for the future tranquillity of the Sikh states, shall secure the British frontier against a repetition of acts of aggression, and shall prove to the whole world the moderation and justice of the paramount power of India.

If this opportunity of rescuing the Sikh nation from military anarchy and misrule be neglected, and hostile opposition to the British army be renewed, the Government of India will make such other arrangements for the future government of the Punjab as the interests and security of the British power may render just and expedient.

By order, &c.

(Signed) F. Currie,
Secretary to the Government of India
with the Governor-General.

No. IV.

Proclamation by the Governor-General of India.

Camp, Lulleana, Feb. 18.

The chiefs, merchants, traders, ryots, and other inhabitants of Lahore and Amritsur, are hereby informed that his Highness Maharaja Dhuleep Singh has this day waited upon the Right Hon. the Governor-General, and expressed the contrition of himself and the Sikh government for their late hostile proceedings. The Maharaja and durbar having acquiesced in all the terms imposed by the British Government, the Governor-General having every hope that the relations of friendship will speedily be established between the two governments, the inhabitants of Lahore and Amritsur have nothing to fear from the British army.

The Governor-General and the British troops, if the conditions above adverted to are fulfilled, and no further hostile opposition is offered by the Khalsa army, will aid their endeavours for the re-establishment of the government of the descendants of Maharaja Runjeet Singh, and for the protection of its subjects.

The inhabitants of the cities in the Punjab will, in that case, be perfectly safe in person and property from any molestation by the British troops; and they are hereby called upon to dismiss apprehension, and to follow their respective callings with all confidence.

By order of the Right Hon. the Governor-General of India.

F. CURRIE,
Secretary to the Government of India
with the Governor-General.

No. V.

Translation of a formal Khureeta, with the seal of the Maharaja, sent on the 8th March.

"All the circumstances regarding the disorganization of the government of Lahore since the demise of the late Maharaja Runjeet Singh until the present time are well known to the British Government.

"The satisfactory settlement of affairs, the discharge of the disturbers of public peace, and the reorganization of the army under the stipulations of the new treaty, are now engaging consideration. But lest, after the departure of the British forces, the evil-disposed should create fresh disturbances, and endeavour to ruin the state, it is the earnest and sincere desire and hope of the Lahore durbar that British troops with intelligent officers should, for some months, as circumstances may seem to require, be left at Lahore for the protection of the government and the Maharaja and the inhabitants of the city. When affairs have been satisfactorily settled, and the period prescribed for the stay of the British force shall have expired, the troops may then be withdrawn."

True note and translation.

F. CURRIE,
Secretary to the Government of India,
with the Governor-General.

No. VI.

Treaty between the British Government and the State of Lahore.

Whereas the treaty of amity and concord, which was concluded between the British Government and the late Maharaja Runjeet Singh, the ruler of Lahore, in 1809, was broken by the unprovoked aggression on the British provinces of the Sikh army, in December last, and whereas, on that occasion, by the proclamation dated 13th of December, the territories then in the occupation of the Maharaja of Lahore on that, the left or British, bank of the river Sutluj, were confiscated and annexed to the British provinces, and since that time hostile operations have been prosecuted by the two governments, the one against the other, which have resulted in the occupation of Lahore by the British troops; and whereas it has been determined that, upon certain conditions, peace shall be re-established between the two governments, the following treaty of peace between the Hon. English East-India Company and Maharaja Dhuleep Singh Bahadoor and his children, heirs, and successors, has been concluded on the part of the Hon. Company by Frederick Currie, Esq., and Brevet-Major Henry Montgomery Lawrence, by virtue of full powers to that effect, vested in them by the Right Hon. Sir Henry Hardinge, G.C.B., one of her Britannic Majesty's Most Hon. Privy Council, Governor-General, appointed by the Hon. Company to direct and control all their affairs in the East Indies, and ou the part of his Highness the Maharaja Dhuleep Singh by Bhae Ram Singh, Raja Lal Singh, Sirdar Tej Singh, Sirdar Chuttur Singh Atareewala, Sirdar Runjoor Singh Majethia, Dewan Deena Nath, and Fakeer Noor-ud-Deen, vested with full powers and authority on the part of his highness.

Article 1. There shall be perpetual peace and friendship between the British Government on the one part, and Maharaja Dhuleep Singh, his heirs and successors, on the other.

Art. 2. The Maharaja of Lahore renounces for himself, his heirs and successors, all claim to, or connection with, the territories lying to the south of the river Sutluj, and engages never to have any concern with those territories or the inhabitants thereof.

Art. 3. The Maharaja cedes to the Hon. Company, in perpetual sovereignty, all his forts, territories, and rights, in the doab or country, hill and plain, situate between the rivers Beas and Sutluj.

Art. 4. The British Government having demanded from the Lahore state, as indemnification for the expenses of the war, in addition to the cession of territory described in Article 3, payment of one and a half crores of rupees, and the Lahore government being unable to pay the whole of this sum at this time, or to give security satisfactory to the British Government for its eventual payment, the Maharaja cedes to the Hon. Company, in perpetual sovereignty, as equivalent for one crore of rupees, all his forts, territories, rights, and interests, in the hill countries which are situate between the rivers Beas and Indus, including the provinces of Cashmere and Hazara.

Art. 5. The Maharaja will pay to the British Government the sum of fifty lacs of rupees on or before the ratification of this treaty.

Art. 6. The Maharaja engages to disband the mutinous troops of the Lahore army, taking from them their arms; and his highness agrees to reorganize the regular, or Ayeen regiments of infantry, upon the system and according to the regulations as to pay and allowances observed in the time of the late Maharaja Runjeet Singh. The Maharaja further engages to pay up all arrears to the soldiers that are discharged under the provisions of this article.

Art. 7. The regular army of the Lahore state shall henceforth be limited to 25 battalions of infantry, consisting of 800 bayonets each, with 12,000 cavalry: this number at no time to be exceeded without the concurrence of the British Government. Should it be necessary at any time, for any special cause, that this force should be increased, the cause shall be fully explained to the British Government, and when the special necessity shall have passed, the regular troops shall be again reduced to the standard specified in the former clause of this article.

Art. 8. The Maharaja will surrender to the British Government all the guns, thirty-six in number, which have been pointed against the British troops, and which, having been placed on the right bank of the river Sutluj, were not captured at the battle of Sobraon.

Art. 9. The control of the rivers Beas and Sutluj, with the continuation of the latter river, commonly called the Ghara and the Punjnud, to the confluence of the Indus at Mittunkote, and the control of the Indus from Mittunkote to the borders of Baloochistan, shall, in respect to tolls and ferries, rest with the British Government. The provisions of this article shall not interfere with the passage of boats belonging to the Lahore government on the said rivers for the purposes of traffic or the conveyance of passengers up and down their course. Regarding the ferries between the two countries respectively, at the several ghats of the said rivers, it is agreed that the British Government, after defraying all the expenses of management and establishments, shall account to the Lahore government for one-half of the net profits of the ferry collections. The provisions of this article have no reference to the ferries on that part of the river Sutluj which forms the boundary of Bahawulpore and Lahore respectively.

Art. 10. If the British Government should, at any time, desire to pass troops through the territories of his Highness the Maharaja for the protection of the British territories, or those of their allies, the British troops shall, on such special occasion, due notice being given, be allowed to pass through the Lahore territories. In such case the officers of the Lahore state will afford facilities in providing supplies and boats for the passage of the rivers, and the British Government will pay the full price of all such provisions and boats, and will make fair compensation for all private property that may be endamaged. The British Government will moreover observe all due consideration to the religious feelings of the inhabitants of those tracts through which the army may pass.

Art. 11. The Maharaja engages never to take or retain in his service any British subject, nor the subject of any European or American state, without the consent of the British Government.

Art. 12. In consideration of the services rendered by Raja Golab Singh, of Jummoo, to the Lahore state, towards procuring the restoration of the relations of amity between the Lahore and British governments, the Maharaja hereby agrees to recognize the independent sovereignty of Raja Golab Singh in such territories and districts in the hills as may be made over to the said Raja Golab Singh by separate agreement between himself and the British Government, with the dependencies thereof, which may have been in the raja's possession since the time of the late Maharaja Khurruk Singh, and the British Government, in consideration of the good conduct of Raja Golab Singh, also agrees to recognize his independence in such territories, and to admit him to the privileges of a separate treaty with the British Government.

Art. 13. In the event of any dispute or difference arising between the Lahore state and Raja Golab Singh, the same shall be referred to the arbitration of the British Government, and by its decision the Maharaja engages to abide.

Art. 14. The limits of the Lahore territories shall not be, at any time, changed without the concurrence of the British Government.

Art. 15. The British Government will not exercise any interference in the internal administration of the Lahore state, but in all cases or questions which may be referred to the British Government, the Governor-General will give the aid of his advice and good offices for the furtherance of the interests of the Lahore government.

Art. 16. The subjects of either state shall, on visiting the territories of the other, be on the footing of the subjects of the most favoured nation.

This treaty, consisting of sixteen articles, has been this day settled by Frederick Currie, Esq., and Brevet-Major Henry Montgomery Lawrence, acting under the directions of the Right Hon. Sir Henry Hardinge, G.C.B., Governor-General, on the part of the British Government, and by Bhae Ram Singh, Raja Lal Singh, Sirdar Tej Singh, Sirdar Chuttur Singh Atareewala, Runjoor Singh Majethia, Dewan Deena Nath, and Fakeer Noor-ud-Deen, on the part of the Maharaja Dhuleep Singh, and the said treaty has been this day ratified by the seal of the Right Hon. Sir Henry Hardinge, G.C.B.,

Governor-General, and by that of his highness Maharaja Dhuleep Singh.

Done at Lahore, this 9th day of March, in the year of our Lord 1846, corresponding with the 10th day of Rubbee-ul-awul, 1262 Hijree, and ratified on the same date.

MAHARAJA DHULEEP SINGH (L.S.)
BHAE RAM SINGH (L.S.)
RAJA LAL SINGH (L.S.)
SIRDAR TEJ SINGH (L.S.)
SIRDAR CHUTTUR SINGH ATAREEWALA (L.S.)
SIRDAR RUNJOOR SINGH MAJETHIA (L.S.)
DEWAN DEENA NATH (L.S.)
FAKEER NOOR-UD-DEEN (L.S.)
H. HARDINGE (L.S.)
F. CURRIE.
H. M. LAWRENCE.

No. VII.

Articles of Agreement concluded between the British Government and the Lahore Durbar, on the 11*th of March*, 1846.

Whereas the Lahore government has solicited the Governor-General to leave a British force at Lahore, for the protection of the Maharaja's person and of the capital, till the reorganization of the Lahore army, according to the provisions of article 6 of the treaty of Lahore, dated the 9th inst.; and whereas the Governor-General has, on certain conditions, consented to this measure; and whereas it is expedient that certain matters concerning the territories ceded by articles 3 and 4 of the aforesaid treaty should be specifically determined, the following eight articles of agreement have this day been concluded between the aforementioned contracting parties:—

Art. 1. The British Government shall leave at Lahore, till the close of the current year, A.D. 1846, such force as shall seem to the Governor-General adequate for the purpose of protecting the person of the Maharaja and the inhabitants of the city of Lahore, during the reorganization of the Sikh army, in accordance with the provisions of article 6 of the treaty of Lahore. That force to be withdrawn at any convenient time before the expiration of the year, if the object to be fulfilled shall, in the opinion of the durbar, have been attained; but the force shall not be detained at Lahore beyond the expiration of the current year.

Art. 2. The Lahore government agrees that the force left at Lahore, for the purpose specified in the foregoing article, shall be placed in full possession of the fort and the city of Lahore, and that the Lahore troops shall be removed from within the city. The Lahore government engages to furnish convenient quarters for the officers and men of the said force, and to pay to the British Government all the extra-expenses, in regard to the said force, which may be incurred by the British Government, in consequence of their troops being employed away from their own cantonments, and in a foreign territory.

Art. 3. The Lahore government engages to apply itself immediately and earnestly to the reorganization of its army, according to the prescribed condition, and to communicate fully with the British authorities left at Lahore as to the progress of such reorganization, and as to the location of the troops.

Art. 4. If the Lahore government fails in the performance of the conditions of the foregoing article, the British Government shall be at liberty to withdraw the force from Lahore at any time before the expiration of the period specified in article 1.

Art. 5. The British Government agrees to respect the *bonâ fide* rights of those jaghirdars within the territories ceded by articles 3 and 4 of the treaty of Lahore, dated 9th instant, who were attached to the families of the late Maharaja Runjeet Singh, Khurruk

Singh, and Sher Singh, and the British Government will maintain those jaghirdars in their *bonâ fide* possessions during their lives.

Art. 6. The Lahore government shall receive the assistance of the British local authorities in recovering the arrears of revenue justly due to the Lahore government from their kardars and managers in the territories ceded by the provisions of articles 3 and 4 of the treaty of Lahore, to the close of the Khurreef harvest of the current year, viz. 902 of the Sumbut Bikramajeet.

Art. 7. The Lahore government shall be at liberty to remove from the forts in the territories specified in the foregoing article all treasure and state property, with the exception of guns. Should, however, the British Government desire to retain any part of the said property, they shall be at liberty to do so, paying for the same at a fair valuation, and the British officers shall give their assistance to the Lahore government in disposing on the spot of such part of the aforesaid property as the Lahore government may not wish to remove, and the British officers may not desire to retain.

Art. 8. Commissioners shall be immediately appointed by the two governments to settle and lay down the boundary between the two states, as defined by article 4 of the treaty of Lahore, dated March 9, 1846.

MAHARAJA DHULEEP SINGH (L.S.)
BHAE RAM SINGH (L.S.)
RAJA LAL SINGH (L.S.)
SIRDAR TEJ SINGH (L.S.)
SIRDAR CHUTTUR SINGH ATAREEWALA (L.S.)
SIRDAR RUNJOOR SINGH MAJETHIA (L.S.)
DEWAN DEENA NATH (L.S.)
FAKEER NOOR-UD-DEEN (L.S.)
H. HARDINGE (L.S.)
F. CURRIE.
H. M. LAWRENCE.

No. VIII.

Treaty between the British Government and Maharaja Golab Singh, concluded at Amritsur on the 16th of March, 1846.

Treaty between the British Government on the one part, and Maharaja Golab Singh, of Jummoo, on the other, concluded on the part of the British Government by Frederick Currie, Esq., and Brevet-Major Henry Montgomery Lawrence, acting under the orders of the Right Hon. Sir Henry Hardinge, G.C.B., one of her Britannic Majesty's Most Hon. Privy Council, Governor-General, appointed by the Hon. Company to direct and control all their affairs in the East Indies, and by Maharaja Golab Singh in person.

Art. 1. The British Government transfers and makes over, for ever, in independent possession, to Maharaja Golab Singh, and the heirs male of his body, all the hilly or mountainous country, with its dependencies, situate to the eastward of the river Indus, and westward of the river Ravi, including Chumba and excluding Lahoul, being part of the territory ceded to the British Government by the Lahore state, according to the provisions of article 4 of the treaty of Lahore, dated 9th March, 1846.

Art. 2. The eastern boundary of the tract transferred by the foregoing article to Maharaja Golab Singh shall be laid down by commissioners appointed by the British Government and Maharaja Golab Singh respectively for that purpose, and shall be defined in a separate engagement after survey.

Art 3. In consideration of the transfer made to him and his heirs, by the provisions of the foregoing articles, Maharaja Golab Singh will pay to the British Government the sum of 75 lacs of rupees (Nanukshahi), 50 lacs to be paid on ratification of this treaty, and

25 lacs on or before the 1st of October of the current year, 1846.

Art. 4. The limits of the territories of Maharaja Golab Singh shall not be at any time changed without the concurrence of the British Government.

Art. 5. Maharaja Golab Singh will refer to the arbitration of the British Government any disputes or questions that may arise between himself and the government of Lahore, or any other neighbouring state, and will abide by the decision of the British Government.

Art. 6. Maharaja Golab Singh engages for himself and heirs to join with the whole of his military force the British troops when employed within the hills, or in the territories adjoining his possessions.

Art. 7. Maharaja Golab Singh engages never to take or retain in his service any British subject, nor the subject of any European or American state, without the consent of the British Government.

Art. 8. Maharaja Golab Singh engages to respect, in regard to the territory transferred to him, the provisions of articles 5, 6, and 7 of the separate engagement between the British Government and the Lahore durbar, dated March 11, 1846.

Art. 9. The British Government will give its aid to Maharaja Golab Singh in protecting his territories from external enemies.

Art. 10. Maharaja Golab Singh acknowledges the supremacy of the British Government, and will, in token of such supremacy, present annually to the British Government one horse, twelve perfect shawl-goats of approved breed (six male and six female), and three pairs of Cashmere shawls.

This treaty, consisting of ten articles, has been this day settled by Frederick Currie, Esq., and Brevet-Major Henry Montgomery Lawrence, acting under the directions of the Right Hon. Sir Henry Hardinge, G.C.B., Governor-General, on the part of the British Government, and by Maharaja Golab Singh in person, and the said treaty has been this day ratified by the seal of the

Right Hon. Sir Henry Hardinge, G.C.B., Governor-General.

Done at Amritsur, this 16th day of March, in the year of our Lord 1846, corresponding with the 17th day of Rubbee-ul-awul, 1262 Hijree.

GOLAB SINGH (L. S.)
H. HARDINGE (L. S.)
F. CURRIE.
H. M. LAWRENCE.

END OF VOL. II.